GW00994247

SEND HER
VICTORIOUS

SEND HER VICTORIOUS

LT–COMMANDER
Michael Apps RN

To my darling Lilian
my friendship, admiration
and love always

Michael

WILLIAM KIMBER : LONDON

First Published by
WILLIAM KIMBER AND CO. LIMITED
Godolphin House, 22a Queen Anne's Gate
London, S.W. 1

Copyright © 1971 Michael Apps
SBN 7183 0102 1

*This book is copyright. No part of it may be
reproduced in any form without permission in
writing from the publishers except by a reviewer
who wishes to quote brief passages in connection
with a review written for inclusion in a magazine
or newspaper or a radio broadcast.*

TYPESET BY SPECIALISED OFFSET SERVICES, LIVERPOOL,
AND PRINTED IN GREAT BRITAIN BY
W. & J. MACKAY & CO. LTD., CHATHAM

CONTENTS

Appendices

Index

MAPS AND DIAGRAMS

LIST OF ILLUSTRATIONS – SEND HER VICTORIOUS

FOREWORD

by
Vice Admiral Ian McIntosh
CB, DSO, MBE, DSC

For more than a quarter of a century HMS *Victorious* formed part of the Fleet and saw action and service from tropical to arctic seas. Her life spanned the period when carrier-borne air power exerted a profound effect on sea warfare. What this meant to the men of the ship and her air group is described in this book in a vivid and intimate manner by Lieutenant Commander Apps who commanded 814 Squadron in HMS *Victorious* during my time in Command of her. To view great events through the eyes of those who were taking some part in them, to comprehend far-reaching technological changes through the effects that they had upon one ship and her men is to be given a unique and enlivening vignette of history. In intimate detail as well as in breadth, it is a fascinating picture. Some readers may find as engaging an interest in tracing and considering another thread which is woven through the backcloth of this tapestry. That some ships acquire a distinct and permanent character has been attested by generations of seamen. Every ship has a character but in the predominant number this is of an ephemeral and fluctuating nature, reflecting the collective qualities, good or bad, of those who, at any one time are serving in her. This is as one would expect. Of greater interest, because it is more rare, is the enduring reputation acquired by some ships.

Such reputations lie normally at the extremes of good or bad. A bad reputation can usually be traced to an early failure in face of a challenge — externally from the elements or the enemies of the Realm or internally from mutiny or technical deficiencies. Acquired quickly, sometimes spectacularly, such a character and its persistence need engage our curiosity no further. It is the enduring good reputation enjoyed by some ships, of whom *Victorious* was one, which deserves closer scrutiny. For when it occurs it has a life-force of its own, enlarged by successive ship's companies who themselves in turn are fortified.

The elements on which this is built are not easily isolated and some, which appear simple or obvious prove to be inessential. Beauty is an example; *Victorious* was singularly attractive to the eye as the reader who unfolds the dust-cover will agree. Yet beauty is not an essential ingredient since some unattractive ships have had most enviable characters. Fitness for purpose is a far more important factor, and no ship deficient in this quality could earn a good reputation. *Victorious* was superbly fitted to her purpose, quirkish at times, but always interesting and responsive, delightful to handle and more than equal to her tasks. A great name can be an important influence felt most strongly when it is repeated, and carried by another ship within living memory. It is clearly not an essential factor, but the influence it exerts suggests the operation of a group memory. And if, over the gap of more than a score of years, memory can exert an influence, its effect should be more powerful still within the life-span of one ship.

It is significant that such reputations attach primarily to larger ships. Smaller ships in any one commission may gain a reputation as efficient and happy but there seems to be no residual memory which carries that reputation forward to provide a foundation for the next commission. The obvious deduction is that this arises from the much larger numbers of men involved, who will inevitably spread the reputation more widely. The argument becomes less convincing when it is more closely examined. A carrier may have over 2,000 men serving in her and a submarine, for instance, under 100. But when these figures are related to the total number of men who by choice and training might serve in the one type or the other, the proportions become similar. One should therefore expect at least a comparable proportion of each type of ship to acquire lasting reputations. Since this is contrary to observation, a different explanation must be sought.

One of the many attractions of serving in small ships is that all are clearly of one company. Each man is a individual, known and recognised, yet all, for success – or indeed for survival – must work closely together. In such an atmosphere it is relatively easy to create an efficient, purposeful and happy ship. The sheer size and labyrinthine complexity as well as the numbers involved tend to blur the sharp outline in any big ship and particularly in an aircraft carrier. For her very essence is her air group and each man and every piece of equipment in her is there to ensure that her aircraft are ready, on time, to carry out the tasks required of them. The closer a man is to the aircraft, the easier it is for him to understand how his duties contribute to the aim. But there are many who see little of the repair and preparation of the aircraft, their fuelling and arming, their launching, control in the air and their recovery. Yet the ship and her squadrons carry no-one who does not, in his own way, contribute an essential element, the lack of which would lower the effectiveness of the whole enterprise. The true foundation of a happy and efficient fighting ship is the realisation by each man that he has a unique and important part to play. This, self-evident in a submarine, requires, in a large ship, a positive and sustained effort by everyone. The task may appear to verge on the impossible. But it is probably the stimulus of this challenge, set at a severe, but not impossible, level of difficulty, which establishes in the first place a persistent memory of a reputation. The achievement becomes a source of wonder, a thing to recount, and in the retelling of it is established a persistent reputation. This in turn allows the following commission to begin, not at the bottom but some part of the way up the slope. If successive commissions can match the challenge, a fortunate reputation is established which becomes an increasingly significant part of the response.

The ship herself acquires, by this process, a character which in time will not be altered by temporary reverses and which will indeed help those in her to surmount difficulties. The affection with which she is treated seems to stimulate an inanimate response from the ship herself. If the condition is rare, it is at least of long-standing and derives support from the records of antiquity. Not indeed in the Bible, for the Israelites, being such firm landsmen that they even crossed the Red Sea on foot, left no record of Noah's relationship with the Ark. But the Greeks, as one might expect from such enterprising sea-farers, give us an excellent example of this interaction between men and ships. The early difficulties which attended the launch of the *Argo* brought together an ill-assorted group of individualists, forcing them to act in concert as a crew and evoked an imaginative response from Orpheus who, with the magic of his lyre, drew crew and ship together and charmed her into the sea. From this start grew that felicitous relationship between the ship and her crew without which the successful exploits of that remarkable and prolonged voyage could not have been accomplished and the names of Jason and his crew and their ship would not have passed into legend. Perhaps, several millenia later, the same elements lay at the heart of the success achieved and the affection called forth by HMS *Victorious*.

ACKNOWLEDGEMENTS

In the writing of the *Victorious* story, I wish to express my very sincere thanks to the many ex-*Victorious* sailors, their wives, mothers, fathers, brothers and sisters, without whose help, co-operation and memories, this book would not have been written. I cannot possibly list everybody and in any case many of those to whom I spoke wish to remain unmentioned, but I must say thank you to them all for their many kindnesses.

In particular I would like to thank Vice-Admiral Ian S. McIntosh, CB, DSO, MBE, DSC who as my Captain in *Victorious* became a personal friend, provided much help and information and has kindly consented to write the foreword to this book. I am also very grateful to Vice-Admiral Sir H.R.B. Janvrin, KCB, DSC, who was Flag Officer Naval Air Command and Commanding Officer HMS *Victorious* 1959-60, Rear Admiral J.A.R. Troup, DSC* (Flag Officer Sea Training and the ex-Commander of *Victorious* in 1959), Rear Admiral D.G. Parker, DSO, DSC, AFC, (who flew from Victorious on the Malta Convoy of 1942 and later in the Invasion of North Africa), Rear Admiral P.M. Austin, (my Cadet Training Officer), Captain E.G. Brown, RN, Captain D.C. Matthews, RN, Captain I.G.W. Robertson, DSC, RN, (who flew on the *Tirpitz* raid and is now Commanding Officer of HMS *Eagle*), Surgeon Captain W.A.N. Mackie, DSC, RN, (Pilot on the Palembang Raid), Kapitan Karl Theodor Raeder, Federal German Navy, (ex Gunnery Officer of *Tirpitz* and now German Naval Attache in London), Captain A.J. Leahy, MBE, DSC, RN, Commander R.C. Hay, DSO, DSC, RN, Rtd., (Air Group Leader for British Pacific Fleet 1945 in *Victorious*), Commander D.P. Norman, AFC, RN, Commander E.R. Anson, RN, Commander Geoffrey

Rotherham, DSC, RN, Rtd., (*Bismarck* Chase 1941), Commander P.B. Reynolds, RN, (the last Commander (Air) of *Victorious*), Commander J. Bagnall, RN, Commander M.C. Clapp, RN, (ex-CO of 801 Squadron), Commander M.J.F. Rawlinson, RN, (ex-CO of 849 Squadron), Commander J.M. Shrives, RN, Commander B.T. Tippetts, RN, (who stood by the ship during Modernisation), Commander L.J.B. Reynolds, RN, Commander J.N.S. Anderdon, RN, (Flight Deck Officer – 1964/65), Commander J.A. Neilson, DSC, RN, (ex-Lieutenant Commander Flying of *Victorious*), Commander R.A. Duxbury, RN, Commander A.D. Levy, RN, Rev. P.J. Burgoyne, DSC, RN, Lieutenant Commander D.J. Melhuish, RN, Lieutenant Commander T.A. Davis, RN, Lieutenant Commander D.A. Pickles, RN, Lieutenant Commander J. Trevis, RN, Rtd, (ex-CO of 825 Squadron), Lieutenant Commander L.A. Cox, RN, Rtd, (Curator of the Fleet Air Arm Museum, Yeovilton), Lieutenant Commander B. Hartwell, RN, (849 Squadron A Flight 1951), Lieutenant Commander I. Gilman, RN, Lieutenant Commander C. Topliss, MVE, DSM, RN, Rtd, (*Tirpitz* Raid 1944), Lieutenant Commander S. Bryden, RN, Rtd, (MOD), Lieutenant Commander N.H. Kerr, RN, (now CO 892 Phantom Squadron), Lieutenant Commander B.H. Stock, RN, (ex-CO 849 A Flight), Lieutenant Commander P.J. Wreford, RN, Rtd, Lieutenant Commander J.H. de Courcy-Hughes, RN, Rtd, (HMS *Victorious* 1948), Lieutenant Commander J.E. Nash, (Present CO of 849 Squadron), Lieutenant Commander Stan Farquar, RN, (British Pacific Fleet 1944/45), Lieutenant Commander R. Massey, RN, Lieutenant Commander B. Giffen, RN, Lieutenant Commander T.R.E. Beabey, RN, Lieutenant Commander J. Johnson, RN, Lieutenant Commander S.R. Batchelder, RN, Lieutenant M.A. Miller, RN, (Sembawang), Lieutenant John Riley, RN, Lieutenant Fred Motley, RN, Lieutenant J.K. Smart, RN, (for all his photographic help), Lieutenant 'Tug' Wilson, RN, Mech 1 Colin Veal, Petty Officer Tony Cox, L.M.E. Baker, HM Dockyard, Portsmouth and Department of Director General Ships, Bath. Commander E. Tufnell, RN, Rtd, for permission to reproduce his paintings of the ship.

In addition my appreciation is due to Mr John Fay for his help with Pacific Interlude, Mr G. Showell (for all his help and photographs), Mr Frank Young (USN Research Material on *Victorious*), His Worship the Lord Mayor of Newcastle, Councillor W. Harding, FCA, Mr G. Gleming Managing Director, Vickers Ltd, Barrow Shipbuilding Works, Barrow-in-Furness, Anthony and Joseph Pavia, Malta. The *Times of Malta*, Mrs Valerie Boyden for her artistic advice and help. Mr Tom Melbourne (served in Battleship *Victorious* 1919). Flight Lieutenant Alfred Price, RAF, who as author of five books was a source of great help and encouragement. The Imperial War Museum, Admiralty Archives, (Mr R.G. Gold and Miss D.H.M. Cummins), Public Records Office, (Mr. D. Ryder) and Miss L. Farrow, (Historical Branch, Admiralty). My three typists, Mrs Yvonne Tribel, Mrs Dorothy Ross and Miss Winifred Pritchard deserve special praise for their painstaking efforts and keeping a sense of humour, and my research helpers Mr. E.J.J. Rennell and Mr. B.V. Cousens. In conclusion I must pay tribute to my great friend Lieutenant David Brown, RN, Rtd. As the author of *Carrier Operations in World War II* (Ian Allan) and an ex-*Victorious* officer, his advice, help, research and considerable knowledge was invaluable to me. Together with my wife who read through the draft, indexed the book and checked the final manuscript, on behalf of our *'Mighty Vic'* — I say thankyou to you all.

1st May 1971

RN Air Station
Yeovilton
Somerset

PROLOGUE

It all started on a cold January night as I flicked over the pages of a grubby and ill-kept Midshipman's Journal and thought back to that day many years ago; it was the 11th October 1949 and as I sat back to re-live those early days of my naval life, my crude scrawl and the constructive abuse of the Course Officer, Lieutenant Peter Austin, leapt at me from the pages and a host of nostalgic memories flooded back into my thoughts. It seems like only yesterday that I said goodbye to my parents and boarded the train for that journey to London, when I set off resplendent in a bright new uniform to join the Navy and my first ship – HMS *Victorious*. Two hours later I joined a group of equally self-conscious cadets on the platform at Waterloo Station, and avoiding the indignity caused by the unenlightened British traveller saying, 'Porter, please carry my bags to platform number five', we boarded the train for Weymouth. 'Hurry up, get a move on then', shouted the stentorian voice of our new tutor and nursemaid, Petty Officer Glanfield, adding the word 'Sirs' as a meaningful afterthought. As we boarded the naval pinnace in Portland Harbour his tone became decidedly more menacing: 'Don't forget to salute at the top of the gangway – right hand if you don't mind, gentlemen'. So at long last we had arrived; we were in the Royal Navy and for better or for worse, *Victorious* would be our home and training ship for the next few months.

Eighteen years later a very changed *Victorious* was steaming up the Channel to Portsmouth, at the end of yet another commission in the Far East. As usual it had been a very happy twelve months, but now Captain Ian McIntosh was bringing her home to a refit, before she sailed away again in 1968 for the last commission of her naval life. It was the 20th June 1967 and most of her aircraft had flown ashore, but the helicopters of 814 Squadron were still on board and preparing to disembark to RN Air Station Culdrose. As I stood on the flight deck and said goodbye to the 'Mighty *Vic*', I did not realise that fate would make this the last commission, that the helicopters flying off would signal the final curtain on her fantastic career and in six months time the order to scrap the ship would be a finality.

In deciding to write this story, I am indebted to the many officers and men who served in the *Victorious*, their wives and widows, mothers and fathers, and the many civilians and friends, who have given me their time, memories and reminiscences, have allowed me to intrude in their lives to build this story and, I trust, to do justice to the men and the ship. To look at, *Victorious* was a large and rather ugly ship, but she was an aircraft carrier that had a personality of her own. A hybrid of a ship that survived the rapid, inexorable march of technical progress and served in the Royal Navy for almost thirty years. The aim of this book is to recount those years and tell her story which spans over a quarter of a century of naval aviation, to recall the exciting moments of history and to re-live the events as they happened with the people who were there. Of necessity, most of the story concerns the activities of her aircraft and of the men who flew them, but it is people who make a ship and the Air Department of *Victorious* formed but a small percentage of her ship's company. This book is a tribute not only to her airmen, but to the thousands of other officers and men who formed the 'team'; the ship's Engineers, Electricians, Cooks, Supply Department, Medical and Dental Staff, Communications and Aircraft Direction teams and all the other unmentioned personnel, without whose loyalty, co-operation and very pleasant company – the 'Mighty *Vic*' would not have been.

The fleet carrier HMS *Victorious* was authorised in the 1936 naval construction programme and was built by Vickers-Armstrong Limited, at the Naval Yard, Walker-on-Tyne. She started life when she was laid down in 1937 and the old saying of 'Tyne Built – Well Built', was to prove true in the years to come. Commissioned in March 1941, her first operational assignment was to ferry aircraft and escort a troop convoy on the initial stage of its voyage to the Middle East, but this was cancelled at the last moment and the unworked up and very new *Victorious* was involved in the *Bismarck* Chase. This was indeed the prelude of things to come, for as a carrier in World War II, she would sail in every ocean, operate with the American Fleet, and take part in every big carrier action. After the *Bismarck* Chase in May of 1941, she spent months in the cold Arctic Oceans on covering duties for the North Russian Convoys, escorted the Malta Convoys and supported the North African landings. She sailed to the Pacific to serve under Admiral Halsey, USN, before returning to strike at *Tirpitz,* then off once more to the Far East and the final phase in the war against Japan. She led an exciting and dangerous life, with near misses from torpedoes, dodging mines and bombs and surviving three Kamikaze hits.

At the end of the war with Japan, she repatriated ex-Japanese Allied Prisoners of War to Australia and finally arrived at Plymouth on 31st October 1945. Between December 1945 and January 1947, she was employed on trooping duties to and from the Far East and Australia, and on one trip came home as a War Brides ship. After a few months in reserve, she became a ship of the Training Squadron of the Home Fleet at Portland and from there, to Portsmouth in 1950 for a facelift that was to last eight long years. Cynics said that many a dockyard worker had grown up, married and raised his family on the proceeds of *Vic's* long modernisation, but when she emerged in 1958 she was Britain's most up-to-date carrier and the symbol of modern naval air power in the sixties. All the latest equipment and modern techniques had been incorporated and, with a new lease of life, she spent most of the next ten years of her service as an operational front-line carrier East of Suez. *Victorious* returned from her last commission in June 1967 and it was the intention to refit her for one more tour of duty in the Far East before the scheduled scrapping in 1971. But a tragic fire during her refit, political pressures and the economic crisis, together with a lack of manpower and resolve within the Navy, conspired to retire this famous lady before her time.

As the dust of yet another Defence Review settles and the planners seek to implement the policies of the Nation, the story of *Victorious* might serve to help us reflect on the past, take heed of the present and perhaps remember for the future. The development of the aircraft carrier heralded the demise of the battleship as the capital ship of the Fleet and, in so doing, challenged the Admirals with their centuries of traditional thought and doctrine. The Fleet Air Arm had to accomplish the impossible, under the burden of past indifference and plain incompetence, to prove that it was a vital part of the navy and not just a more potent and flexible extension of the gun. As sail was replaced by steam and battleships gave way to aircraft carriers, so too will they go and progress take its course. But as we rush headlong towards the end of the twentieth century, faced with the prospects of missiles, weapons in space and the ever increasing speed of technological advance, is it possible that the need for air power at sea is an outdated concept.

As the workmen of the Clyde tear *Victorious* to bits, it is fitting that we pay tribute to a fine ship that has become a legend in her lifetime, that we salute and remember with pride the thousands of men who worked, lived and died to build that legend. In the present climate of a rapidly changing world it would seem that for Britain *Victorious* and her kind are a luxury that we can no longer afford. Money and priorities must dictate Defence Policies and hence our capabilities, but have the lessons of World War II, Korea, Suez and Vietnam no place in our deliberations?

Victorious is no more, but the need for air power at sea is as important today as it was yesterday and after reading this story, perhaps the options are less attractive.

Chapter I

THE LEGEND IS BORN

The Fleet Air Arm of the Royal Navy is a relatively young branch of the service, but is nevertheless an integral part of the Navy which has matured under the traditions and influence of the sea. Its aircraft provide an extension and development of the cutlass, cannon, musket and gun of earlier times, while the aircraft carrier replaces the sailing ship of Trafalgar and the battleship at Jutland. 'Let us show ourselves to be all of a company', Drake exhorted his men in the *Golden Hind* – a sentiment that was a reality to the ship's companies throughout the life of the carrier *Victorious*. One cannot be so certain about the ship's companies of her four predecessors, but even so the following history is a fascinating catalogue of achievement, progressive maritime development and of Long Service and Good Conduct in the Royal Navy.

The name *Victorious* first appears in the year 1785, but it probably goes back further than that. It may have originated from the French *Victorieuse*, the name of a captured prize added to the British Fleet after a successful engagement, but if the supposition is correct and such a ship existed, then the original *Victorieuse* has long since passed into obscurity. What is certain is that a Brig Sloop of that name was captured by the Fleet off Texel on the 31st August 1795 and served in the British Navy until she was broken up in August 1805. The incorporation of captured enemy ships into one's own fleet was common practice by navies during the eighteenth century and if the name was not a tongue-twister, it was left unchanged or sometimes translated into its English equivalent.

To trace the early history of the first really known *Victorious,* our story must go back to the latter end of the eighteenth century when expansion was the key-word, and new classes of ships were added to the Navy. Already considerable in numbers, by the year 1800 this expansion had created a fleet of no less than 900 ships of all sizes, and gave England by far the finest and most formidable navy the world had ever seen. It certainly came at the right time and was a morale booster for, after a century of maladministration and inefficiency, it marked the stirrings of a new life and provided the necessary impetus for which the Navy had been waiting since the legendary days of the great Hawkins, Howard, Drake and Frobisher.

The Battle of Trafalgar which finally set the seal of the superiority of English sea power, was still some twenty-seven years away when Mr Perry, a London shipbuilder, started work on the first *Victorious*. On the 27th April 1785, she was launched as a third-rate two-decker of 74 guns. These ships had proved themselves to be by far the most useful class and in numbers alone, formed the greater part of the new British Fleet. After being fitted out, she sailed to take her place as a ship of the line and was next heard of at the Cape of Good Hope in 1795.

When Holland was over-run by the French Armies of the Revolution and the Stadtholder — the Prince of Orange — fled for safety to England, a naval squadron was hastily gathered together and dispatched to occupy the Cape of Good Hope. It was imperative to prevent the French from getting possession of the Cape and securing a base for operations against the vital trade to India and the Dutch possessions in the East Indies. It was hoped that any intervention by the naval force in the Cape would be with the consent of the resident Dutch authorities, but the Admiral leading the expedition was briefed to use force if all else failed.

As the sun was setting on Thursday 11th June, HMS *Victorious* sailed into Simon's Bay. She formed part of the squadron under the command of Vice-Admiral Sir George Keith Elphinstone, flying his flag in another 74-gun line-of-battle ship HMS *Monarch*, together with the *Arrogant* (74), the *America, Stately* and *Ruby,* all 64s, and two sloops, the *Echo* and *Rattlesnake* each carrying 16 guns. As soon as the ships had anchored, Admiral Elphinstone lost no time in getting ashore to explain to the authorities the reason for his presence with such a powerful force.

During the next two weeks while negotiations were being carried on in Cape Town, the British ships were treated with the normal hospitality accorded to visiting men-o'-war – it was rather Hobson's Choice for in the face of such an armada, the few Dutch officials in Simon's Bay (with their meagre defences) could scarcely do otherwise. The ships of the squadron were allowed to take on water and received beef, fruit and vegetables from the shore. The latter were especially welcome, as many of the ships' companies were suffering from scurvy. The *Victorious* in particular had become almost useless as a fighting ship, having no less than 187 men afflicted with this terrible disease. To alleviate the suffering, some of the worst cases were sent to a hospital established ashore, and were looked after and accommodated 'at the advanced but unavoidable cost of six shillings per man per day'.

Life at sea for the eighteenth century sailor was not the romantic escape portrayed by twentieth century Hollywood, or conceived in the mind's eye of the office-bound landlubber. In reality, it was a hard life of discomfort, danger and purgatory and for most sailors – a hateful existence. Volunteers were hard to come by and press gangs roamed the streets of our major ports, to recruit the necessary sailors to man the fleet and compensate for the lack of volunteers. Doctor Samuel Johnson observed that: 'No man will be a sailor who has contrivance enough to get himself in jail; for being in a ship is being in a jail with the chance of being drowned. A man in jail has more room, better food and commonly better company'.

The Dutch official Resident, Mr Christoffel Brand, was predisposed to welcome the British ships, but the negotiations did not proceed very quickly. The true situation in Europe was very confused and in any case, Commissioner Sluyskens and the Council of Policy felt that they were quite capable of defending the Cape against outside aggression without British help. Admiral Elphinstone got more than a little impatient with the protracted negotiations and, somewhat injudiciously, took the matter into his own hands. He issued a general proclamation to all the inhabitants of the Cape, exhorting them to accept a temporary

British occupation. This attempt to over-ride its authority irritated the Council so much that on 26th June it ordered all further supplies of provisions to the ships to be stopped forthwith and all cattle to be driven inland out of reach of the fleet. However, the sick were allowed to remain in the hospital ashore, because apart from the humanitarian aspect, they could do no harm and were a source of considerable profit at a time when ready money was very short in the colony. The scurvy had abated somewhat with the improved diet and good nursing ashore, but in *Victorious* a great many were still afflicted and a number of her ship's company had died.

The stoppage of supplies to the fleet was a very serious matter, as the ships were woefully short of food. This was the principle reason which finally compelled Admiral Elphinstone to break off the negotiations and resort to force. On the 14th July, Simon's Town was occupied by the few troops available and preparations were begun for the advance along the coast to Muizenberg and on to Cape Town. For the next two and a half months, the *Victorious* remained at anchor in Simon's Bay. With nearly two hundred of her crew incapacitated by the scurvy and another two or three hundred among the thousand seamen landed in support of the troops for the advance to Cape Town, there would scarcely have been enough men left on board out of her normal complement of 584 to take the ship to sea, much less to take part in any fighting. It was a full fortnight after the capitulation on the 16th September, before the seamen had returned on board and the *Victorious,* together with the other larger ships, *Arrogant, Stately* and *Ruby,* was in a fit state to sail round to Cape Town, where she arrived on the 3rd October.

Victorious did not remain long in Table Bay. With *Stately,* she sailed away on the 27th October with orders to cruise off the French Islands and Bourbon — now known as Mauritius and Reunion. After three weeks of cruising, she was to proceed to Madras to join the Admiral who, with *Monarch, Arrogant, Echo* and *Rattlesnake,* sailed from Cape Town on the 15th November. During the next few years the fleets of England were pitted against those of France, Spain, Denmark and virtually the rest of the world, culminating in the disappearance of all serious rivalry to Britain as the ruler of the seas. With the capture of territories

in all four corners of the world, the influence of England was
greater than that of Rome at the very zenith of her power.

Seven years passed before *Victorious* again returned to the
Cape. It seems probable that throughout this period she was on
active service in Eastern waters. In September 1796 in company
with the *Arrogant,* she fought an action with five French frigates
off the coast of Sumatra. The action was very fierce and the
two British ships suffered considerable damage, especially to
their masts and sails. Thereafter, nothing more was heard of the
Victorious until the 12th December 1802, when she arrived in
Table Bay on passage from India to England. Peace had been
declared in March of that year and the majority of British
warships in India and the East Indies were returning home. The
Victorious would not have put into Cape Town, but she was in
such bad shape that she was compelled to do so for the repair
of various defects. She was now twenty years old and for seven
years she had been serving on a station where few facilities
existed for repairing damage and refitting. The defects were
made good and she sailed again on the 27th December, taking
with her part of the 81st Regiment of Foot, which was being
returned to England on the evacuation of the Cape by the
British. After her return to England, she was eventually broken
up in Lisbon in 1803.

At the beginning of the nineteenth century, the Wooden Walls
of England were to be found on every ocean of the world. They
were lower built and stronger than those of the previous
century; the square stern, and decoration had almost disappeared
and the rig of the three-masted ships was fairly well
standardised. In seamanship and gunnery the British Navy was
unequalled and, as the year 1805 dawned, the day was not far
off when that superiority was to be proved.

Messrs Adams and Company was a well established shipbuilder
at Portsmouth. Many years experience and skilled shipwrights,
riggers and other craftsmen combined to construct a new
Victorious on 7th February 1805. At a cost of only £41,796,
this third rate 74-gun ship of the line began to take shape.
Although the Admiralty had ordered in 1796 that no decoration
was to be incorporated in future ships, the unpopular order was
partially ignored to the extent that *Victorious* retained her

figurehead and, tactfully, a little decorative work on the stern. She was painted 'Nelson fashion' with a black hull and broad yellow bands between the tiers of guns, while inside, on the gun decks, the area around the guns was painted a bright red. The idea was that blood spilt in action would be less conspicuous on a red deck and thus less distracting to the more squeamish mariners of the time. With a complement of 590 men, the second *Victorious* was launched at Buckler's Hard on 20th October 1808.

It took just under six months to fit her out for sea and 'copper her bottom'. Bottom-fouling by marine growth is a problem that even modern science cannot solve completely – particularly for ships operating in warm tropical waters. Today, great improvements have been made by the use of modern anti-fouling paints and even high frequency vibrators, but even so ships must undergo periodic and costly dockings to remove the growth, which reduces their speed and hence increases running costs. About the middle of the eighteenth century serious attempts were made to solve this problem; the old lead sheeting was abandoned and in 1761 the frigate *Alarm* was sheathed in copper. Unfortunately the metal was fastened with iron bolts, which corroded through electrolytic action and the copper fell off. Not to be daunted however, the shipbuilders then used copper bolts and the problem was solved. By the end of the century all the warships and most of the merchantmen were 'copper bottomed'.

Victorious left Portsmouth on the 2nd March 1809 and her first venture with the fleet was to take part in the disastrous Walcheren Expedition. At 10 am on the morning of the 14th August *Victorious* was one of the ships of a naval squadron bombarding the town of Flushing – an indifferent action in which the naval ships lost a total of seven men killed and twenty-two wounded and a large number of invading troops went down with swamp fever. Later that year under the command of Captain John Talbot, the *Victorious* was sent to serve in the Mediterranean. Action does not appear to have been very predominant in the life of the ship during her spell in Mediterranean waters in the early stages, for apart from intercepting and sinking the Italian schooner of war *Loeben* of 10 guns and sixty men, loaded with ordnance stores and bound for Corfu from Venice, very little other activity was recorded. Just before her return to Chatham on 24th July 1812 however, the *Victorious* had the opportunity to distinguish herself in an extremely successful engagement off Trieste.

Captain Talbot in *Victorious* and the 18-gun Brig *Weazel* commanded by Commander John William Andrew were ordered to proceed to the Port of Venice, to keep an eye on the *Rivoli* – a new French 74-gun ship which had recently been completed and was reported to be ready for sea. He arrived off the port on 16th February and because of the miserable, foggy weather, he was unable to see anything. After five days the weather cleared and the enemy was sighted. That evening, Commodore J.B. Barre sailed in the *Rivoli* in company with the *Jena* and *Mercure,* each carrying 18 guns, the *Mamelouck* with 10 guns and two gunboats. The enemy force shaped course in line of battle for Pula in Istria and the *Victorious* and *Weazel* set off in pursuit.

Early on the morning of the 22nd February, Captain Talbot noticed that the *Mercure* had dropped behind her consorts and that the *Rivoli* had shortened sail to allow the brig to close up. This was the chance that he had been waiting for and he immediately ordered *Weazel* to attempt to pass *Victorious* and 'bring the laggard to action'. This Commander Andrew promptly did and opened fire on the *Mercure* and, for a time, the *Jena.* After an action lasting some forty minutes the *Mercure* blew up and *Weazel* picked up only three survivors, leaving *Jena* to make off and escape. Meanwhile the *Victorious* was busily engaged with the *Rivoli*; after a battle lasting nearly five hours, during which the Frenchman became 'dreadfully shattered in both hull and rigging', the *Rivoli* was forced to surrender. Out of her complement of 810 officers and men she had upwards of 400 killed or wounded, while the *Victorious* lost 27 men killed and a further 99 wounded. During the running engagement which was interrupted from time to time by fog and smoke, Captain Talbot was nearly blinded by a splinter and had to hand over much of his duties to his First Lieutenant, Lieutenant Thomas Ladd Peake who fought the ship magnificently against a most gallant, skilful and experienced enemy. Ship engagements in those days were fought at very close quarters and thus tended to be more personalised and gruesome. Frequently ships would be locked together like fighting bulldogs, grappling with each other and blasting broadside after broadside into each other's hull. The carnage could be terrible and in one action in 1794 what was probably the most devastating and destructive broadside in history was fired: Admiral Lord Howe in his flagship the *Queen Charlotte* punched a hole in the stern of the French 120-gun flagship *Montagne* and the hole was so great that a coach and four could comfortably have been driven through. In that one massive broadside no less than 300 men including the Captain were killed outright. Today it is not uncommon for the opposing fleets to be many miles apart and in almost all of the carrier actions in the Pacific in World War II, the outcome was decided by aircraft strikes from the two forces, which did not even sight each other.

As the result of this most successful action, Captain Talbot of *Victorious* was awarded a gold medal and knighted, while his First Lieutenant was promoted to Commander. The *Rivoli* was added to the Royal Navy and *Victorious* came home to England. After a refit at Chatham and still commanded by Captain Talbot, she sailed for the West Indies on the 7th November 1812. From there she headed for the coast of North America and the Davis Strait between Greenland and Baffin Island. Her task was to give protection to the Whaling Fleets operating in northern waters during the summer months, but unfortunately she struck a rock and sustained so much damage that she had to return to Portsmouth for repairs, arriving on 11th August 1814. She was paid off and very little more was heard of her activities until she was broken up in Portsmouth on 27th September 1861 and the sale of her scrap realised £2,508.

It is indeed irony that Admiral Lord Nelson was apparently one of the few Naval Officers to appreciate the future of steam for ship propulsion. After a presentation by Mr Henry Bell to draw attention to his ideas and 'the practicability of, and utility of, steam as a propelling power against winds and tides', he was politely told that 'my Lords Commissioners, after careful consideration of the proposal, had concluded that it was of no value in trans-marine navigation'. Lord Nelson protested:

My Lords and Gentlemen, if you do not adopt Mr Bell's scheme other nations will, and in the end vex every vein of the Empire.

It was the year 1800 and five years before Trafalgar.

His plea did not fall on deaf ears and although development was slow, the eighteen hundreds saw the rise of the steamship and the gradual demise of the famous clipper ships, sail and ultimately the wooden walls of England. Legendary names sign-posted the progress of those early days, with the *Great Western* in 1837, Brunel's *Great Britain* in 1844 and his ill-fated *Great Eastern* in 1852. To the superstitious the *Great Eastern* was an unlucky ship, to her owners a commercial failure, but to maritime development, an architectural triumph that was born before her time.

By 1850 armour and metal ships had come to stay. The French *La Gloire* was the world's first iron-clad ship and prompted the Admiralty into building and launching the *Warrior* — Britain's first iron-clad — in 1860. Progress in ship design, size, engines and armament continued until the end of the century, when a new and very different *Victorious* made her debut with the Grand Fleet.

Rated as a first-class battleship and one of six of the new 'Majestic' Class, *Victorious* the Third was built at Chatham and launched on the 19th October 1895. Just two months earlier, an identical battleship was built and launched at Portsmouth Dockyard and named *Prince George,* these two ships being destined to cause a certain amount of confusion in the Admiralty. But to return to *Victorious,* this 14,900-ton battleship was completed in 1896 at a cost of £885,212, prepared to start her career in the Channel Squadrons. After a spell on the China Station she went to the Mediterranean at the turn of the century, before returning to Home Waters in 1903. After a refit she became the Flagship of the Second-in-Command, the Channel Fleet from 1904 to 1906. Very little seems to have happened to her during this time, and she continued to operate in the Channel areas until the outbreak of World War I. The only excitement in her life occurred on the 5th June 1910, when she was involved in a minor collision in fog with her sister ship HMS *Majestic.* With the *Majestic's* 'bow up her stern' she sustained minor damage to her stern-walk and disabled her starboard engine, but happily at the subsequent Board of Enquiry all was forgiven and no one was held to be blamed.

This coal-burning battleship was intended for the 9th Battle Squadron at the outbreak of war, but with flexibility as the keynote, operational plans were changed and she was sent under the command of Captain R. Nugent, RN, to defend the Humber from possible enemy attack. In 1914, after a somewhat quiet war, she was relieved of her Humber Defence duties and was attached to the Third Division Reserve Fleet where she remained for the next two years. It was then decided to fit her out as a Dockyard Repair Ship and, from 1916 to 1919, *Victorious* became the base ship at Scapa for dockyard workers. Her war career could not be described as having been spectacular for as one of the penultimate pre-Dreadnoughts, she was small, slow and carried only four 12-inch guns. Nevertheless, she had the Victorian profusion of supporting weaponry for beating off anything from torpedo-boats to seagulls.

Whether somebody just plain forgot, or whether it was part of some deeper and more subtle plot will never be known, but on the 3rd March 1918 the battleship *Prince George* was renamed *Victorious II*. For the next two years the two battleships *Victorious* continued to be part of the active fleet and one can visualise long investigations into how the battleship *Victorious* could be in two places at once. Clearly this state of affairs could not be allowed to continue, and in 1920 the First *Victorious* who finished her active service wearing the flag of Vice-Admiral Commanding Orkneys and Shetland, was renamed *Indus II*. She was sold to Mr A.J.P. Purves on the 19th December 1922 and four months later, resold to the Stanlee Shipbreaking Company of Dover to go the way of all good ships and be broken up. Meanwhile *Victorious* the Second soldiered on in harbour service, but her career in that illustrious name was to be shortlived. On the 29th January 1921 she was sold to a Mr Cohen who promptly resold her – presumably for profit – and she was stranded in tow off Kamperdium, while being taken to a breaker's yard in Germany.

Hardly had the battleship *Victorious* commenced her uneventful life, when the world was shaken by an historic event which would have far reaching consequences. At Kill Devil Hill, a range of sandy hills near Kitty Hawk, North Carolina, the Wright Brothers achieved man's greatest ambition and on the 17th December 1903, made the first ever flight of 820 feet in an aeroplane under its own power. In the years that followed these two pioneers worked hard and slavishly to perfect the technique, lengthening the time in the air and improving the safety factor. In September 1904 they made their first curved flight, and one month later flew a circular course of three miles in five minutes. By September 1905 they were able to fly a distance of 24 miles, and by that date had made nearly 300 flights. Despite their achievements, the Wright Brothers received little encouragement or recognition in their own country and in 1907, offered the patent of their revolutionary invention to the Admiralty. But as in their letter to Mr Bell in 1800 regarding his proposal to use steam for the propulsion of ships, the Admirals were to show that they were equally unimpressed by this new, lunatic invention of the aeroplane. History was to repeat itself as they replied: 'Their Lordships are of the opinion that they [aeroplanes] would not be of any practical use to the Naval Service.'

Three years later, the first four naval pilots were taught to fly and by 1912 both Naval and Military Flying Wings of the Royal Flying Corps had been established. The Royal Naval Air Service was officially formed on the 1st July 1914 and during World War I pioneered much of the basic carrier operations, provided bombardment spotting and reconnaissance for the Fleet. They were unsurpassed when 'mis-used' as land-based fighter units and by developing the long-range bomber, formulated the basis of strategic bombing philosophy which was expounded later by the RAF.

These were the golden years of opportunity and progress, but from 1918 when the Royal Air Force was founded until the summer of 1937, the opportunities were to be ignored. Responsibility for the naval aviation was divided between the Admiralty and the Air Ministry and for nearly twenty years, naval aviation was handicapped, restricted, ill-equipped and frustrated by the policies and machinations of dual control. It is not necessary to dwell on that sorry tale of wrangling between the two services, suffice it to say that the Fleet Air Arm was the loser and in 1939 should have been better prepared for modern war. One section escaped the influence of joint administration and though, to some extent, it shared in the legacy of those years of neglect and indecision, the carrier design and construction department provided the spur for a belated war-time expansion.

By 1930 the Navy had six carriers of which only the *Hermes* had been built as a carrier from the start. Under the Washington Treaty of 1922, only 20,000 tons was available for carrier building, but in fact the stringent economic policies of the British Government further restricted a carrier building pro- gramme and until 1935 new carriers for the navy were mere drawings on a board and dreams in the Admiralty. Drawing on the experiences of the First World War, the enthusiastic carrier design and construction branch of the Admiralty was able to experiment and develop with a relatively free hand and, by the early 1930s, they had produced an excellent design of ship, the fore-runner to the present day fleet carrier. Their chance came in 1935 when the decision was taken to build one new carrier — *Ark Royal*; but even as she was being built the ominous signs of impending war were casting shadows over Europe. The need to build carriers became urgent and under the Defence Estimates of 1936, four more carriers of the 'Illustrious' Class were ordered. This new class of armoured fleet carrier was based on the *Ark Royal* design of ship and they were to be named *Illustrious, Victorious, Formidable* and *Indefatigable*.

Victorious was the third of the new class to be ordered and the fifth ship to bear the proud name. Before a warship is built the Naval Staff at the Admiralty lay down certain requirements which the new ship must meet. They include such details as tonnage, speed, range, the type of armament to be fitted, radars and other special equipments and so on. When all the various specialised departments have had their say as to what the ship should carry, the naval staff draw up a document which is known as a Staff Requirement.[1] This document is the basic

[1] The Staff Requirement for HMS *Victorious* appears as Appendix Page.

blueprint for the new ship and formed the starting point in the life of *Victorious.*

Once the Staff Requirement has been agreed, a sketch design is then produced embodying all these requirements and it is submitted to the Board of Admiralty for approval. If the Government have allotted the necessary money and the Board approve, the sketch design and detailed Staff Requirements are then given to the contractor selected to build the new ship. In the case of *Victorious,* the firm selected was Messrs Vickers-Armstrong Limited and the contract for the ship was signed at the Naval Yard, Walker-on-Tyne on the 18th January 1937. Briefly the new ship was to be some 753 feet long overall and have a beam of 95¾ feet, while three steam turbines designed to provide 110,000 shaft horsepower on three shafts would drive the displacement of 23,000 tons of ship at a speed of 30 knots.

The keel was laid on the 4th May 1937 and over the next two years an army of workmen from the yard drilled, riveted and welded the mass of steel sheeting and plates that would be named *Victorious.* Day by day and slowly but surely the great ship started to take shape and to assume an identity. The double bottom was constructed to give the ship protection against underwater damage, ribs to give it strength and form the skeleton for the sides on which to hang the armour plate to defeat the torpedo. Then came the stern castings, propellers, rudder and the huge internal 'boxes' that would form the boiler and engine rooms, housing the three large Parsons geared steam turbines that would drive the ship along. All these were built into the ship as the months went by, and the hull started to take shape climbing higher and higher from the keel plate at the bottom of the building berth.

Soon it was time to start constructing the many workshops, machinery spaces, living accommodation for the crew and officers. Internally the ship was a vast honeycomb of small compartments and overall was placed the boxlike hangar topped by the enormous flight deck as its lid. Every intricate detail was carefully attended to, every stage planned, considered and then built into this complex fighting ship, that would be home and mobile airfield to her 1,600 officers and men. To give added protection against possible damage from enemy surface gunfire, the designers provided for armour plating to be placed round the hull, hangar sides and on the flight deck. The hangar was completely enclosed in an armoured shell with double (or flash-proof) access doors, independent fire-fighting systems and an exhaust system to vent dangerous petrol fumes out of the ship. This armoured construction gave *Victorious* tremendous strength and the ability to withstand considerable damage, whilst the enclosed hangar construction was a brilliant concept and a great step forward in carrier design. Both these advantages were to be severely tested and well-proven in the following war years. On the 10th January 1941 her sister ship *Illustrious* was hit by six 500-Kg armour-piercing bombs while covering a convoy to Malta. Incredibly she remained afloat and was able to steam at 21 knots; she could claim to have survived more damage than any other carrier in World War II, although she required extensive repairs as the result of this plastering. Even the savage and chilling fury of the Japanese Kamikaze pilots bent on an orgy of destruction made little impression on these very strong and well protected ships. Unlike the damage inflicted on the wooden flight decks of their American counterparts, firefighters and flight deck personnel could sweep off the bits and the ship could continue operating aircraft within hours of sustaining a hit.

The cavernous hangar was designed to stow some 36 aeroplanes, but in reality *Victorious* embarked up to 52 aircraft during her operational life in World War II, though this increase in complement meant that she had to carry a deck park and tended to impair her operating efficiency. Two electric lifts were built into the flight deck, one at either end of the ship to provide for the rapid ranging and striking down of aircraft from the hangar below. As soon as flying was scheduled, serviceable aircraft would be trundled to the two lifts and raised to flight deck level. Here, a flight deck party would push the aircraft into position in the deck park ready for the launch. To assist heavily loaded aircraft to get airborne, one hydraulic accelerator was fitted into the port forward end of the flight deck, while to enable the plane to land back on, the aircraft's hook would engage one of six arrester wires strung across the after end of the flight deck. If the pilot was unlucky enough to miss all the wires, then the aircraft would fly into one of two large wire crash barriers abreast the island.

The construction of the ship was going well and was on time; a small paragraph in the *Times* Newspaper for 1st March 1939 read:

> Construction of the *Illustrious* and *Victorious* at the works of Messrs Vickers Armstrong Limited, at Barrow-in-Furness and High Walker respectively, is proceeding satisfactorily, and they are expected to be launched in April and September next, respectively.

A quaint reassurance, but before the launching in September, another event would steal the headlines and capture world attention. In Europe, the war clouds that had been gathering on the horizon for many months moved overhead and suddenly erupted in the long awaited storm. At 0530 on the morning of the 1st September 1939 German troops surged over the borders to invade Poland and in fulfillment of their pledge Britain and France entered the war against Germany just two days later. For the next five and a half years the world would be torn by a long and bitter struggle against Fascism, a war in which Naval carrier air power was to come into prominence and the new carrier *Victorious* would play an important and leading role.

On the 14th September the great day dawned and the mighty hull of *Victorious* was 'ready to be launched. The arrangements for the ceremony were all completed and the crowds of workers, company officials and guests assembled to witness the occasion. The sponsor chosen for the honour of launching the new ship was Lady Augusta Inskip, the wife. of a famous man well-known and much respected in Fleet Air Arm circles; it is reported that Lady Inskip had a soft spot for the Fleet Air Arm and her husband Sir Thomas W.H. Inskip had served the Navy well. As the minister responsible for the co-ordination of defence under Prime Minister Stanley Baldwin, his great claim to fame was the 'Committee of One', when he reported his findings to the Cabinet on 21st July 1937 over the question of 'The Navy and its relation to the Fleet Air Arm and shore-based aircraft'. This far-reaching report known as the 'Inskip Award' finalised once and for all the question of responsibility for the provision of air power at sea. It severed naval reliance on the Royal Air Force and gave the Fleet Air Arm its proper terms of reference.

The launching went as planned and as the champagne bottle shattered against the stem to the words of Lady Inskip: 'I name this ship *Victorious* and may God protect her and all who sail in her' the huge carrier began to move down the slipway. The weather was dull and misty but nothing could dampen the delight and pride of the men who had spent nearly two years toiling for this day. To the accompaniment of the cheers of hundreds of dockyard workers, officials and the handful of naval officers and guests, slowly and majestically she started on her first journey to the sea. A low rumbling roar drowned the cheers as she gathered speed down the slipway and her stern parted the murky waters of the Tyne, then the huge drag chains strained to take the weight and bring the now floating hull to a safe stop. The ceremony was over and as the busy, fussy little shipyard tugs crowded protectively round her, the crowds turned away and began to disperse. They had seen another launching, but there can have been few if any of the spectators present who could have visualised and forecast the fame and glory that was to be hers, and the contribution that this one carrier would make to the war at sea and to naval aviation in the years to come.

Although the early days of World War II on land were described as the 'phoney war', at sea the Germans at once opened a campaign by submarine and mine to destroy Allied and neutral shipping. As the war gathered momentum and German troops occupied country after country, England became more and more isolated and within a few months, solely dependent upon seaborne links for survival. Because of this and the fact that German successes in their U-boat campaign being waged in the North Atlantic were taking a terrible toll of our merchant shipping, and the vital convoys of much needed food and war materials were being badly mauled by an increasingly hard hitting and enterprising enemy, it was decided to afford a high priority to the construction of escort vessels so urgently required to combat the U-boats. *Victorious* could and did have to wait. The losses, already unacceptably high from both sumarine and air attacks, could be further increased by surface raiders. Heavily armed enemy battleships and battle cruisers were roaming the seas of the North and South Atlantic Ocean seemingly at will, intercepting our convoys and causing very great damage to the severely out-gunned and out classed convoys and escorts. In Europe the Germans stood across the channel and seemed poised to make their final thrust to cross the 'ditch'; although the Battle of Britain had been won, it seemed only a matter of time before they would make their inevitable move. It was into this depressing and dangerous situation that *Victorious* made her maiden voyage as she slipped the last securing line on that morning in mid April 1941.

The ship commenced her sea trials on Wednesday 16th April with a maiden voyage from her birthplace and home on the Tyne round to Rosyth. She had commissioned for the first time at 1130 on 29th March on the Tyneside under the Command of Captain C.H. Bovell, RN, and after a last few hectic days of getting the ship cleaned up and learning their way around, the new ship's company were busily preparing to work up *Victorious* into an efficient fighting unit.

It was decided by the Admiralty that the ship's first task would be to sail to the Mediterranean with a consignment of Hurricanes for Malta. Continuous air attacks together with a surface and submarine blockade of the island were having a profound effect, making our position in the island and our presence in the Eastern Mediterranean virtually untenable. It soon became apparent that the relief of Malta was of paramount importance and that the situation could be eased by flying in additional aircraft. The only practical way to do this was by sending the aircraft in a ferry aircraft carrier and *Victorious* was therefore ordered to be ready to sail from the Clyde on the 22nd May, in company with the battle cruiser *Repulse* and troop convoy WS8B bound for Gibraltar.

Early in May 1941, a temporary squadron of 18 Fulmars was formed at Royal Naval Air Station Donibristle in Scotland. The task of this squadron was to provide fighter protection to those carriers engaged in ferrying aircraft to the Mediterranean and then to fly as escorts to the RAF aircraft flown ashore from the carriers. The Squadron was divided into three separate flights and allocated to the ferrying carriers as required: 800X consisted of nine Fulmars and was allocated to accompany *Furious*; 800Y was detailed to embark in *Argus* with three Fulmars; and 800Z was ordered to embark in *Victorious* with six aircraft, under the command of Lieutenant Commander J.A.D. Wroughton, RN.

After two weeks in No. 1 Dry Dock at Rosyth, the dock was flooded up and she carried out a tilt test before coming out on the 4th May, fuelling from a small tanker rejoicing in the name of *British Tommy* and preparing for her first assignment. As if to emphasize that there was a war on, Rosyth had an air raid that night and for two minutes her 4.5-inch guns joined with those of other ships and shore batteries, in a colourful though noisy 'firework display'. A hectic week followed in which she embarked more stores, ammunition, 800Z Flight Fulmars, an RAF maintenance party and last but not least – 48 crated Hurricanes for Malta. Finally all was ready and thankfully at 0530 on the morning of 15th May, she slipped her last line from B6 Berth and slid quietly out of harbour en route to Scapa Flow.

Before *Victorious* had finished her preparations, events were taking place on the other side of the Channel and were going to change all the Admiralty plans. The German Naval Staff were highly encouraged by the successful cruise of their surface raiders *Scharnhorst* and *Gneisenau* against British supply routes between January and March 1941. Between them, these two ships had successfully intercepted and sunk some 22 ships totalling 115,622 gross tons. The combined effect of the German submarine campaign and the surface raiders was having a disastrous effect on our supply routes and the war was going most profitably in their favour. The German Naval Staff met to plan further sorties by their surface raider groups and decided that the newly completed *Bismarck*, 'The Pride of the German Navy' as Hitler had called her during his visit in May 1941, together with the cruiser *Prinz Eugen* should re-inforce the powerful Brest Squadron, and join in this profitable and highly satisfactory trade war being waged in the North Atlantic.

Chapter II

THE BISMARCK CHASE

There is a narrow, navigable channel of water known as the Great Belt that lies between the Danish Islands. Fortunately for the British, two large German warships and six destroyers were sighted steaming out of the Belt into the Kattegat at 1500 on 20th May. Their course led them northwards, then west through the Skaggerak north of the Jutland Peninsula and finally, north once more to a quiet fiord near Bergen to refuel on 21st May. For the Germans it meant that Operation 'Rheinbung' or 'Rhine Exercise' had started, but for the Admiralty it meant trouble and for *Victorious* – the inevitable change of plans.

The German plan was simple; the two ships were to proceed via the Belt and North Sea out into the North Atlantic. There they were to intercept and attack Allied shipping when opportunity offered, replenishing stores and ammunition as required from either a port on the west coast of France or suitably positioned tankers and supply ships. They would be supplied with intelligence information on our convoys by an elaborate special reconnaissance link between the raiders, U-boats and cunningly disguised merchant ships. The Germans had already sailed the support forces of two scout ships, two supply ships, five tankers and six submarines. Operation 'Rheinbung' differed from the earlier operation of the *Scharnhorst* and *Gneisenau* in one important respect; they had been restricted to attacking unescorted merchant shipping only, whereas the *Bismarck* group was ordered to attack all shipping including protected convoys, unless a 15-inch battleship was present.

The fourth *Bismarck* was by far the biggest warship ever built in Germany. Laid down in the Blohm and Voss shipyard in

Hamburg in 1936, she was not launched until 14th February 1939. She was given out to be a battleship of 35,000 tons standard displacement – that is exclusive of fuel and reserve feed water for her boilers – but she was actually 50,900 tons fully loaded. This monster battleship was 791 feet long at the waterline, had a beam of 118 feet and a draught of 28 feet. Her impressive armament boasted eight 15-inch guns, twelve 5.9-inch guns and sixteen 4.1-inch anti-aircraft guns as well as a large number of small AA weapons. Together with the *Prinz Eugen,* this formidable pair of hunters would patrol our convoy routes looking for prey, and woe betide the unfortunate merchantmen or luckless escorts who crossed their path.

The sighting and intelligence information which reached Admiral Tovey on the 20th came as no surprise. Increased enemy reconnaissance flights in the Denmark Strait area had led him to station cruiser patrols in both the channels between Greenland and Iceland and Iceland and the Faeroes. At noon on the 20th he visited the *Victorious* and addressed the ship's company, telling them that the two enemy surface raiders had been reported heading for the North Sea and that he expected them to break out into the North Atlantic. If his assumptions were proved right, then he would need every ship to seek out and neutralise the enemy threat, and the new ship *Victorious* would be a vital addition to his force. In anticipation of early developments, the Hurricanes which could be flown off were landed ashore, the ship topped up with fuel and ammunition and 825 Squadron of nine Swordfish were ordered to embark. It was short notice and the aircrews had no opportunity to work up with the ship, but the Squadron under the command of Lieutenant Commander (A) E. Esmonde left Campbeltown, refuelled in the Orkneys and landed aboard *Victorious.*

The action really began on 21st May when an RAF reconnaissance Spitfire found itself high over Korsfiord, a short distance to the south of Bergen. Flying Officer M. Suckling the pilot of the aircraft photographed two large warships steaming in company and one of these ships turned out to be the *Bismarck.* One can imagine the impact of this particular photograph at the Admiralty. The big search was over, but the implications were only too obvious: firstly that the enemy was moving his surface raiders for yet another sortie against our shipping; and secondly that British forces had better do something about it. This then was the situation which faced the Commander-in-Chief Home Fleet, Admiral Sir John Tovey, flying his flag in the battleship *King George V* at Scapa Flow on 21st May. He prepared to 'do something about it'; the next few hours were packed with frantic activity and changes of plan as signals flashed back and forth between the Admiralty, Air Ministry, Commander-in-Chief Home Fleet, *Victorious* and *Repulse*. The Admiralty cancelled the sailing of the two ships with the WS convoy and put them at the disposal of Admiral Tovey, who ordered them to join his force. C-in-C knew that his quarry was in Korsfiord, but how long would they stay there and which way would they go? The stage was now set for one of the most dramatic and thrilling games of nautical chess in maritime history.

The RAF photograph confirmed that the *Bismarck* was at Korsfiord and later that day a force of Whitley and Hudson bombers was dispatched to try to deal with the threat, but in the awful weather conditions over the Norwegian coast, only two aircraft made it to Bergen and they could see nothing on a coast completely shrouded in fog. The next day the weather was even worse with heavy rain, cloud down to 200 feet and a visibility of about half a mile. It was under these conditions that Captain Fancourt, the Commanding Officer of the Royal Naval Air Station, Hatston in the Orkneys asked for volunteers and sent on his own initiative, a target-towing Maryland aircraft of 771 Squadron to try and sort things out. The Captain realised the importance of clarifying a confused situation and providing the Admiralty with the latest accurate position of the enemy force. Piloted by Lieutenant Noel Goddard, RN, under the most hazardous conditions, the Maryland set off for Norway.

The weather conditions were really terrible [Commander Geoffrey, or 'Hank', Rotherham said], with 'clag' right down to the surface of the sea. We had to keep coming down to check the wind speed for navigation and on one occasion, I saw the surface of the sea only 30 feet below the aircraft and the pilot hadn't seen it. Fortunately the weather cleared before we hit the Norwegian Coast.

The aircraft entered the Korsfiord, searched and found it empty, so the pilot then flew on to search Bergen Fiord and the aircraft's observer, Commander Geoffrey Rotherham, RN, was able to confirm beyond any doubt that the enemy had sailed. The enemy AA fire was very intense and though the aircraft wasn't hit, unfortunately the radio packed up. Telegraphist Air Gunner Milne got through on Hatston's private target-towing frequency, and the long awaited message was relayed to the Admiralty. At 2000 the news was passed to C-in-C and later that evening on the 22nd, after a telephone conversation between Commander Rotherham and the Chief of Staff to C-in-C to confirm the results of the search, the C-in-C sailed from Scapa with four cruisers, seven destroyers and his only available carrier *Victorious,* which was reckoned to be about thirty per cent efficient and carried the unworked up squadron of Esmonde's nine Swordfish.

Between Greenland and Iceland there is a dreary expanse of Arctic which is frozen and icebound for a considerable distance from the coast of Greenland. Known as the Denmark Strait, it is an inhospitable part of the world and is frequently shrouded in swirling banks of fog and mist. It was here on the evening of the 23rd May that the cruisers *Norfolk* and *Suffolk* first sighted and reported the enemy ships as they skirted around the edge of the ice pack. The news was received by the C-in-C in *King George V* with *Victorious*; it was received by an Atlantic covering force consisting of the battle cruisers *Hood, Prince of Wales* and six destroyers who were sailing from a position to the south of Iceland to intercept; and finally, it was received by Force H, consisting of the aircraft carrier *Ark Royal,* the battle cruiser *Renown* and the cruiser *Sheffield* who had left from Gibraltar thousands of miles to the south to assist.

The armada of ships was gathering in an attempt to close a net round the enemy and seal their fate, although it would be many hours before the ships would be in a position to pull the net tight. The two British cruisers shadowed their quarry at a respectful distance, nipping in and out of the many rain and sleet squalls which gave them a very necessary degree of protection. As the Arctic twilight gave way to the Northern day, the *Bismarck* could be seen some 12 miles away to the south making about 27 knots on a south-westerly course. At 0500 on the morning of the 24th while C-in-C and the *Victorious* group were still some 400 odd miles to the south-east, the two shadowing cruisers sighted the *Hood* and *Prince of Wales* who had steamed all through the night on a north-westerly course to intercept. An hour later the action was commenced as *Hood* opened fire on the enemy at a range of 25,000 yards. The enemy ships quickly replied and the *Bismarck's* second or third salvo – and possibly one also from the *Prinz Eugen* – hit the *Hood* and started a fire amidships near the port after 4-inch gun. This fire quickly spread until the whole of the midships section of the *Hood* seemed to be in flames, burning as one eye witness stated, 'with a pink glow and dense white smoke'.

Just as the British ships were being turned to enable the after turrets to join in the engagement, the *Hood* was hit again and rent in two by a huge explosion between the after funnel and the mainmast. The forepart began to sink immediately bows up, while the after section remained shrouded in an enormous pall of dense smoke. Three or four minutes later she had vanished completely beneath the waves leaving only one midshipman and two ratings to survive from a ship's company of 95 officers and 1,324 men and a vast cloud of smoke drifting downwind to leeward.

The enemy now turned his undivided attention on to the *Prince of Wales,* but she was no match for the combined firepower and accuracy of the two German ships and when she was hit by four 15-inch shells, and three from *Prinz Eugen's* 8-inch guns, it was decided to break off the engagement and retire under cover of a smoke screen. One 15-inch shell hit the bridge of the *Prince of Wales* and killed or wounded all the officers and men with the exception of the Captain and a signalman. It would seem from the later reports of the enemy survivors that the *Prince of Wales* had secured two hits on the *Bismarck* before withdrawing from the action. One of her shells had in fact penetrated the enemy's starboard side under water and had flooded three sections, causing her to lose valuable fuel oil and contaminating other fuel with sea water. Thus ended the brief – and for us tragic – engagement on the morning of 24th

May 1941, but it was not without some compensation, for a little later on in the day a shadowing Sunderland reported that the *Bismarck* was leaving a trail of oil in her wake and the two cruisers, still hanging on but keeping our of harm's way, reported that she appeared to be damaged and had reduced speed.

The first round had clearly gone to the enemy and the hunt was being closely watched by an anxious Admiralty. Every available warship totalling some nineteen major units had been thrown into the arena and it now remained to see whether the *Bismarck* could shake them off. Admiral Tovey was still some 330 miles away and loss of contact by the shadowers or evasion in the worsening weather were distinct possibilities unless the enemy's speed could be still further reduced. It was the possibility of escape which finally persuaded the C-in-C to call on the aircraft and aircrews of *Victorious* to help him in his task. At 1600 on the afternoon of the 24th he detached Rear Admiral A.T.B. Curteis commanding the Second Cruiser Squadron, with *Galatea, Aurora, Kenya* and *Hermione* to proceed with *Victorious* to a position within 100 miles of the enemy ships. From that position the carrier would be able to launch a strike of Swordfish torpedo-carrying aircraft and attempt the all-important task of sinking, or at least slowing down, the enemy raiders. That evening, according to the latest reports of the shadowing cruisers, Admiral Curteis found that he was within 120 miles of the *Bismarck* and decided that he could afford to wait no longer.

As the day had worn on and the *Victorious* had battled her way at 30 knots to the north-west, the weather which had been bad to start with had noticeably worsened. The flight deck of the carrier presented a most forbidding picture as it pitched up and down in the angry sea, whipped into a 32-foot swell by a howling wind from the north-west. Esmonde led his aircrew out on to the rain and spray covered decks to man their aircraft and, up above, the low scudding clouds raced past as the wind increased and the rain became more continuous. The nine Swordfish aircraft started up and prepared to take off and, slung under each belly, the aircraft carried an 18-inch torpedo set to go off on contact at 31 feet. As the cumbersome, heavily loaded aircraft gathered flying speed and trundled down the flight deck, the hopes of the Fleet went with them. Commander Ranald, RN, who was the Commander Flying of the ship looked at his watch, it was fourteen minutes past ten on a cold, windy and very miserable evening.

In the high latitude of the Denmark Strait, sunset was not until an hour after midnight, so it was still daylight when the aircraft took off to avenge the *Hood.* As soon as they were airborne the Swordfish disappeared into a rain squall and were lost to view, but without too much difficulty the Squadron formed up and, flying through broken stratus cloud at 1,500 feet, Esmonde set course of 225 degrees at a speed of 85 knots. Forty minutes after the launching of the strike three Fulmars of 800Z Flight were flown off for shadowing duties, to be relieved two hours later by another pair. The shadowing Fulmars were briefed to maintain contact at all costs so that if necessary another strike could be launched at dawn.

In the terrible weather conditions prevailing, a visual search for an enemy ship was like looking for a needle in a haystack, but the Swordfish of 825 Squadron were fitted with a new and very recent innovation – an airborne radar set of very limited range known as ASV, short for Air to Surface Vessel Radar. At 2327 it was this device which gained a contact some sixteen miles ahead of the formation and *Bismarck* was sighted briefly through a gap in the clouds; only to be lost again seconds later. The strike leader relocated the still shadowing cruisers and the *Norfolk* directed the aircraft towards their target some fourteen miles ahead on the starboard bow. It was ten minutes to midnight when the leader sighted a vessel below them, but it turned out to be the United States cutter *Modoc* lying stationary in the Atlantic swell. The *Bismarck,* who was then only six miles to the south, spotted the aircraft as it came down to look and, alerted to the impending attack, immediately opened up with a very heavy anti-aircraft barrage. This unfortunate mistake cost the attackers the vital element of surprise for as the Swordfish closed the reception by the enemy's short range armament was 'very vigorous and accurate'. In fact so accurate was the *Bismarck's* fire, that Lieutenant Commander Esmonde's Swordfish was hit at a range of four miles from the

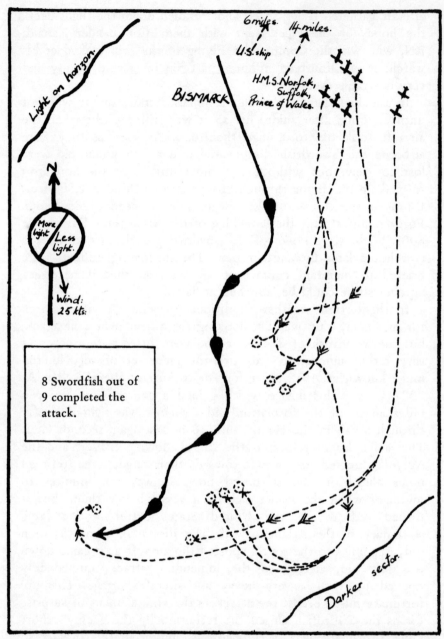

Torpedo attack on *Bismarck* by 825 Squadron from HMS *Victorious*, midnight 24/25th May, 1941, showing aircraft tracks and position of release.

enemy ships. One of the Swordfish lost contact in the dense cloud covering the ships, but the remaining eight aircraft pressed home their attack with dash and verve.

At exactly midnight Esmonde led the first sub-flight of three heavily laden and lumbering Swordfish into a simultaneous attack. His starboard lower aileron was hit and he abandoned his original intention to attack from starboard, deciding to drop there and then, whilst he was still in a good position on the target's port beam. The *Bismarck* was steaming at high speed in a heavy sea and nicely silhouetted against the glow of the setting sun. Three more Swordfish of the second sub-flight were led in by Lieutenant P.D. Gick and, not satisfied with his first approach, he worked his way round to a better position, coming in to attack low down on the water on the enemy's port bow a minute after his leader. One aircraft came in from the starboard bow, while the last one took the long way round to attack from the starboard quarter. As the aircraft turned away, the air-gunners sprayed the *Bismarck's* superstructure and gun positions with machine-gun fire at almost point-blank range. As one of the air-gunners remarked:

It didn't sink the *Bismarck,* but it certainly kept their heads down and in any case, it relieved our feelings.

Although 825 Squadron had had no opportunity to practise this form of co-ordinated attack, one torpedo hit was obtained amidships. Unfortunately it caused little damage to the heavily armoured *Bismarck,* which had been alerted to the attack and was manoeuvring violently and taking evasive action throughout the attack. Nevertheless, the hit was confirmed by a shadowing Fulmar, who reported a 'great, black column of dense smoke rising from the starboard side', and also that the battleship's speed was reduced.

A German account of the attack is summarised from an eye-witness report and states:

They came in flying low over the water, launched their torpedoes and zoomed away. Flak was pouring from every gun barrel but didn't seem to hit them. The first torpedo hissed past 150 yards in front of the *Bismarck's* bows. The second did the same, and the third. Helmsman Hansen was operating the pressbuttons of the steering gear as, time and time again, the *Bismarck* manoeuvred out of danger. She evaded a fifth and then a sixth, when yet another torpedo darted straight towards the ship. A few seconds later a tremendous shudder ran through the hull and a towering column of water rose at *Bismarck's* side. The nickel-chrome-steel armour plate of her ship's side survived the attack, but Bos'un Heiners was flung against a bulkhead and did not – he died of severe internal injuries and was the first of over 2,000 deaths aboard the 'Pride of the German Navy'.

With the attack over and his aircraft heading for home, Esmonde reported back to *Victorious*: 'Have attacked with torpedoes, only one observed.' Night was now falling and the weather worsened as the striking force returned to their ship. It must have been a worrying time for Commander Ranald, the Commander Flying in charge of the Air Department aboard *Victorious,* but it was far more worrying to the aircrews who had to make a night deck-landing on a violently pitching deck. The wave height was now 33 feet and, to add to their already considerable difficulties, the homing beacon in *Victorious* suddenly went unserviceable. Almost as if fate were playing a game with the airmen, the ship was temporarily hidden in a rain squall and the returning Swordfish missed the carrier. Captain Bovell realised that the position was becoming serious and although the aircraft would have to be homed by radar, he ordered the powerful signal projectors to be switched on shining vertically upwards – a useful visual aid to help the planes get back.

The sea state was causing the flight deck to rise and fall extremely violently and one can imagine the thoughts of a tired pilot as he made his approach at night onto a heaving, bucking deck. Add to this the not improbable damage to the aircraft from enemy action and the ingredients add up to an accident looking for somewhere to happen. This state of affairs frequently provided a somewhat macabre form of entertainment to the peculiar group of spectators known throughout the Fleet Air

The 14,900 ton battleship *Victorious* wearing the flag of the Second-in-Command, the Channel Fleet, 1904–1906; she was later re-named *Indus II*. She carried four 12-inch and twelve 6-inch guns, but she was a slow, coal-burner and was quickly out-dated.

The aircraft carrier *Victorious* starting her first journey to the sea at the Naval Yard, Walker-on-Tyne, 14th September 1939.

Lieutenant Commander (A) Eugene Esmonde, DSO, RN, the Commanding Officer of No. 825 Squadron of Swordfish in HMS *Victorious* for the *Bismarck* chase. Esmonde later lost his life on 12th February 1942 when his Squadron attacked the German battleships *Scharnhorst* and *Gneisenau*, escorted by the cruiser *Prinz Eugen*, as they made their famous channel dash. For this action he was awarded a posthumous VC.

Swordfish aircraft of Esmonde's 825 Squadron on *Victorious'* deck armed and waiting to take off to strike the German *Bismarck*. The aircraft are armed with torpedoes and in fact scored one hit.

Arm as 'Goofers': they are the people who crowd every available vantage point to witness the excitements of a land on, to see the spectacular results of a crash on deck. But always in their heart of hearts they are with the pilots, praying, hoping and willing them to make it safely down – with perhaps just one small mishap to add to the fun.

The situation on *Vic's* flight deck at 0200 that night was not a Goofer's benefit, it was far too cold and wet for even the most enthusiastic non-participant to turn out. One by one the aircraft circled the ship and awaited their turn to land on. When the second Swordfish landed on and taxied up the flight deck past the barriers and into the deck park for'ard, a large wave broke over the bows of the carrier and filled the cockpit with sea water. 'It was all right,' said the pilot later; 'the bottom of the fuselage had been shot away by the *Birsmarck's* gunfire, so it soon drained.' By 0200 all the aircraft of the striking force had returned safely and had landed on, a remarkable achievement by an unworked up ship and an untried air group.

Not so fortunate were the shadowing Fulmars of 800Z; aircraft that were neither designed nor equipped for the task they were called upon to perform. The two Fulmars which had taken off as relief shadowers at 0110 had had bad luck, for in spite of the utmost perseverance and great gallantry flying in very bad weather, they were unable to hold onto the enemy ships and had to be landed on with the returning strike force at 0200. The two Fulmars airborne with the strike at 2300 had not returned and were out of contact so *Victorious* kept her projector beams switched on until 0250. By this time it was very dark and reluctantly Admiral Curteis ordered them to be switched off. The ever present submarine menace made the continued use of the lights too hazardous and by now there was little hope for the overdue aircraft. Both the aircraft were lost, but fortunately one crew was rescued by the SS *Ravenshill,* a passing merchantman – after spending many chilly hours of meditation in the cold North Atlantic.

Just after the last aircraft had landed aboard *Victorious,* the shadowing cruisers lost contact with *Bismarck* and for the next thirty-six hours a vast network of airborne and surface ship searches attempted to relocate the elusive enemy ships. As

British forces combed the most likely routes open to the *Bismarck,* an official Admiralty communique told an anxiously waiting world the outcome of events so far:

> After the engagement yesterday in the North Atlantic, the enemy forces made every effort to shake off the pursuit. Later in the evening an attack by naval aircraft resulted in at least one torpedo hit on the enemy. Operations are still proceeding with the object of bringing the enemy forces to close action.

All through the 25th and 26th *Victorious* continued to fly off her Swordfish aircraft for anti-submarine patrols and air searches. Nothing was found, but at half past ten on the morning of the 26th Flying Officer D.A. Briggs sighted the *Bismarck.* He was flying a Catalina of 209 Squadron on the southernmost of the Bay patrols, when he was engaged by heavy and accurate fire from the enemy ship. His report put *Bismarck* 690 miles to the west-north-west of Brest and gave the pursuers less than 24 hours in which to intercept before she could reach friendly Luftwaffe protection and the sanctuary of port. Clearly Admiral Tovey would need to slow down his quarry with yet another air strike, and the only carrier within striking distance was *Ark Royal* coming up from the south. By 1115, *Ark Royal's* aircraft were shadowing the enemy and although *Victorious* played no part in the final chapter of this dramatic chase, the Fleet Air Arm was to provide the Commander-in-Chief with his long awaited opportunity to come to grips with the enemy.

Ark Royal came within range of the enemy at 1450 on 26th May and launched her first Swordfish strike. This was to provide a lesson that the Fleet Air Arm and the Royal Navy will never forget, for eleven torpedoes were released at a ship before the aircrew realised to their horror that their target was the cruiser *Sheffield.* Unfortunately Admiral Tovey failed to brief *Ark Royal* that the cruiser *Sheffield* was shadowing and the aircrews were told that only *Bismarck* was in the area. Appreciating that it was a case of mistaken identity and to the eternal credit of Captain Larcom in the *Sheffield,* he ordered his guns to remain silent and on no account to fire. Then, quite calmly, he rang for full speed ahead and successfully dodged the torpedoes.

Later that night at 1915 the *Ark* launched her second strike of fifteen Swordfish. Mostly they were the same aircraft, but this time the aircrew were determined to redeem themselves and there was no mistake. Two hits were obtained on the *Bismarck,* one on the armoured belt and the other right aft — it was this hit that was to seal her fate. The second torpedo destroyed her steering gear, badly damaged the propellers, jammed the rudders and made her virtually unsteerable. Although her main armament remained intact, she was reduced to steering an erratic course and was harried all night by the destroyers. At 0710 the next morning *Bismarck* made her last signal — '*Send U-boat to save War Diary.*' The end came for this mighty ship at 1040 on the 27th May as the heavy ships of the Home Fleet poured broadside after broadside into her at almost point-blank range, before forming up in line ahead and steaming away to the northward, with only just enough fuel to get them home. They left her with her upperworks reduced to a tangle of blazing wreckage and, below, a scene of almost unbelievable devastation. Hatches were jammed by concussion, pipes were twisted and bulkheads buckled and smashed — bodies and debris lay everywhere. Although a third strike of 21 Swordfish were over the smashed hulk of *Bismarck,* they were ordered to jettison their torpedoes and return. The coup de grace was given by a torpedo from the cruiser *Dorsetshire* and at twenty to eleven, with her flag still flying, she turned turtle, floated keel upwards for a moment and then slid gently beneath the waves — *Hood* was avenged!

Throughout the long chase some 71 torpedoes had been fired at the *Bismarck* and eight hits obtained, although it would seem from subsequent reports that they had little or no effect against the armour. *Rodney* fired two torpedoes in the latter stages of the action and became the first battleship to fire this type of weapon against another battleship. Although *Dorsetshire* was the last ship to engage the enemy with a torpedo hit on the port side, *Bismarck* was inevitably doomed. The crew had already opened the sea valves, exploded the scuttling charges and were abandoning ship.

Very heavy seas were running, but immediately the *Dorsetshire* and *Maori* commenced rescue work to try to pick up the helpless, stranded sailors from a bitterly cold water. The ships wallowed in a heavy swell and men were smashed against the ships' sides – many were too weak or injured to climb the ropes thrown to them or get up the scrambling nets. All the time the two rescue ships presented an easy target to any enemy submarine and then it happened: *U74* was sighted by *Dorsetshire* and the two British ships beat a hasty retreat with 110 survivors. The submarine had been ordered to assist *Bismarck* or at least save the War Diary, but bad weather had delayed her and then prevented her from attacking the British ships. As she cruised through the battle area of oil, debris and bodies she managed to rescue three more survivors – a final total of 113 saved out of a ship's complement of over 2,300 men.

Prinz Eugen had parted company from the ill-fated *Bismarck* after nightfall on the 24th, to proceed independently while the *Bismarck* attempted to make for Brest. She reached the safety of port on 1st June and there learned of the fate that had befallen her consort.

Meanwhile *Victorious* returned once more to the Clyde to load up for the second time with her consignment of Hurricanes for Malta; then she set sail on the first leg of her journey to Gibraltar. In company with *Norfolk* and *Neptune* she passed the boom astern of convoy W58X at midnight on 31st May, flying off air searches and A/S patrols en route. On the 4th June, a Swordfish of 825 Squadron sighted and stopped the German supply ship *Gonzenheim*. This luckless vessel was waiting to rendezvous with the *Bismarck* some 200 miles north of the Azores, but although *Neptune* was detached to assist the aircraft, the German gracefully submitted and scuttled herself in anticipation of her ultimate fate.

Ark Royal and Force H met *Victorious* on 9th June and two days later *Ark* was back in Gibraltar to embark 24 Hurricanes from *Vic*. On the 13th the two carriers with *Renown* and seven destroyers slipped out of La Linea Bay, turned left and headed towards a position to the south of the Balearic Islands. At the appointed time four twin-engined Hudsons duly arrived at the rendezvous from Gibraltar, with the task of escorting the 48

Hurricanes on the last stage of their journey to the besieged island of Malta. Between them, the two carriers managed to launch 47 Hurricanes, but in the event only 45 aircraft made it to Malta and two of those crashed on landing. One of the Hurricanes got into trouble, broke formation and was last seen heading for the coast of North Africa, while another fell into the sea en route.

Back in Gibraltar once more for a short six-hour spell, she embarked 11 German officers and 52 ratings as Prisoners of War — survivors from the ill-fated *Gonzenheim. Victorious* transferred 825 Squadron Swordfish to *Ark Royal* and then flew on *Ark's* 820 Squadron for the passage home. At 0925 on the morning of the 19th June she took her leave of *Ark Royal* for the last time and set course for the United Kingdom and Greenock. Within five months *Ark Royal* and all the aircraft from Esmonde's 825 Squadron would be lost off Gibraltar — victims of a successful torpedo attack by *U81*. For the present the 63 prisoners of war marching off to captivity marked the successful completion of her first operational sortie, and the final curtain on the *Bismarck*.

Chapter III

KIRKENES AND PETSAMO

June 22nd 1941 is a day that will live in the German history books as one never to be forgotten, for on that day the German High Command launched 'Operation Barbarossa' — the German invasion of Russia. It was an ironical and an ominous choice of date, for it was on this day exactly one hundred and twenty nine years earlier, that Napoleon had launched his ill-fated campaign against the Russians. That evening the Prime Minister broadcast the policy of His Majesty's Government: 'Any man or State who fights against Nazidom will have our aid.' It was not long before the Russians asked for assistance from the Allies and plans were put in hand immediately to provide practical help wherever and whenever possible. On the 6th July the C-in-C was informed by the Admiralty that 'everything possible was to be done to assist the Russians', who had asked specifically for naval assistance. They requested that British forces should attack enemy transports, which were reported to be in Kirkenes in North Norway and in the former Finnish port of Petsamo — both now in German hands. Between them, these two ports were of great importance to the Germans attacking Russia in the north, since Petsamo was the major channel of supplies to the Germans for all logistic support arriving in North Norway via Kirkenes.

To carry out an attack on Kirkenes and Petsamo, the force would have to sail many hundreds of miles to the north and through the frozen Arctic Ocean on the top of the world, where there is no darkness in summer and the sun shines at midnight — to the harsh, bleak wastelands where it snows on August Bank Holiday Monday — at least it did in 1941. They would be out of range of friendly shore-based air support, in an area where the enemy were known to have airfields close at hand and the opposition would be considerable. To challenge a powerful enemy on his own doorstep, and he equipped with fast Me Bf 109 and 110 fighters – and us with a couple of carriers and a handful of obsolete and slow naval aircraft was on the face of it – tempting providence!

Victorious and the aircraft carrier *Furious* were ordered to carry out this operation, but in spite of her recent blooding in the *Bismarck* action, *Victorious* was still not worked up and would require at least another fortnight's preparation. The Commander-in-Chief Home Fleet, Admiral Tovey, pointed out that he was not at all happy about this venture. He considered that a daylight attack on enemy ships in harbour, close to the enemy airfields where heavy fighter opposition could be expected, was not a proper employment for obsolete Swordfish and Albacore aircraft. Furthermore, to undertake operations some thirteen hundred miles from their base, in conditions of almost continuous daylight, would in his opinion involve very serious risks to the carriers, oilers and the aircrews. In any case, he considered that the risks were out of all proportion to the most optimistic estimates of the results they could achieve. His alternative proposal was, therefore, that they should concentrate their attacks against coastal shipping and shore targets on the Norwegian coast further to the south. This very sensible argument and forceful plea fell on deaf ears, for in a climate of heavy political pressure the Admiralty insisted on the operation and the sailing date for the two carriers was fixed for the 21st July.

Victorious operated off Scapa and embarked twelve Albacores of 827 Squadron under the command of Lieutenant Commander J.A. Stewart-Moore from Macrihanish on the 2nd July, Lieutenant L.A. Cubitt's nine Albacores of 828 Squadron from Hatston on the 3rd and, finally, twelve Fulmars of 809 Squadron from St Merryn under Lieutenant Commander V.C. Grenfell on the 12th. Both ship and aircrew trained hard for what they knew was going to be a tough operation and every other day the ship put to sea for intensive deck landing practice and weapon training. In particular, 827 and 828 Squadrons co-operated closely with each other, training in co-ordinated

attack procedures with both bombs and torpedoes. By the time
that the force was ready to sail, Commander Ranald was certain
that his squadrons had done all they could to prepare for the
operation — training time had run out and now success was in the lap
of the gods.

Force P consisting of the two carriers, the cruisers *Suffolk*
and *Devonshire* and six destroyers finally set sail from Scapa on
the 23rd July under the command of Rear Admiral W.F.
Wake-Walker flying his flag in the *Devonshire*. The passage to
the north east was uneventful except that on the 25th August,
Achates, one of the escorting destroyers went over the corner of
a British minefield off Iceland and her bows were seriously
damaged. The unfortunate ship lost 65 men and was eventually
towed into Seidisfiord by the destroyer *Anthony.*

In *Victorious,* the aircrew listened intently as the various
briefing officers outlined the details of the strike. 'Vic' aircraft
would strike at shipping at Kirkenes, while *Furious* would send
her aircraft to look for the enemy at Petsamo. If no transports
or shipping of any kind were found, then alternative targets
were to be the iron ore plant at Kirkenes and the oil storage
tanks at Petsamo.

The Force called at Seidisfiord in Iceland on the 25th July
where both cruisers launched their Walrus amphibian aircraft for
local anti-submarine patrols. An enemy U-boat had been
reported just outside the entrance to the fiord, but nothing was
sighted and on completion of fuelling at 2300 on the 26th, the
ships sailed again that night. On the run up to the launch area,
the aircrews received their final orders. 827 Squadron of
Albacores were to attack targets to the east and west of the
Tower of Kirkenes and up the Langfiord while 828 Squadron
Albacores were to concentrate on any targets found in
Holmengraafiord and to the east of Renoy Island. Both
squadrons would be escorted by the Fulmars of 809 Squadron
who were ordered to act entirely as defensive fighters and not to
attack targets themselves. After the attack all aircraft were to
return to the ship by the shortest possible route.

Victorious and *Furious* reached the flying off position about
80 miles to the north-east of Kirkenes at 1330 on the afternoon
of the 30th and the cloud cover which persisted until noon

dispersed and the weather cleared. The aircrews looked up at the sun now shining from a clear blue sky. They didn't say much, but each realised the increased odds as conditions turned against them. The flight deck looked crowded as the aircraft stood ready and ranged for the attack. Some had torpedoes slung underneath while others carried bombs, but on each warhead the propaganda boys and humorists had been busy. Chalked slogans relieved their feelings with such phrases as *'From all at Plymouth Hoe'* or the optimistic *'I hope you see the point of this'* to the more humorous *'As this is your meatless day, here's a fish.'* Fifteen minutes before launch time and just as the aircrew were manning their aircraft, there was a sudden shout of 'Hostile aircraft, Green 80.' A German Heinkel 111 reconnaissance aircraft appeared on the scene and for the second time in *Victorious'* short life, the vital factor of surprise was lost. All eyes turned to watch the escorts engage the enemy but he escaped. Now he would warn the Germans to expect an attack, and the odds were even more heavily stacked in favour of the enemy. Because of the political importance attached to the mission, it was considered too late to cancel the operation so, at 1400 precisely, both carriers flew off their air strikes.

Furious launched four Sea Hurricanes for fighter defence of the carrier force and nine strike aircraft followed by *Victorious,* who launched 20 strike aircraft and eighteen minutes later the 12 Fulmars to defend the strike. All the strike aircraft circled the carriers and formed up on the far side of *Furious* before heading for their respective targets. In the case of the Kirkenes contingent, the course to their target was straight into bright sunlight as 827 Squadron led the force towards the Norwegian coast keeping between 100 and 200 feet above the sea. The glaring sun made it extremely difficult for the escorting Fulmars to locate the bombers as well as giving the initiative to any enemy fighters as far as light was concerned. The Fulmars climbed to get a better view and this action may have given the enemy the opportunity to make a radar detection. In the event, this mistake didn't really affect the issue, because, as expected, the enemy shadower had reported his sighting and the enemy were ready and waiting.

At Ribachi Light the force climbed to 3,000 feet and swung

towards their targets; within seconds of reaching the coast, the Fulmars were engaged by very heavy flak near the approaches to Kirkenes. In an effort to deceive the German defences, our aircraft had been instructed to fire four red Verey lights, the German recognition signal of the day, but according to the records of Kommandant der Seeverteidigung, the Commanding Officer of the German Seaward Defences, his gunners noticed that the red was of a distinctly darker shade and they were never in any doubt as to the identity of the attackers. On the other hand, the Commanding Officer of *Victorious* mentions that 'on three occasions enemy aircraft approaching to attack broke off the engagement when this signal was fired' and that 'one German aircraft even replied by pyrotechnic signal.'

A lethal curtain of anti-aircraft fire met the attackers as they approached the target, twisting and turning to avoid being hit. Once over the target area the protecting Fulmars orbited at 4,000 feet, with the idea of drawing off the flak from the striking Albacores. Suddenly and without any warning the anti-aircraft fire ceased, there was a short pause and then the German fighters appeared. The enemy employed mainly a mixed bag of Ju 87 and Me Bf 110 types of aircraft and the ensuing battle took place in excellent weather with exceedingly fine visibility. During intermittent combats two Me Bf 110s and one Me Bf 109 were shot down for certain, one by the CO of 809 Squadron and the other by Sub Lieutenant (A) J. Cooper and Sub-Lieutenant (A) A.E. Wilkinson, RNVR, for the loss of two Fulmars — one of which had force-landed. In another combat between a Fulmar and an Me 110 the rear-gunner Leading Airman Ford beat off the German's quarter attack with his personal Thompsons hand-held machine gun, a weapon supplied to these aircraft more to support the aircrew morale than for lethal use in aerial combat.

In the meantime, the Albacores were seeking suitable ship targets in the fiords adjoining Kirkenes. The gunnery training ship *Bremse* and two small merchant ships of about 2,000 tons were attacked with torpedoes and the latter two were hit and observed to be on fire. As soon as the attack was over the strike aircraft headed for the coast and home, but on the way they were jumped by enemy fighters which suprisingly included Ju

87 Stuka dive bombers. The Stuka was reported to be armed with extra machine guns and possibly canon as well, which made it an extremely formidable adversary for the Albacore and Swordfish. From German records, it is now known that they did not carry cannons, but had just returned or been recalled from operations over the Russian lines and had not even refuelled before wading into our aircraft. This may account for their reluctance to follow our battered squadrons out to sea on their return to the carriers, and much less to attack the carriers themselves. A lucky escape for both aircraft and ships!

Some extraordinary escapes from destruction at the hands of German aircraft were recorded by our aircrews, perhaps the most noteworthy being that of Albacore 4K piloted by Lieutenant J.N. Ball with Lieutenant B.J. Prendergast as his Observer. This aircraft was on its way home and flying right down on the water when it was jumped by a Stuka. The enemy made about 30 passes and attacking runs at 4K, but with skilful conning of the pilot by the observer the avoiding action was successful and the enemy failed to secure a hit or shoot him down. Impatient at not getting any results from his runs from astern and the quarter, the Stuka pilot decided to try something different, so with his dive brakes and flaps selected down to reduce his speed, he took up a position ahead and slightly above his quarry. This invitation to disaster could not go unanswered and, seizing his chance, Lieutenant Ball pulled up the nose of his aircraft and let fly with his one front gun. Eighty-seven rounds were enough to break up the Stuka which plunged into the sea and ended an exciting few minutes of combat. This was certainly the first and probably the only time that an enemy aircraft fell to the front gun of an Albacore. When Lieutenant Ball landed back on board *Victorious,* not a single bullet hole or scratch was found on his aircraft and it was the only aeroplane to return undamaged from this otherwise disastrous sortie.

The CO of 827 Squadron in his report on the Kirkenes attack says of Albacore 4K's fine effort:

This is a classic example of cool thinking and complete co-operation between pilot and observer ... The enemy were undoubtedly waiting for us in force; the fact that Ju

87s were employed as fighters against the TSRs while their faster aircraft held off our small fighter escort shows that they had a fair idea of what was coming. They seem to have put every available aircraft into the air.

To turn now to the *Furious* striking force which attacked the Petsamo area: on arrival there they found it practically empty of enemy shipping and their weapons practically useless – they had to expend torpedoes on easily repairable wooden jetties. But some of the aircraft carried bombs and found these more useful, for they were able to bomb their secondary objectives, namely the shipyard and oil storage tanks. Minor damage to the former and at least one oil tank hit were claimed, in addition to two small craft partially destroyed. Fighter opposition over the Petsamo area was on a smaller scale than at Kirkenes and consisted mainly of Me Bf 109s. In consequence, our casualties were less severe and only one Fulmar and one Albacore were shot down. One other Fulmar aircraft force-landed just before reaching the target, but the crew of Sub Lieutenant (A) E.S. Burke and Leading Airman J. Beardsley climbed into their dinghies and 48 hours later, after some minor excitements, they managed to reach Russian held territory safely.

The German Luftwaffe records issued on 31st July 1941 contain one or two items of interest and are worth mentioning. They state that a total of four Me Bf 110s, nine Me Bf 109s and nine Ju 87 aircraft were used against our forces that day. Of these they admitted one Me Bf 110 and one Ju 87 shot down, but claimed a total of 27 of our aircraft destroyed. Two small merchant ships had been torpedoed, but again the German report admits only one small ship in ballast sunk and a pier slightly damaged. Of their failure to attack our carriers the German report explains tersely: 'The British warships could not be found again later owing to fog', and concludes that the BBC was unusually frank in admitting the loss of 16 British aircraft.

In the certain knowledge that all chance of surprise had gone and that they would have to face heavy opposition, the gallantry of all the attacking aircrews was in the highest traditions of the Fleet Air Arm. But for *Victorious,* still feeling her way as a very new and inexperienced carrier, the price had been high. Her squadrons had been decimated by the loss of 11 Albacores and 2 Fulmars and Admiral Tovey had been proved right. Five officers and four ratings had been killed in the operation, whilst 20 officers and 7 ratings were posted as prisoners of war. As the result of this action four officers were awarded the Distinguished Service Cross, one Petty Officer gained the Distinguished Service Medal and one officer and one air gunner were mentioned in dispatches.

One by one the survivors returned to their parent carriers and the two ships recovered aircraft. In *Victorious,* the land on was watched with great concern for only one of the nine surviving Albacores was undamaged. At 1845 the last aircraft touched down, caught a wire and came to a safe stop, and the carriers withdrew to the south to lick their wounds. As they were making for Scapa Flow and home the next day, a Dornier 18 flying-boat was detected shadowing the force. Two of 880 Squadrons 'A' Flight Sea Hurricanes from *Furious* piloted by Lieutenant Commander Judd and Sub Lieutenant Howarth shot the enemy down – the first victim to fall to the guns of a Sea Hurricane. This minor success was the last incident and closed the curtain on what can only be described as a disastrous debacle.

Rear Admiral Wake-Walker summed up the failures of this operation, by concluding that the operation was carried out in a hurry with neither the *Victorious* nor *Furious* really ready for it. Furthermore, there was a need for far better intelligence than was available in this operation. When there was no information and the small amount of enemy shipping was strung out between Narvik and Kirkenes, the simile of looking for a needle in a haystack was apposite. 'Nevertheless,' he stated, 'I trust the encouragement to the morale of our Allies was proportionately great.'

Chapter IV

NORTH RUSSIAN CONVOY DUTY

A disaster like Kirkenes and Petsamo affects everyone in a close knit community and the wounds take time to heal. To *Victorious,* so newly commissioned, the loss of half her air squadrons was a bitter blow and much hard work would be needed to offset the adverse effect on morale. Fortunately her reputation as a happy ship and the leadership of Captain Bovell stood her in good stead, for with minor interruptions such as 'Pedestal' − the famous Malta Convoy, and 'Torch' − the North African landings, *Victorious* was destined to stay with the Home Fleet until the end of 1942. The barren, dreary and windswept Scapa Flow would be her base and 'run ashore' for the ship's company, while the cold, inhospitable seas off the Norwegian coast became the familiar and dangerous area for her operations in defence of the convoys to Northern Russia.

At the outset, the Germans seem to have underestimated the importance of these convoys for no interference was attempted except by a few submarines and destroyers, and an under-strength Luftwaffe based on Bardufoss and Banak in Northern Norway. Nevertheless, Admiral Tovey and the Home Fleet, already committed to containing and neutralising the German surface raider threat, had the added problem of providing convoy defence. The solution to yet another extra commitment was simple and effective. Admiral Tovey formed a Distant Cover Group of capital ships and escorts, whose job was to contain enemy surface raiders, provide additional cover to the convoys on the scheduled routes and, when the situation allowed, carry out independent strikes with his force against enemy strategic or other targets along the coast of Norway.

Victorious was the only carrier in the Home Fleet, or

anywhere else for that matter, available for duties in the distant covering force and accordingly she was made a founder member. Almost as if to give this election the official stamp of approval, the Ceremonial Guard and Band were paraded for Divisions and His Majesty King George VI visited the ship for an hour on the afternoon of the 9th August. This was indeed a great honour much appreciated by the whole ship, but with the visit over and the first convoy sailing sometime towards the end of August there was no time to lose. The first priority was to replace the decimated 827 and 828 Squadrons and on 14th August, she embarked 12 Albacores of 832 Squadron from Campbeltown under the command of Lieutenant Commander A.J.P. Plugge, followed the next day by 9 Albacores of 817 Squadron under Lieutenant Commander D. Sanderson from Hatston.

Under the operation code name of 'Dervish' the first convoy of six British tramp steamers and one Soviet vessel left Reykjavik on 21st August and started on its way for Archangel. Combined with 'Dervish' was an operation code-named 'Strength', in which 48 Hurricanes were to be carried for delivery to the Russians. Twenty-four of the aircraft were partly assembled and carried in the old aircraft carrier *Argus,* while the remaining 24 Hurricanes were crated and carried in the merchant ships of the convoy.

To cover and protect both operations, Force M under Rear Admiral Wake-Walker and consisting of *Victorious,* the cruisers *Devonshire, Suffolk* and three destroyers left Scapa two days later. They met up with the convoy on the 26th to the west of Bear Island, fuelled the escorts from an oiler in the convoy and then detached it to wait in Bell Sound, Spitzbergen, while the merchant ships and escorts proceeded north of Bear Island to Archangel. On the 30th, Rear Admiral Wake-Walker and the escorts parted company from the convoy off the entrance to the White Sea and returned to meet the *Argus,* which, escorted by *Shropshire* and three more destroyers had left Scapa the same day. No enemy reconnaissance aircraft or submarines had been encountered up to this time and so the Admiral felt that it would be safe for the convoy to continue the short journey to its destination without the protection of the covering force. In fact, the convoy with its vital war materials and stores reached its destination of Archangel without incident.

As the covering force had two days now in hand before meeting *Argus,* the Admiral decided to carry out an air attack with *Victorious'* aircraft on shipping in the Leads to the north of Tromso. Intelligence indicated that convoys were now leaving the port for Kirkenes every three days and there might be some good pickings, so the force re-fuelled from the oiler which had been left waiting at Spitzbergen and in high hopes, set sail for their destination early on 2nd September.

Just after midnight on the 3rd, two air striking forces were flown off *Victorious.*[1] The aircrews were briefed to attack shipping and the oil storage tanks at Hammerfest', but received explicit instructions not to attack unless there was cloud cover. There was a large number of Ju 88 aircraft stationed at Banak and in any case the Command and surviving aircrews in *Victorious* had not yet recovered from the Kirkenes mauling a month before. Although ' this sortie was conducted exactly as briefed, in the event it was a complete waste of time and effort. Without cloud cover it would have been suicidal to attack in the face of modern and superior enemy air opposition, and another object lesson was learnt which re-emphasised the limitations of our old, outdated and outclassed naval aeroplanes. 817 Squadron which was the more northerly of the two striking squadrons sighted a small convoy in Svaerholthavet, but as the sky had cleared near the coast and they had been challenged when still fifteen miles from land, they wisely about-turned and headed back to *Victorious* without attacking. The other striking force of 832 Squadron found nothing and also returned. One Albacore force-landed in the sea though, happily, the crew were picked up wet, cold and a bit fed up, but otherwise unharmed!

We had achieved precisely nothing except to tell the enemy that we were in the area and, prompted into activity, he obliged by shadowing the force throughout the 3rd and 4th September. Many interceptions were attempted by the Fulmar fighters

[1] Six Albacores of 817 Squadron armed with torpedoes and six Albacores of 832 Squadron each carrying six 250-lb Semi Armour Piercing and eight 40-lb General Purpose bombs.

Top: the mighty *Bismarck*—described by Hitler as 'the Pride of the German Navy'.

Right: Scapa Flow, 2nd July 1941: the Commanding Officer of 827 Squadron, Lieutenant Commander J. A. Stewart-Moore, makes the first land-on in his Albacore prior to the ill-fated Kirkenes and Petsamo raid.

Bottom: the *Tirpitz*—sister-ship of the *Bismarck*—which was attacked by aircraft from *Victorious* on operation 'Tungsten', 3rd April 1944.

Tirpitz and *Friedrich Ihn* sighted from an Albacore of 817 Squadron just before the attack.

North Russian Convoy Duty in the Arctic 1942: Albacore 4B of 817 Squadron makes an overshoot with his hook and flaps down, while the starboard crane moves another Albacore casualty from the starboard catwalk. A third Albacore can be seen joining the landing circuit top right.

during the two days, but only one was successful and a Dornier 18 flying-boat was splashed at 0930 on the 3rd. In nearly every other case, the superior speed of the enemy aircraft enabled them to keep out of harm's way and still shadow — much to the disgust and frustration of the Fulmar pilots. To add injury to insult and even the score, a Fulmar crashed into the sea during the afternoon sortie on the 3rd, but again the crew were recovered unharmed.

Next day the Admiral met *Argus* and her escorts and, still shadowed by German aircraft, the combined force set course to the north of Hope Island where they hoped to meet fog. Fortunately they did and at long last were able to shake off the persistent shadowers, but it must have been embarrassing to require nature's aid to protect a force of two carriers, both carrying and able to operate defensive fighters. *Argus* had in fact embarked two Martlet 111s of 802 Squadron for her own defence, but these were transferred to *Victorious* on the 6th. One must conclude that the Germans were unimpressed with the pinprick raids by our carrier aircraft at this time and were content to regard them merely as a passing nuisance and keep an eye on them. On the other hand, however, we now know that over half of the operational strength of the Luftwaffe was concentrated in Russia during the initial stages of their attack, and thus they had very few aircraft to spare; in fact the next six Arctic convoys sailed unmolested from either surface, air or submarine attack.

To return to Force M: in the early morning of the 7th September a short interval of good weather enabled *Argus* to reassemble the 24 Hurricanes and fly them off unobserved. The flying-off position was about 100 miles from the nearest friendly territory and 200 miles from the destination of Vaenga, but from 0520 in the morning the Hurricanes took off in four waves of six aircraft each and all landed safely. As *Argus* and her escort headed via Seidisfiord to Scapa, where they arrived on the 14th, *Victorious* and Force M set course via Spitzbergen once more for the Bodo area. This time, she was to have a little better luck and by and large things went according to plan. The carrier reached the flying off position about 40 miles west of the Lofoten Islands just after midnight on the 12th and launched her strike.[1] No. 817 Squadron aircraft hit and sank a ship of about 2,000 tons in Vestfiord, and then managed to sink another small vessel and damage a quay in their attack. German sources confirmed the losses and admitted the sinking of the Norwegian coastal passenger steamer *Baro,* with 160 German and Norwegian casualties. 832 Squadron had been ordered to go for the power station and aluminium works at Glomfiord and carried out a reasonably good attack. They managed to start fires in the aluminium works as well as destroy a D/F station on Rost Island; as before, there was no air opposition and all the aircraft returned to *Victorious* and landed on safely.

The Admiral intended to withdraw his force to the westward and then run in again for a second attack, but German reaction forced a change of plan when at 0930 the next morning an He 111 appeared on the scene and commenced to shadow. After a hectic 50-mile chase by Martlets at full throttle it was successfully shot down by the two aircraft which had been transferred from *Argus.* Piloted by Lieutenant J.W. Sleigh and Sub Lieutenant H.E. Williams, these two young officers took great satisfaction in chalking up their first joint kill. Although the shadowing success of the Heinkel was short-lived, obviously he had remained in the air long enough to report details of his find for, shortly afterwards, a replacement in the form of two Blohm and Voss flying-boats appeared on the horizon to keep watch and report. Though attacked repeatedly by sections of Fulmars, they evaded all attempts to shoot them down and finally the British aircraft ran out of ammunition. The constant shadowing coupled with our inability to shoot them down prevented any possibility of the force making a second attack that night, so *Victorious* headed back for Scapa and arrived there on the 13th, after steaming over 8,000 miles on this one operation.

Nearly a month passed before the next operation and, yet again, *Victorious* was ordered back to her happy hunting ground to attack enemy shipping ·on the coastal route between

[1] Seven Albacores of 817 Squadron armed with torpedoes and five Albacores of 832 Squadron each carrying six 250-lb Semi Armour Piercing and eight 40-lb General Purpose bombs.

Glomfiord and Vestfiord in the vicinity of Bodo. *Victorious* joined the battleship *King George V*, the cruiser *Penelope* and the 11th and 12th Destroyer Divisions outside Seidisfiord, reaching the flying off position to the west of the Lofoten Islands at dawn on the 9th. This time weather damaged five out of thirteen aircraft on deck and drove five more back to the ship before they could attack their targets, but the three remaining stalwarts hit a ship of about 1,500 tons and returned without loss.

During the forenoon there was a repeat performance in better weather and just ten miles north of Bodo; eight Albacores armed with bombs found a small convoy of two 5,000-ton merchant ships escorted by a couple of flak ships. In a combination of low level and low dive-bombing attacks, 817 Squadron scored a hit on one of the merchantmen and a probable on the other, while 832 Squadron aircraft hit and damaged the Norwegian SS *Haakon Adelstein* of 1,500 tons and had the satisfaction of seeing the crew take to the boats. During the whole of the day's flying there was little opposition and no enemy aircraft appeared – a fact which the Admiral considered 'encouraging'. With the anti-shipping strikes successfully completed, *Victorious* and her escorts headed for Scapa once more where she arrived on the 10th October 1941, to complete the last of her North Russian convoy outings for the year.

The Admiral wanted to mount more air strikes against German shipping on the Norwegian coast, but with the surface raider threat looming large again in the form of *Tirpitz,* all such plans were shelved and the carrier was held in readiness. From November until the end of the year, she patrolled and exercised with units of the Home Fleet, watching and waiting for the powerful German ships to make a move. They spent much of their time in the waters between Iceland and Scapa where the weather was usually atrocious and gales were commonplace at that time of year. Operating aircraft in the high winds and enormous seas necessitated steaming at slow speed into wind and sea, but deck movement was considerable and caused aircraft to overturn on landing, crash in the catwalks or go over the side. The mounting number of deck-landing accidents was a serious matter, but even the ship itself was not immune and suffered two lots of weather damage. On the second occasion the damage to her bow plates was so bad that she had to disembark the air group while she undertook a week's self refit in Scapa.

Notwithstanding aircraft deck accidents, squadrons were having a large number of casualties from engine failures and, like the aircrew, the Admiral was becoming very concerned about it. When Albacore 3R ditched on the 17th November the situation had got so bad that the makers sent an engine expert and test pilot to sort things out. A quiz soon revealed that few of the pilots aboard knew the correct method of starting, warming or running up their Bristol-Taurus engines in cold weather, but that was a failing that was soon put right by the company representatives to the satisfaction of all concerned.

From this brief account of her operational life from the *Bismarck* chase in May to the end of 1941, the reader will appreciate some of the problems that faced this very new carrier. *Victorious* had been thrown in at the deep end and the first few months of her first commission proved a hard, testing time for both the ship and her squadrons. For most of the period she was steaming in northern waters, defending the convoys to Russia in atrocious weather conditions, carrying out the occasional strikes against a variety of coastal targets and enemy shipping; operations for which she had to put in a lot of effort, gained few rewards and suffered disproportionate aircraft losses.

Suddenly and dramatically the war was to change and the focus of attention to shift for on 7th December 1941, away from Europe on the other side of the world, the peace was shattered when the Japanese made a treacherous and devastating attack on United States warships, aircraft and installations at Pearl Harbour, the American naval base in the Hawaiian Islands in the Pacific Ocean. The attack by midget submarines and carrier-borne aircraft took place before the Japanese declaration of war, and while the Japanese envoys in Washington were still negotiating with the American Government. On this 'Day of Infamy' as it was later called by President Roosevelt of the United States, about 360 fighters and bombers from the six Japanese carriers took the defenders by surprise. In one crippling blow they sank the US battleships *Arizona* and *Oklahoma*, severely damaged six others and also sank or damaged three cruisers, four destroyers and several auxiliary vessels. Apart from much damage to airfields and port installations 2,403 Americans were killed 1,178 were wounded and 347 aircraft on the station destroyed, while the total Japanese casualties amounted to twenty-nine aircraft, one I-Class submarine and five midget submarines. This attack brought the United States into the Second World War, prevented any immediate linking of the US and British Far Eastern naval forces and, more important, gave Japan complete air and sea supremacy in the Pacific.

The bombs that fell on Pearl Harbour signalled the start of simultaneous Japanese attacks which ranged from Hawaii to Thailand, from Hong Kong to Singapore. Inspired by success, the Imperial Japanese Army rolled south with seemingly uninterrupted progress and by the beginning of March, Java, Rangoon and Singapore had fallen to the military might of the Rising Sun, while farther eastward they had landed in New Guinea with an implied threat to Australia. Nearer home the situation was equally disturbing, for having virtually taken over control from the Italians in North Africa, the Germans were advancing through Cyrenaica and looked as though they might well take Egypt and the whole of the Middle East.

By the spring of 1942 the situation in Arctic waters had changed greatly to our disadvantage. The arrival of new enemy surface raiders, cruisers and destroyers placed an added strain on our already slender resources. Even more disastrous, Allied shipping losses for the first quarter of 1942 were the highest of the war and remained at about the same figure of over 450 ships for the quarter following. The United States were slowly recovering from the stunning blow dealt them at Pearl Harbour, but we had lost the *Ark Royal, Barham, Prince of Wales* and *Repulse,* with *Valiant* and *Queen Elizabeth* badly damaged by a new war weapon – the limpet mine. In summary, then, the prospects in early 1942 were gloomy for the Allies and the war situation the world over was fast becoming critical.

The Russian success against the Germans on land was the only encouraging feature to brighten a picture of otherwise unrelieved gloom. Reminiscent of 1812, the severe winter and the skill of the Russians in using it to their advantage was causing heavy losses to the enemy, but to maintain this success, Allied supplies to Russia had to continue without serious interruption. The enemy on his side had at last woken up to this fact and was determined to stop the traffic with all means at his disposal. The opposition and danger increased and meant that each convoy would now have to be fought through all the way. With the battleship *Tirpitz* at Trondheim in January, followed by the pocket battleship *Admiral Scheer* and heavy cruiser *Prinz Eugen* in February — ostensibly to repel any attempted attack on Norway — it was also evident that, contrary to our earlier practice of patrolling, we should have to give heavier support to future convoys — at least in the opening days of their passage.

Within a week of *Tirpitz* arriving in the Trondheim area British counter action was taken. A Bomber Command force of nine Halifax and seven Stirling aircraft based on Lossiemouth attempted to carry out an attack on her on 30th January, but severe icing conditions in the 10/10ths cloud prevented any of these aircraft finding the target. Although other attacks were repeated on 31st March, 28th April and 29th April, with the last two under good moonlight conditions, none was successful in damaging *Tirpitz*. Moored close under the cliffs in Foetten Fiord and with elaborate camouflage arrangements, effective anti-aircraft defences and the means of producing an effective smoke screen, she provided a difficult target and thirteen bombers were lost in these operations. The mere presence of *Tirpitz* on our flank had a considerable influence on Allied naval strategy for, without steaming a mile, she was keeping a completely disproportionate number of our heavy ships in Atlantic or Arctic waters; to us, the necessity of destroying or crippling her became paramount.

As we have seen, the bad weather seriously affected *Victorious* during the winter of 1941-42, but with the prospects of an improvement in conditions and lengthening hours of daylight, her aircraft began to play an ever increasing part in the defence of the Russian Convoys. On the 19th February *Victorious* in company with Admiral Tovey in the battleship *King George V, Berwick* and seven destroyers left Scapa. This was scheduled to be the last independent sortie for *Victorious* and her aircraft and once again shipping in the Tromso area was to be the target for her strikes. However, two days out en route for Hvalfiord in Iceland, the C-in-C received an important signal. A Coastal Command aircraft had reported that the German heavy ships *Admiral Scheer* and *Prinz Eugen* were steaming north in company off Jutland, presumably with Trondheim as their most likely destination. On receipt of this news the Tromso project was forgotten and the fleet immediately altered course south and increased speed.

The two surface raiders, *Admiral Scheer* and *Prinz Eugen,* realising that they had been reported by the reconnaissance aircraft turned back. After some hesitation they finally decided to anchor in Grimstadtfiord, south of Bergen, with both ships entering the Leads at Skudesnes at dawn on the 22nd. The C-in-C heard the news and was heading back towards Iceland when he received another Admiralty signal which informed him that the German ships were expected to continue their passage northward after night-fall, so he about-turned his force once more, detached *Victorious, Berwick* and four destroyers at 27 knots, while the battleship and the remaining three destroyers followed in support at a more leisurely and fuel conserving pace. *Victorious* was ordered to proceed to a flying-off position about 100 miles off Stadtlandet and launch her torpedo-carrying aircraft to sweep down the Norwegian coast, then both forces were to rendezvous subsequently north-west of the Shetlands the following morning. To provide as it were a long-stop and increase the chances of success, four submarines were disposed off the entrance to Trondheim.

The barometer was falling slowly and before *Victorious* reached the flying-off point she passed through a front, but her meteorological officer was optimistic and forecast much better weather on the Norwegian coast. A rising wind, sleet and an exceptionally heavy snow shower with visibility of only 200 yards delayed the take-off. The Commanding Officer remarked in his report, 'that the long period between ranging the aircraft was due to the difficulty of getting signals through and turning the force back into the wind in the prevailing conditions of visibility.' All was now ready and *Victorious* turned into wind, reduced her speed to 12 knots in the face of a 31-foot wave height and waited for the snow to stop falling.

It was bitterly cold and miserable and, as one officer re-marked, 'Hardly flying weather because even the seagulls were walking', but the severe snow squall passed eventually and an hour after midnight, Lieutenant Commander A.J.P. Plugge and his ten Albacores of 832 Squadron were flown off. Armed with torpedoes and meteorological promises of better things to come, they set off in formation keeping low on the water. Only one of the aircraft was fitted with the new ASV radar with which they hoped to gain contact on the enemy, so this set was vital to their chances of success and the height at which they flew was also important. Having made a landfall on the west coast of Stadtlandet, they were to carry out a sweep and search to the southward, keeping ten miles out and parallel to the coastline and flying as far as their aircraft's endurance would allow. Because they would have insufficient fuel to enable them to return to the carrier, all aircraft were briefed to cross the North Sea on completion of the sweep and land at the RAF base at Sumburgh in the Shetlands. They were ordered to remain in formation, but if any aircraft became separated it was to carry out the sweep independently. In fact this is exactly what happened to Albacore 4C. Sub Lieutenant (A) K.D. Landles was the last aircraft to take off from the carrier and flew straight into a heavy snowstorm and when he got clear of it, the rest of the formation had vanished. Together with his observer Sub Lieutenant D.J.R. Harvey and air gunner Leading Airman Thomas Armstrong, he circled *Victorious* and took departure to carry out the operation alone. After a most difficult and dangerous flight in the most appalling weather conditions, Albacore 4C landed safely at Sumburgh some four and a half hours later. Led by Lieutenant Commander D. Sanderson, a second range of seven torpedo-carrying Albacores of 817 Squadron left the deck at 0145 with orders similar to those of 832 Squadron, except that their sweep to the southward was to be 20-30 miles out from the coast and they had two radar fitted aircraft in the formation.

As the formation approached the coast, the weatherman's optimistic forecast hit the all-time low. The weather conditions were so bad that even on the surface, three of the five destroyers escorting the *Admiral Scheer* and *Prinz Eugen* lost contact during the night. At about 0200 the radar-fitted aircraft in the first formation obtained three echoes at a range of eight miles and some eighteen miles off the coast. The formation altered course to pass over them, but owing to the bad visibility nothing was sighted. As the Admiral remarked later:

It is now known that the radar echoes were certain to have come from the *Admiral Scheer* and *Prinz Eugen* or their screen. It is unfortunate that the ships were concealed in one of the snow storms reported by the senior surviving officer of this Squadron, instead of being in the fine weather between.

Some 20 miles west of Utvoer Light the aircraft reached the limit of their endurance and set course across the North Sea for home, though by now the visibility had closed right down and the wind had increased in strength. To the slow Albacores this was a serious problem as it reduced their ground speed; to lighten the aircraft and conserve precious fuel some of them jettisoned their torpedoes. Aircraft were icing up and nearly all became separated in the appalling weather. Hands and feet were frozen and the pilots struggled to keep their machines in the air and in sight of each other. Then disaster struck: a large orange flash lit up the sky as two of the aircraft collided; then some thirty miles from home the Squadron Commander's plane dropped a flare close to the water and was not seen again. It was thought that Lieutenant Commander Plugge may have been dropping a marker to find the strength of the wind and crashed into the sea. At any rate the Navy lost a first class squadron commanding officer and an excellent observer, and of the seventeen Albacores that left *Victorious,* only fourteen landed in the Shetlands between quarter to five and six o'clock that morning. Three had been lost on the fruitless mission and, of the lucky ones, some had only twenty gallons of petrol left in their tanks when they landed — just about enough petrol to taxi their aircraft.

The only offensive action taken during the sweep was by one aircraft of 817 Squadron, who on emerging from a cloud at 200 feet close to Sando Light dropped his torpedo on a possible

E-boat without apparent result. The German ships did not have it all their own way, however, for the carefully laid trap in the form of the submarine barrier paid off. Almost simultaneously with the last Albacore landing at Sumburgh, the submarine *Trident* hit *Prinz Eugen* with a torpedo which tore away her stern and rudder. She managed to limp into Trondheim Fiord for examination and temporary repairs before returning to Kiel some ten weeks later for a refit that was to last nine months.

Reporting on this operation, the Captain of *Victorious* complained with some justification of the poor weather forecasting, and the lack of up-to-date reports for the Norwegian coast supplied in the Fleet Synoptic Messages. This lack of accurate reports is even more surprising, since RAF aircraft were over the Norwegian coast for several days immediately prior to the operation.

> Had I known the conditions over the coast, [Captin Bovell added] I would never have flown off the striking force. Long odds must be taken in war and losses accepted, but I submit that the Service cannot afford to squander its slender capital of trained Fleet Air Arm personnel, when information is available that there is no chance of success.

This very forceful complaint produced the desired results but even so many future operations planned by the Home Fleet in Northern waters had to be cancelled, for even the improved standard of weather reporting with RAF help could not always anticipate nor predict the treacherous, changeable Arctic weather.

The other major criticism raised by the Captain was on the question of enemy intelligence information:

> One of the chief lessons in this war has been that if an air attack is not to be a costly 'blow in the air', recent and accurate reconnaissance is essential. In no operation (except that which resulted in the sinking of the *Bismarck*) do I feel that I have received the quantity, or quality of information necessary to success.

Having read the account of his first year in commission and

learned of the operations and experience of the carrier's air
squadrons, it is difficult not to sympathise with his *cri de coeur*.
A post-war examination reveals that this lack of up-to-date
intelligence from air reconnaissance was the main reason for the
comparative ineffectiveness of her air strikes in relation to the
tremendous scale of effort required to back them up. Of course,
it could be argued that surprise might well be prejudiced by
prior reconnaissance, but if the enemy isn't there, then the
element of surprise hardly matters!

Few people can appreciate the sheer hell and misery of those
convoy trips in winter. Although they enjoyed the protection of
the long dark nights, the sailors had to contend with constant
storms, freezing temperatures, the ever present danger of pack
ice in the Arctic circle and, if sunk, survival was a matter of
minutes in the freezing seas.

The voyage was usually one of some 2,500 miles. At the
height of summer it was almost constant daylight apart from an
hour or two of dusk, but in the depth of winter the situation
reversed — with conditions of constant night broken only by an
hour or two's grey daylight. But these extreme conditions are
arrived at through weeks of change. A ship's captain put it thus:

> From February onwards it is lighting up quickly. At the
> end of January there are four hours' daylight; end of
> February eight hours' daylight; end of April 20 hours'; and
> July and August virtually 24 hours' daylight, with sun all
> the time, which works along the horizon. From April to
> August there's no really bad weather; conditions are ideal
> for enemy day attack. Winter starts in September, and from
> October to the end of December there's a lot of fog and
> heavy snowstorms but not much wind. From the end of
> December you may get gales of hurricane strength which
> can last five days, but between gales the weather may be
> flat.

Icing can vary a good deal. A captain who returned from
Archangel in the winter of 1941 said it took him 16 days to
move 70 miles, and that every night his men were able to leave
the ship and walk across the ice to neighbouring ships. They
turned the propeller every ten minutes to keep it free from ice.

On the other hand, a Master describing a later voyage to Russia said that his ship got very little ice on her, though the naval escorts looked like sugar boats, as though they had sailed off a cake.

Aboard *Victorious,* temperatures on the flight deck registered from 20-45 degrees of frost and everything became encrusted with ice, tons and tons of ice. As one officer recalled:

> Even inside the ship, scuttles could be frozen solid and ice on interior bulkheads sparkle like a ballroom – put your bare hand on the metal surface of a gun or aircraft and it stuck there and if you pulled it free then you pulled the skin off.

By the early spring, the PQ and QP convoy cycle had been established and they continued to run at roughly three week intervals to the end of June 1942, between Hvalfiord or Reykjavik in Iceland to Archangel or Murmansk in North Russia. Indeed up to March 1942, of the 158 ships in 12 eastward and 8 westward bound convoys sailing to and from North Russia, only one merchant ship, SS *Waziristan,* and one escorting destroyer, HMS *Matabele,* were lost – both by enemy submarine attack. At the outset, the Germans were confident that the Russian campaign would be a repetition of their earlier successful Polish invasion in 1939, but after a hard winter and a few reverses even the Nazi optimists re-appraised the situation. The sea-borne supplies were the vital lifeline by which the Russians could survive and strike back; and so inevitably, German forces started to take a more aggressive interest in the PQ convoys.

The sailing of PQ12 from Reykjavik on 1st March and QP8 from Murmansk for the United Kingdom on the same day, marked the end of the phoney war and the beginning of a new and bitter phase, in which the German High Command organised a bigger air, surface and U-boat offensive to sever the supply link to Russia. Thus the spring of 1942 opened for *Victorious* as part of Admiral Tovey's re-inforced escort, which sailed from Scapa on 4th March to protect convoy PQ12, a convoy of 15 merchant ships and one oiler which had sailed from Iceland three days earlier. The covering force consisted of the battleships *King George V, Duke of York, Renown, Victorious, Berwick* and nine destroyers, while ocean escort for the convoy itself consisted of *Kenya* (carrying two Walrus), and two destroyers. Five days later, on 6th March, the covering force was cruising about 50 miles to the southward of the convoy, which had been located and shadowed for some hours the day before by an enemy aircraft. That evening a report was received from the submarine *Seawolf* that *Tirpitz*, or a heavy cruiser, had sailed to the northward from Trondheim, but that the exact identity was doubtful owing to the bad light and the distance at which the sighting took place.

To give warning of the movement of any heavy German units from their bases in Norway, Coastal Command flew special 'prowl' patrols in the vicinity of Trondheim, during the period when the Russian convoys were in the western half of their passage and vulnerable to surface attack. Unfortunately, during the first six months of 1942, Coastal Command's aircraft strength was at a very low ebb and on many days the sorties had to be cancelled due to unserviceability and lack of aircraft. Thus it was that the Coastal Command patrols scheduled for the afternoon of the 6th did not take place, and it was not until the evening of the 7th, that a Photographic Reconnaissance flight established that *Tirpitz* and three destroyers had in fact left Trondheim. For the next few days the weather was very variable with snow storms, sea smoke[1] and gales, as *Tirpitz* sought to intercept the two convoys PQ12 and QP8 and the Home Fleet looked for *Tirpitz*. It was the nautical equivalent of blind man's buff for at noon on the 7th, unknown to Admiral Tovey, the convoy PQ12 to Russia and a returning convoy QP8 from Russia passed literally through one another in a snowstorm. They were about 200 miles south-west of Bear Island and unknown to everyone, *Tirpitz* was then only 70 miles away.

That evening at 1720 *Kenya* catapulted her Walrus aircraft to search out to 45 miles south-west of the convoy PQ12 but to no avail. In fact, the Walrus only just missed seeing *Tirpitz* who was then about 60 miles to the west of the convoy and steaming in

[1] Sea Smoke — a very dense low lying fog usually 20 to 50 feet in height caused by very cold air blowing over warmer water and causing evaporation. Found particularly off coast of Northern Norway and at the edge of the pack ice off Greenland.

a southerly direction. Earlier that day, Admiral Tovey had intended to send an air search from *Victorious* out 120 miles to the south of the two convoys, but in the words of his report:

> By great misfortune – for this search would almost cert-ainly have located the *Tirpitz* – severe icing conditions were experienced and no air reconnaissance was possible all day.

In *Tirpitz,* Admiral Ciliax had no idea that the Home Fleet was at sea and like Admiral Tovey – two minds with but a single thought – he also intended to fly an air search, but again the weather caused both his and the German land-based recon-naissance flights to be cancelled.

About the same time that *Kenya's* Walrus was searching to the south-westward, the *Friedrich Ihn,* one of *Tirpitz's* screening destroyers sighted and sank a straggler from the returning westbound convoy QP8. The unfortunate Russian Merchantman *Ijora* did manage to signal an accurate position and that she was being 'gunned by a man-of-war', so naturally Admiral Tovey thought the attacker could well be *Tirpitz* and sent his destroyers off in pursuit. Subsequent bearings confirmed that a German unit was moving south from· the luckless *Ijora's* last position.

We now know that the vital convoy PQ12 and *Tirpitz* were manoeuvring within 120 miles of each other during most of the next day 8th March and, in spite of aerial reconnaissance by a FW 200 aircraft and our own searching, neither side knew the whereabouts of the other. At about 2030 that evening, thinking that he had missed the convoys or that they had turned back, Admiral Ciliax in *Tirpitz* decided finally to return to base and set course for the Norwegian coast. After some delay, inform-ation from the Admiralty made it clear that *Tirpitz* was now steering southward for home, and the Admiral realised that the only way to catch the enemy raider was with *Vic's* aircraft. He decided to launch an air strike at dawn, but prior to the strike he would dispatch six of his Albacore aircraft on diverging courses out to a depth of 150 miles. With luck, these aircraft would find the enemy raider and guide the following strike aircraft onto their target.

Meanwhile swift Admiralty reaction ordered four cruisers and every available destroyer into positions south and east of Jan Mayen Island in the hope of intercepting *Tirpitz*. Coastal Command moved nine Beaufort Torpedo Bombers with four Beaufighter escorts to Sumburgh (Shetlands), with seven more Beauforts at Wick and eight at Leuchars (Fife). Bomber Command also had six Halifax and six Lancaster bombers ready at Lossiemouth to attack the *Tirpitz*. In addition to all these offensive preparations Coastal Command instituted two special patrols to intercept *Tirpitz's* estimated track to Trondheim. In the event none of these aircraft affected matters, but they bear excellent testimony to the nuisance value of this one enemy ship.

On the morning of the 9th March, in weather conditions of low cloud and icing down to sea level, *Victorious* flew off six Albacores to search for *Tirpitz*. Fifty minutes later Lieutenant Commander W.J. Lucas took off with a striking force of 12 torpedo-carrying Albacores from 817 and 832 Squadrons, together with a signal from C-in-C which read: '*A wonderful chance which may achieve most valuable results. God be with you.*' At 0800 Albacore callsign Duty F flown by Sub Lieutenant (A) W.H.G. Brown, RNVR, identified a suspicious vessel as the *Tirpitz* in a position which put her about 80 miles away from the fleet. He was quickly joined by another Albacore and two minutes later the Observer of Duty F, Sub Lieutenant (A) T.T. Miller gave the news that everyone had been waiting for in the Fleet, that *Tirpitz* and one destroyer were steaming south at high speed.

At 0815 the *Tirpitz* sighted the two shadowing Albacores who were shortly joined by a third, catapulted her own Arado seaplane and headed for the safety of the Norwegian fiords at 29 knots. Slowly the strike aircraft closed the gap and at about twenty minutes to nine the strike leader sighted his target 20 miles to the south-east. The Albacores altered course towards the target and clambered up to 3,500 through the clouds, gaining firm radar contact on *Tirpitz* and her escorting destroyer *Friedrich Ihn* at 16 miles. The intention was to remain in the safety of the cloud cover and to bring the formation unseen to a position ahead of the raider before diving to attack, but at ten

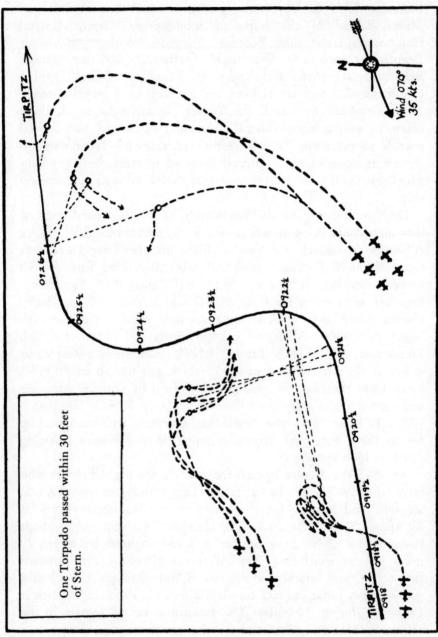

One Torpedo passed within 30 feet of Stern.

Torpedo attack on *Tirpitz* by 12 Albacores of 817 and 832 Squadron, 9th March, 1942.

minutes to nine, for some unexplained reason but probably to reduce the risks of prolonged cloud flying, the strike leader instructed the sub-flights to act independently. Looking back now, it is obvious that he was having more than his fair share of problems, for the wind speed had increased to about 35 knots at 3,500 feet and this in turn reduced the rate of closing on the *Tirpitz* to about 30 knots. To add further complication, there was a severe risk of icing if the formation remained in cloud for more than about 30 minutes. After what must have seemed an eternity, *Tirpitz* was seen below through a break in the cloud and because she failed to open fire, the Strike Commander assumed she had been surprised and went into the attack – a tempting but disastrous mistake.

At nine-twenty he gave the order 'Dive to attack' and the aircraft swept in. Unfortunately they were almost on top of their target instead of being ahead and upwind, thus they forfeited the advantage of high relative speed on the final run in. It is perhaps also unfortunate that the Squadron CO had just taken over command, had not flown with the Squadron before and had little or no practice in torpedo attacks since 1937. The dreadfully slow approach into wind meant that by the time the second and following sub-flights had reached the water, *Tirpitz* had had time to take effective avoiding action and was engaging the aircraft with heavy, and fairly accurate anti-aircraft fire.

The slow closing rate of the Albacores to the *Tirpitz* was to reveal another miscalculation, for evidence provided by one torpedo-aiming camera showed that this aircraft was at double the range intended by the pilot when he dropped his torpedo, and also that it was released outside possible hitting range. Later evidence from German records after the war, however, seems to show that this underestimation of the enemy battleship's range may not have been so general. Extracts from *Tirpitz's* log mention that the attack was pressed home with dash and determination, with aircraft dropping their torpedoes at from 400 to 1,200 yards range and that one torpedo actually passed within ten yards of her stern. Furthermore, after dropping their torpedoes, some of the aircraft attacked the ship's bridge with guns! Two Albacores were shot down; they were probably hit by short-range AA fire, presumably inside torpedo dropping range, but be that as it may, no hits were obtained on the enemy and, as the aircraft withdrew, she was last seen making smoke and proceeding at high speed for the Norwegian coast. Leutnant zur See Karl Theodor Raeder was the Gunnery Officer in *Tirpitz* in 1942, and was watching from 'Dora' (aft) 38 cm gun turret as the Albacores came in. He remembers the bravery of the British crews, who pressed home their attack through a volcano of fire. *Tirpitz* had some 88 guns in action, of between 20 mm and 150 mm calibres.

> Just after the attack finished we passed an Albacore which had crashed in the water, and I remember seeing one of the airmen sitting helpless on the top wing. In that ice-cold water there could be no doubt that in a few minutes he would be dead. But we had just survived one attack, another might be in the offing, and there could be no question of stopping the battleship to pick up an enemy airman.

Since all aircraft torpedoes were set for impact at 25 feet and assuming the absence of a lucky hit on shafting, propellors or rudder as in the case of *Bismarck*, a hit might have reduced her speed and just allowed our surface forces to reach her before she obtained the shelter of the Norwegian fiords, which at the time of the attack were only about 60 miles distant. Again we had demonstrated that without considerable luck, the chance of success is indeed remote using inexperienced aircrew and 12 obsolete aircraft; by comparison, over fifty torpedo and bomber aircraft were used by the Japanese against *Repulse* and *Prince of Wales* four months earlier. The failure of the attack on *Tirpitz* was a great disappointment to the aircrews of *Victorious*, but they were not to know that their attack could claim one important success; on Hitler's orders, no German heavy ship was to put to sea if carrier-based aircraft were in the vicinity.

Very shortly after turning for home, the fleet was shadowed by a Blohm and Voss 137 and a section of three Fulmars was flown off. After several attacks from beam, quarter and astern it was driven off with an engine apparently on fire, but German records make no mention of its failure to return to base. Other enemy aircraft continued to shadow however, and in the late afternoon three Ju 88s were sighted. Two of the watchers were kept at arm's length by fighters and gunfire, but the third managed to drop some bombs fairly near *Victorious,* although she escaped without damage.

After the abortive attack, the Commanding Officer of *Victorious* summed up the general feeling:

> The gravity of the failure to take full advantage of this opportunity which may never recur, and its far-reaching implications are fully realised. No one is more disappointed than the crews of the aircraft who took part in the attack; it was the chance they had dreamed of and prayed for.

Another opportunity for a carrier-borne air torpedo attack on *Tirpitz* never did occur, but the narrowness of her escape on this occasion had a profound effect on the enemy. The *Tirpitz* episode impressed on the Germans the need for an aircraft carrier of their own. Hitler gave orders for the immediate completion of the *Graf Zeppelin* and the construction of the requisite carrier aircraft, but these could not be ready before the autumn of 1944 owing to labour shortages. As a further reinforcement, however, Hitler ordered that the cruiser *Seydlitz* and the liner *Potsdam* should be converted into auxiliary carriers.

Victorious continued to accompany the Home Fleet as a member of the heavy covering force, and in the last week of March while covering the passage of PQ13, she ran into a force 9 gale with an estimated wave height of 65 feet. The sea buckled her bow plating and forward bulkheads and caused so much weather damage that she had to have yet another short refit in Rosyth. During this particular trip, a nasty accident occurred that would be repeated on occasions in other carriers: an anti-submarine patrol aircraft crashed over the side during take-off and the depth charges exploded as the aircraft sank. Although very little damage was done to the ship, the unfortunate aircrew didn't stand a chance.

With the weather damage repaired, *Victorious* left Rosyth on the 7th April 1942 for covering operations on the next four convoys both to and from Russia, PQ14 to PQ17 eastward and

PQ10 to PQ13 westward. The pair to run in March 1942 were savagely attacked and their story is well known, for the U-boat arm and air forces in northern Norway were heavily strengthened, three more destroyers were sent to Kirkenes and, together with the heavy surface raiders at Trondheim, the re-inforcements showed that the enemy meant business. Before sailing with the Home Fleet to cover the convoy designated PQ16, *Victorious* was at sea to assist the damaged cruiser *Trinidad* en route from Murmansk. HMS *Trinidad* had been torpedoed in PQ13, but had managed to limp into Murmansk for temporary patching up. On her return trip to the UK, she was heavily damaged again by a bomb which hit her between 'B' turret and the bridge, causing her to be abandoned and sunk by a British torpedo.

Nearly a month was to elapse between the arrival of PQ16 and the sailing of the tragic PQ17, so *Victorious* was available to carry out important Admiralty trials of the new Seafire. This aeroplane was a very different cup of tea to anything that the Fleet Air Arm had had before, and came into naval service as the direct result of two factors: one, the skilful handling of RAF pilots and, two, the persistence of one high ranking naval officer – Admiral Lumley Lyster. The majority view currently held was that high-performance single-seat fighters couldn't be operated from the deck because their speed was too high. Yet in the final stages of the ill starred Norwegian campaign, fourteen out of sixteen RAF Hurricanes had managed to land on board the carrier *Glorious* – without arrester hooks! Where an RAF Hurricane could lead, a Naval Spitfire could follow argued Admiral Lyster. The Seafire story was a far from happy one and re-emphasised the point that, however good or successful a land plane turns out to be, naval aircraft must be designed as such from the start: the role is very different and compromise will end inevitably in failure. The Seafire suffered from a very spindly and weak undercarriage, which under deck-landing conditions created very serious problems. The chronically short endurance meant that it had to be used almost exclusively in the role of Fleet protection and finally, the long nose provided a poor view for the pilot for his landing and necessitated a new curved approach. Even so the Seafire was far from easy to deck-land and her debut with the Fleet was not a happy one. Although they had an easy blooding covering the Allied landings in North Africa, records show that for every plane lost or damaged in the air, over twenty aircraft were lost or damaged on the deck – an unhappy record that was to be maintained during the latter stages of the British Pacific Fleet operations against Japan.

To return to the Arctic convoys: after the completion of the trials, *Victorious* went back to her old task and in spite of the unfavourable time of year from the point of view of long daylight hours and better flying weather, Convoys PQ16 and QP12 got away on time in the third week in May. The usual heavy covering force of old faithfuls was at hand and, for the first time, all merchant ships flew balloons to afford some protection against air attack. For their part, the Russians had promised to stage a big air strike on German airfields in northern Norway with two hundred Army bombers during the convoy's passage. The Russian aircraft available for normal everyday assistance to the PQ and QP convoys were of the order of eight torpedo bomber aircraft and thirty to forty Hurricane and Tomahawk fighters. Obviously this was going to be a special effort on their part, but predictably there was the usual hitch in the drill and the Russians failed to keep to their side of the bargain. As the Commander-in-Chief reported, 'this undertaking went the way of all Russian promises, the offensive being limited to one attack by twenty aircraft after the main series of German air attacks on the convoy had been completed.' PQ16 was attacked by large formations of enemy aircraft and lost seven freighters and had several more badly damaged.

PQ17 sailed from Iceland on 27th June 1942 with a close escort of four cruisers, three destroyers and a distant cover of *Victorious*, *Duke of York*, USS *Washington*, two cruisers and fourteen destroyers. *Victorious* embarked additional fighters in the form of 885 Squadron Sea Hurricanes and, hoisting the flag of Vice Admiral Sir Bruce Fraser, Second in Command Home Fleet, she sailed from Scapa on 29th June 1942. This convoy was well protected, but the disaster that followed led to a complete revision of the convoy system and a change in our tactics.

As soon as German intelligence learned of the departure of PQ17, they massed their forces. A formidable concentration of enemy ships including *Tirpitz*, the *Admiral Hipper*, two pocket-battleships — *Lutzow* and *Admiral Scheer* — and twelve destroyers met at North Cape, the northernmost point of Norway, to be ready to strike at the convoy as it went by. They were to attack the convoy only if enemy aircraft carriers were eliminated and were under strict orders that no unnecessary risks were to be taken. As the hours went by, an extraordinary sequence of events occurred which was to have the most tragic consequences. On 4th July, the Admiralty received a report that a Russian submarine had sighted the German ships heading for the convoy. This report which turned out to be completely false, coupled with reports that the German air force had been shadowing the convoy since it left port, led the Admiralty to withdraw the escorts and to scatter the convoy. The German fleet sailed on the afternoon of the 5th July, but was recalled because the convoy had scattered to make for Russian Ports individually.

German aircraft and submarines capitalised on the British action and twenty-two of the thirty-three merchantmen were sunk. The slaughter went on for five days and the equipment of an army went down: 210 aircraft, 430 tanks, 3,350 vehicles and just under 10,000 tons of other war material for a German cost of five aircraft. The direct result was that the Murmansk run was stopped for two months, because the vital aircraft carrier support was needed elsewhere. *Victorious* would take part in a grim life or death struggle for the survival of Malta.

Chapter V

MALTA CONVOY

In the Mediterranean, Rommel was hammering on the gates of Cairo and by the beginning of June 1942 Malta's supply position was very, very precarious. For some time past, only submarines and fast minelayers had been able to beat the enemy surface and air blockade, but the quantities that they could carry were small and were limited to essential supplies. The 'double convoy' run from both ends of the Mediterranean simultaneously at the beginning of the second week of June had got into trouble. Under the code name of 'Harpoon', the plan was to run five freighters and one tanker from Gibraltar and, at the same time, to send in no less than eleven freighters from Alexandria as Operation 'Vigorous'.

The east-bound convoy was harrassed by all forms of enemy air attack, but was given the heaviest possible protection, with the carrier *Eagle* and a few Fulmar fighters in the ferry carrier *Argus*. The two carriers withdrew at the Sicilian Narrows or 'Bomb Alley' as it was called, and up to that time only one merchant ship and one destroyer had been sunk. The convoy continued on its way through the Narrows under cover of darkness, but the next day the Axis threw the full weight of their air effort into the battle, and in spite of the fact that the convoy was within range of the Malta-based fighters, three more merchant ships went down — all sunk by air attack.

The passage of the west-bound convoy from Alexandria ended in a dismal failure. Subjected as it was to continuous air attack, lacking the protection of an aircraft carrier and faced with an inevitable clash with the Italian Fleet, the convoy had to turn back. It was a difficult decision, but with only light cruisers, no air cover and only a third of the AA ammunition remaining, the losses in proceeding would have been calamitous. As it was, the enemy had sunk two merchant ships and two destroyers before the convoy turned back and, of the seventeen ships which had started out to relieve the Island of Malta, only two reached their destination.

On the island itself the position was now critical, for only 15,000 tons of cargo had arrived with the two ships from 'Harpoon' and the people were on starvation rations. The enemy air forces were pounding the island daily and the defences were feeling the strain. To counteract the enemy air bombardment only 80 aircraft were now left out of the 275 fighters delivered since March and as they were being written-off at the rate of seventeen per week, the arrival of another convoy was essential to the survival of Malta.

With the whole of Cyrenaica in Axis hands, the experience of 'Vigorous' showed that it was not possible to run a convoy through to Malta from the east; any relief would have to come from the western end of the Mediterranean. We had to assemble a force strong enough to oppose the Italian battlefleet and the combined Axis air forces, and then fight the convoy through. At the same time, the air forces at Malta had to be strongly re-inforced from the United Kingdom and Egypt. The whole operation was given the code-name of 'Pedestal'.

To provide the necessary support, we had to withdraw the Home Fleet from their Russian convoy duties and every available warship was assembled for this operation. No fewer than three carriers were provided for the escort of this vital convoy, *Victorious* flying the flag of Rear Admiral Lyster, *Indomitable* and the veteran carrier *Eagle*. In the ferry role was *Furious*, with 38 Spitfires as well as her half-dozen Sea Hurricanes. In addition, the escort consisted of a formidable array of ships, with no less than two battleships, seven cruisers and twenty destroyers, all to escort the fourteen fast merchantmen comprising the convoy. In the small hours of the 10th August 1942, the convoy and its large fleet escort passed through the Straits of Gibraltar and headed eastward. The passage of this impressive armada through the Straits was known immediately to the Italian High Command and, appreciating its importance, they lost no time in implementing the necessary countermeasures. No

less than five ambushes had been planned by air, submarine and
surface forces, intent upon destroying every ship and thus
preventing the vital relief.

All the carriers had embarked extra fighters for this operation,
with *Vic* disembarking six Albacores of 832 Squadron, to make
room for six Fulmars of 884 and six Sea Hurricanes of 885
Squadrons. This brought her complement of fighters to twenty-
four, which included the 'resident' 809 Squadron of Fulmars. So
crowded was the ship for this operation, that the Sea Hurricanes
had to be stowed as permanent deck-park. To add to the
complications, they had non-folding wings and so were placed
on outriggers over the starboard side. This allowed for easier
aircraft operation as well as enabling the ship to carry the
necessary extra aircraft. The force carried a total of some
seventy fighters to combat the huge fleet of over 600 German
and Italian aircraft, assembled and waiting to meet them on the
airfields of Sardinia and Sicily.

Thick fog which had formed overnight cleared at dawn, and
day one passed quietly enough. There was a hot sun in a clear
blue sky as the ships threaded their way slowly eastward. In the
three carriers, ·the fighters were ranged in readiness on the
flight-decks, while deck and aircrews stood around watching and
waiting expectantly. The aircrews of the anti-submarine
Albacores had a new task during the early stages of the voyage,
they had been detailed off to man the ship's guns, causing the
fighter pilots to beg the more enthusiastic of these amateurs to
confine their attentions only to hostile aircraft.

Thirteen of the merchant ships carried a mixed cargo of flour,
ammunition. and petrol stored in five gallon drums, while the
last ship, the large tanker *Ohio,* carried 11,500 tons of fuel. By
the next morning, this convoy had come within range of enemy
reconnaissance aircraft and, inevitably, they started to focus
their unwelcome eyes on the movements of the force. A fighter
patrol was flown off at first light and a standing patrol of four
was kept airborne over the convoy all day. Halfway through the
morning at ten minutes past ten the first of the shadowers was
detected. Aircraft were scrambled and fighters from the carrier
Indomitable drove it off shakily losing height with one of its
two engines on fire. *Victorious* lost one of her Fulmars in the

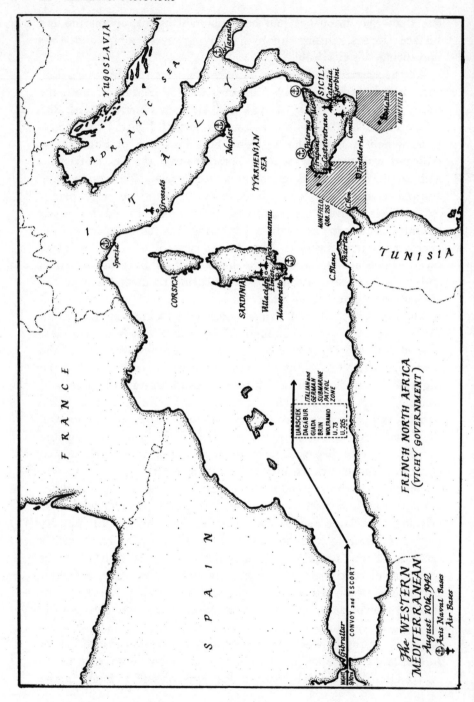

The WESTERN MEDITERRANEAN
August 10th, 1942
⊕ Axis Naval Bases
⊕ " Air Bases

sea but the crew were rescued by the escort *Wishart*. To the watchers on deck, this was the first indication that the convoy had been sighted; as the morning wore on, several more shadowers appeared. Carriers follow the sound naval custom of telling the ship's company below decks what is happening and from time to time, the loudspeakers in *Victorious* would sound: 'D'ye hear there, a small group of aircraft, presumed hostile is approaching the convoy from the north-east. Our fighters have been sent to intercept.' As yet there had been no air attack, but at sea, there are dangers other than from the air. Unknown to anyone but the enemy, the convoy and escort were already threading their way through the first of the five ambushes awaiting them – nine submarines spread out across the convoy route north of Algiers.

U73 was a 750-ton, type VIIB U-boat operating out of La Spezia and had heard the approach of the surface ships. To clarify the situation the U-boat commander came up to get a visual look, and the periscope cut a fine white feather of spray as the German submarine closed in for his attack. Kapitan Leutnant Helmut Rosenbaum saw that he was admirably placed to fire at the merchantmen, but his attention was focused on far bigger game. Through the powerful lens of his periscope he could see an aircraft carrier at the rear of the starboard outer column. Providing that a zig-zag by the force didn't rob him of his chance, the carrier would pass right into his sights at a range of about 500 metres. He was delighted to find that he was also well inside the screen of protecting destroyers, so he wouldn't have to worry about them for a while. He identified his target as the carrier *Eagle*, and he decided to take the gamble and wait. His luck held. At quarter past one he fired a spread of four torpedoes at a point blank range of 500 metres, went very deep and made good his escape. Sub Lieutenant Chancey Parker was in the landing circuit in Fulmar DR 724 and turning cross-wind to land on *Victorious* at the time. 'I looked over the side', he recalls, 'and saw three or four torpedo tracks very close together and heading straight for *Eagle*, so I shouted to my telegraphist Leading Airman Ford to broadcast a warning, but they probably hit as the message was received.' *Eagle* was in a starboard turn astern of *Victorious* at the time and continued on. The torpedoes hit her amidships and she took on even bigger list as she started to sink. Within eight minutes, she had gone.

One minute after *U73* fired his four torpedoes a series of explosions shook *Victorious* and *Indomitable*. 'God!' said someone, *'Eagle,* look at *Eagle!'* Smoke was pouring from the carrier and already the large flight-deck was listing over to port. Immediately the other two carriers rang on and increased to full speed, zig-zagging as they took violent torpedo avoiding action. The escorting destroyers rushed in, darting this way and that as their asdic beams probed the depths, looking for the hidden, elusive enemy submarine. Soon the sea was torn apart as great columns of water shot skywards, and crash after crash shuddered through the hulls of the surface ships, as the depth charges sought to kill the intruder.

The loudspeakers aboard *Victorious* crackled again: 'D'ye hear there, the *Eagle* has been hit by a number of torpedoes fired by a submarine and is sinking. The explosions you can hear are the depth charge attacks being made by our destroyers. The air raid that was approaching the ship has been turned away by our fighers and at least one enemy aircraft shot down. That is all.'

The report was very matter of fact and almost routine, except that *Eagle* had been struck by three or possibly four torpedoes and sank within eight minutes. Happily 77 officers and 862 of her ship's company were saved including her Commanding Officer, Captain L.D. Mackintosh, DSC, destined to be the next captain of *Victorious*. Much more serious however was the loss of the aircraft which sank with her, for at one stroke, submarine *U73* had deprived the force of twenty-five per cent of its valuable and irreplaceable fighters. The story could have been worse because *U205* was also in the area at the time, but fortunately for the convoy she was unable to make contact.

Four of *Eagle*'s Hurricanes were airborne when she sank and while one landed on *Indomitable,* the other three headed for *Victorious*. One of *Eagle*'s pilots orbiting *Victorious* made an emergency landing signal, but continued to circle the ship until his companions and the returning fighter patrol from *Victorious* were safely aboard before making his final approach. With his windscreen covered with oil and almost out of petrol, he feared he might crash on landing and so foul up the deck.

A few minutes after *Eagle* had gone, the anti-aircraft cruiser *Charybdis* reported sighting torpedoes and almost immediately a torpedo crossed the bow of *Victorious*. Ten minutes later a submarine periscope and the tell-tale plume of wake was seen by a *Victorious* lookout, followed shortly afterwards by a torpedo – again on the starboard side. That afternoon as the convoy and escorts forged their way through the submarine barrier, no less than six U-boat sightings and two torpedoes were reported, in addition to numerous underwater asdic contacts. From German records, it would appear that *U73* who sank *Eagle* was the only submarine to get in an attack that afternoon, for as we have heard, *U205* failed to make contact with our forces. It is interesting to note that neither *U73* nor *U205* fired again that afternoon and it poses the question, if torpedoes were fired at *Victorious*, where did they come from and who fired them? As the afternoon wore on, reports of enemy submarine contacts came in thick and fast. It was obvious that the enemy were after the carriers, but as the Captain of *Victorious* stated in his report of 15th August, 'suitable avoiding action was taken for each.' The ships continued on their zig-zag course and the escorts dropped more depth charges; over all, the hot Mediterranean sun continued to beat down from the cloudless sky. During the afternoon the ferry-cruiser *Furious* flew off her consignment of 38 Spitfires to augment the Malta squadrons and provide the much needed replacements and additions. As soon as the last aircraft had left the deck, she thankfully altered course for Gibraltar, her mission completed.

For a while there was an ominous lull. The late afternoon dog watches dragged on and only small groups of enemy aircraft approached, careful to keep at a respectful distance and quite content to watch and wait. On the approach of our fighters, they would not stay to fight, but flew off seeking to return at some more opportune moment and perhaps catch the force off-guard. As the evening approached and the shadows length-ened to darken both the sea and the sky, the carriers waited patiently for the attack they knew must come. The scene aboard *Victorious* was vividly described by one of the officers at the time:

The standby squadron was all set on deck, with the aircraft armed, fuelled and waiting and the pilots in their cockpits gazing upwards and perhaps munching a biscuit. Men stood by the lanyards which secured the wingtips of the air-craft — others lay by their chocks and yet more men sat astride their starter motors. The flight-deck officers fiddled with their flags and Commander Flying nursed his flight-deck microphone. There was a tenseness in the air, expectancy and waiting, all waiting for those vital 17 seconds which would follow the Boatswain's Mate's call 'Fighters stand-to.' The mad scramble to get the aircraft off and then the eighteenth second should see the ship return-ing to her station with her fighters safely airborne over the sea.

Blips appeared on the radar, warning of the first enemy air attack, and suddenly the call came. It was nearly 2100 and a quarter of an hour after sunset as the Fulmar aircraft flew off and merged into the gathering darkness. Hurricane fighters from *Indomitable* were already engaging the raiders, a group of some 36 Heinkel 110s and Ju 88s. Some they managed to drive off, but the failing light made interception and combat difficult. Two of the bandits managed to break through and, flying at a height of 8,000 feet, they passed down the port side of *Victorious*. The multiple pom-poms and eventually the shorter range Oerlikons poured out a barrage of flying steel at the two aircraft as they dived to bomb *Victorious* from astern. In the twilight sky the bombers were nicely silhouetted and the AA guns continued to blaze away. The *Victorious* twisted and turned as she strove to avoid the enemy's bombs which, although they fell close astern, missed their target and did no damage. As the enemy pulled away, both aircraft were seen to be hit and crashed into the sea — one of them, according to an eye witness, looked like 'a torch of fire in a sheaf'. The remainder of the enemy aircraft dropped their loads of bombs ineffectually, then tried to escape both the wall of AA fire and the fighters waiting for them outside the barrage umbrella.

It was now dark and as the attack was over there was haste to land on the fighters which had been longest in the sky. So critical was the situation that a Hurricane from the *Indomitable*

had to make an unscheduled landing aboard *Victorious*. Apart
from the fact that it was pitch dark, the only difference
was that the aircraft was out of petrol and *Victorious* was still
out of wind and under wheel at the time. Coming in to land
while the flight deck was still slewing hard to starboard did not
help the pilot and the aircraft skittered up the deck, hit another
Hurricane stowed abaft the island and went on to crash into the
barrier and burst into flames. The pilot made an undignified and
very hasty exit from the burning aircraft and happily escaped
unhurt. Led by the Air Technical Officer, the Flight Deck Party
dashed in to extract the unexpended ammunition before it
exploded, while one of the Albacore pilots manning a nearby
Oerlikon gun grabbed a hose and sprayed it over them all — a
credit to the night vision and flexibility of naval aircrew! Such
was the speed and efficiency of the flight deck personnel, that
the flight deck was cleared within six minutes allowing the
remainder of the fighters to land on. Another aircraft crashed on
landing but, after the last plane had 'hooked on', it was found
that five more aircraft were missing from *Victorious*. There were
no more aircraft in the sky and so reluctantly, the ship turned
out of wind to regain her station with the convoy. At length a
tiny blue signal lamp flashed from *Indomitable* to say that the
five aircraft had landed safely aboard — one of the pilots is said
to have sat for twenty minutes spinning tales to an enthralled
audience before he discovered that he was in the wrong ship.
Thus ended day two . . .

So far, no ship in the convoy had been damaged, but the Axis
powers had four more ambushes in store. They had a lot of
their 600 aircraft still intact, many U-boats and then twenty-
three MTBs to put against the convoy on the morrow. On the
convoy's side that night when the count was finally made, there
were only 50 serviceable Hurricanes, Fulmars and Martlets to see
them through the critical third day. There would have been even
fewer aircraft had not the Captain of *Indomitable* switched on
his flight deck lighting and steamed at 26 knots for over an hour
to help his aircraft land on. The convoy was now about 180
miles north-east of Malta and this put it within 100 miles of
Cape Spartivento and the German airfields in Sardinia. It was to
be a sleepless night of hard work and vigilance as guns' crews

scanned the skies for possible enemy sneak attacks, while the asdics probed the depths for enemy submarines. Below in the hangar and workshops, the maintenance crews sweated and strained to make every available aircraft serviceable. One Hurricane had to have a complete tail unit and its airscrew changed, as well as requiring a serious leak in the hydraulic system to be repaired. Work which might have taken 48 hours to repair on an airfield ashore had to be completed that night and before daybreak.

Day three lived up to its expectations and proved to be a real test of endurance. *Victorious* went to Action Stations at 0520 and from dawn the two carriers kept twelve fighters in the air continuously, with the remainder at readiness. With the coast of Africa now a mere 50 miles away and also well within spitting distance of the airfields of Sardinia and Sicily, enemy fighters could accompany their bombing formations right to the doorstep and very determined raids could be expected. An Italian S79 shadowing aircraft was the first victim that day as it fell in a flaming spiral to the guns of a Fulmar, to hit the sea without ceremony half a mile off the North African shore. From then onwards 'there were few moments' said Admiral Syfret, 'when neither aircraft, submarines, torpedoes nor asdic contacts were being reported.'

At nine o'clock, as reinforcements went up to meet the threat of the first big raid, the leader of the *Vic's* formation saw Hurricanes from the *Indomitable* diving into a formation of 20 Ju 88s at 8,000 feet. Two of the enemy plummeted into the sea like stones, ten more jettisoned their bombs and beat a hasty retreat, while two more unenthusiastic raiders were caught by the *Vic* formation as they shot past en route for home. The first raid had been broken up successfully and in less than two minutes the sky was clear again and the convoy steamed on. So the day continued, with ships and air group working non-stop as the carrier turned into wind to launch, land on, refuel and re-arm and launch again. Without let-ups throughout that long day the enemy came in wave after wave and in the Air Direction Rooms of the carriers, the radar screens were never clear of enemy aircraft. Hour after hour, the Hurricanes, Fulmars and Martlets clawed their way into the sky to meet yet another

This famous photograph was taken from *Victorious* on the 9th August 1942 as they passed into the Mediterranean on their way to Malta. The Hurricanes of 885 Squadron can be seen on deck and one is on its starboard outrigger. The convoy is not yet in range of the enemy and the carriers *Indomitable* and *Eagle* can be seen astern.

Journey's end: the damaged tanker *Ohio* reaches Grand Harbour Malta on 15th August 1942. She is being 'carried in' lashed to the escorts *Penn* and *Braham* on either side; the bravery of her Master, Captain Mason, and the crew remains one of the finest exploits in the annals of maritime history.

A camera-gun picture of a Junkers 88 hit and damaged, with its starboard engine on fire, during Operation 'Torch'. Sub Lieutenant Parker was flying in Seafire IIC (MB 122) of 884 Squadron from *Victorious* on the 11th November 1942 and was credited with a probable.

The Prime Minister, Mr. Winston Churchill, and the Lord Privy Seal, Sir Stafford Cripps, pay a surprise visit to *Victorious* on the 15th October 1942 prior to sailing for Operation 'Torch'.

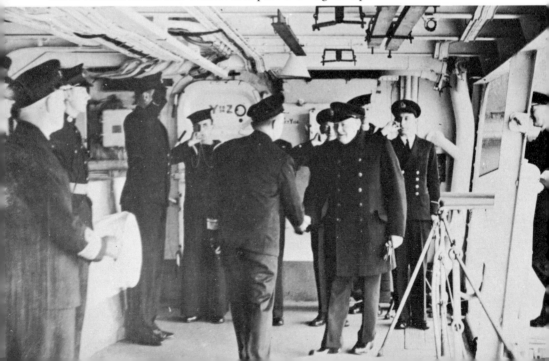

threat. To force the enemy aircraft to combat, to make the bombers drop in haste and, with luck, to shoot them down. One pilot said that he found it hard to decide whether the crews were baling out before or after he had pressed the firing button. One large formation of Cant Z 1007 torpedo bombers found the opposition so stiff that they could do no more than circle round hopefully like a pack of jackals – well out of range as our fighters did not let them get within five miles of the convoy.

The enemy's great effort – over 70 bombers, escorted by many fighters – took place at noon, and after this second major raid of the day came a nasty shock for *Victorious*. Two Italian Reggiane 2001 fighters were orbiting the carrier as though waiting to land on, when they suddenly broke from the circuit and dived down on the ship's port quarter, levelled off two miles away and came roaring in from astern over the flight deck just a few feet up. *Vic* was landing on Hurricanes at the time – not dissimilar in appearance – and 'everyone thought that they were Hurricanes', quoted an officer from *Victorious*. 'How they love to play', remarked another. Just then, the two aircraft pulled up over the flight deck, dropped their bombs and, to quote the under-statement of the year, 'achieved complete surprise.' Fortunately one burst harmlessly in the water close to the port bow and, even more fortunately, the other hit the armoured flight deck on the centre line, broke up and fell over the side without exploding. The aircraft got away without a shot being fired and apart from some shattered nerves and a pair of broken binoculars belonging to a very surprised anti-submarine lookout no other damage was done. During this very heavy and concentrated enemy attack, British reports state that enemy aircraft dropped mines ahead of the force, but official enemy reports make no mention of such an incident, though the Italians did drop a new circling torpedo called the 'Motobomba FF' – without apparent success. Unfortunately the enemy bombing attack claimed its first victim, when the 7,514 ton SS *Deucalion* was hit and stopped. She had to leave the convoy and was later attacked and sunk near Cani Rocks Lighthouse off the Tunisian Coast.

During the afternoon there was a welcome lull in the air activity, but as Captain Bovell of *Victorious* wrote in his report:

'Frequent submarine alarms kept the interest alive.' This was certainly the case, for as the convoy passed some 20 miles to the north of Galita Island, they steamed through another ambush of Italian submarines. Many submarine contacts were made during the afternoon and eventually the defenders met with success, when the Italian submarine *Cobalto* (Tenente di Vascello Raffaele Amicarelli) was brought to the surface by depth charges, and was rammed and sunk by the destroyer *Ithuriel.* Although torpedoes were fired by the Italian submarine *Emo* (Tenente di Vascello Giuseppe Franco) the watchfulness and efficiency of the escorts prevented any casualties and to thwart the attacking submarines the convoy made no less than 48 emergency turns during the two days up to the 12th August.

> Soon after 5 p.m. [Captain Bovell of *Victorious* reported] the air woke up again and every available fighter was in the air and operating continuously, engaging shadowers, intercepting groups of incoming raiders and breaking up enemy formations.

Around six-fifteen that evening, the enemy threw everything at the force. Large groups of aircraft were detected and every available fighter was at once put in the air. These groups consisted of many types; Ju 87, Ju 88, Cant Z1007b, SM 79, Messerschmitt Bf 109G, Bf 110C-4, Re 2001 and Mc 202 – a veritable flood of enemy aircraft – bent on the saturation of the defences and the destruction of the convoy. Though at a serious disadvantage, all our fighters intercepted and engaged the enemy, shooting down and damaging many and generally breaking up the groups. Aircraft from *Victorious* were in the thick of it and Sub Lieutenant A.J. Thompson of 885 Sea Hurricane Squadron intercepted a group of four Ju 87s. In a short but spirited battle, he set one of the attackers on fire and watched it roll over and crash into the sea, while the remainder jettisoned their bombs and made for home. The attack was well planned and synchronised and, although heavily engaged, one formation of four Ju 88s and eight Ju 87 bombers broke through and dived onto the carrier *Indomitable.* Hidden in columns of water from erupting bombs and spray, she was hit by three bombs and her flight deck was put out of action. Although she continued under her own steam she could not operate her aircraft, so those that were in the air had to land on *Victorious.* One of these pilots, Sub Lieutenant M. Hankey — already a survivor of *Eagle*'s 801 Squadron — though he had just landed and was advised to rest, insisted on going up again as soon as his Sea Hurricane had been refuelled. With great bravery he flew off, shot down an enemy aircraft and was last seen with another on his tail. Another of *Indomitable*'s aircrew operating from *Victorious* gave the carrier's flight deck party a most thrilling spectacle when he chased and splashed a Stuka close to the carrier; Lieutenant B. Richie of 800 Squadron had just taken off from *Victorious* when he saw the enemy plane at low altitude. Chasing it through a barrage of AA fire, he succeeded in catching the German with a burst of machine gun fire and sending it into the sea in a ball of fire. By 1930 after more than an hour of ceaseless combat the enemy broke off the attack. Miraculously the convoy was still virtually intact and now only 130 miles from its destination. Beaufighters of the RAF took over the patrol and by daylight there would be Spitfires. The *Vic* and the wounded carrier *Indomitable,* their task completed, turned towards the setting sun and headed once more for Gibraltar. It had been the naval fighters' greatest battle and their greatest victory. Some 70 fighters, only one of them armed with cannon, had been opposed to a force of at least 600 bombers, torpedo aircraft and fighters. Yet in spite of the losses of aircraft in the *Eagle,* in spite of being out-distanced and out-gunned, the Martlets, Hurricanes and Fulmars had shot down 39 enemy aircraft and nine probables, damaged many more and all at a cost of only thirteen British aircraft. Writing of their magnificent work, Vice Admiral Syfret said:

Flying at great heights, constantly chasing the faster Ju 88, warning the Fleet of approaching formations, breaking up the latter, and in the later stages doing their work in the face of superior enemy fighters forces — they were grand.

Nor must the work of those who kept the aircraft in the sky be forgotten. Composed mostly of young Able Seamen, the flight deck parties had been on duty from dawn until dusk ranging the aircraft, placing the chocks in position and removing them on the signal, releasing the aircraft's arrester hooks from the arrester wires, folding the wings and striking the aircraft down. On day three the party in *Victorious* made 86 journeys up and down the flight deck, a distance of some 20 miles. In the hangars the maintenance ratings worked like galley slaves in their cramped spaces. The decks were covered with grease and running with oil and petrol. The heat was intense and they had to work all the time under the glare of electric light taking their food when and as they could in the hangar.

The operational problem of convoying merchant ships to Malta was not dissimilar from that of convoying them to Murmansk or Archangel. As in the Mediterranean, the route through the Barents Sea lies within reach of the enemy heavy bombers, but beyond the reach of British shore-based fighters, so that once again the only means of giving effective air cover was by carrier borne aircraft. Perhaps an interesting reflection for the future!

There was no fuel oil available to replenish the capital ships in Malta, and so they had turned back. No sooner had the carriers departed than things started to go sour and, from the convoy point of view, their incredible luck ran out. Apart from one ship, the *Deucalion*, the fourteen merchant ships were still intact thanks to the air defence afforded by the carriers, but within an hour things were to change. As the ships steamed on with only the token air protection that could be provided by the RAF from Malta, the story of 13th August was to be tragically different. The convoy was thrown into disorder by a remarkably effective submarine attack, followed by an equally effective series of air attacks, which inflicted serious damage and losses on both convoy and escorts. The straggling ships then afforded easy prey to the new threat of motor torpedo boats which were awaiting them to the south of Cape Bon. Only five ships reached Malta, one of which included the *Ohio*, a very disabled tanker with her vital 11,500 tons of oil. After an epic struggle to save this ship, the efforts of her crew and escorts were rewarded: lashed between the two naval escorts *Braham* and *Penn* and aided by the minesweeper HMS *Ledbury,* the very brave and battered hulk of *Ohio* entered Grand Harbour at 0930 on 15th August. Between them the five merchantmen survivors carried nearly 40,000 tons of vital supplies, naval stores, aviation fuel, aircraft spares, ammunition, meat, grain and other commodities; the 'Santa Maria' convoy as it was called in Malta had brought enough to replenish the stocks of the island for another two months. Malta was out of danger and by the time more supplies were needed, in November, the Allies had landed in North Africa and the battle of El Alamein had been won.

Victorious arrived at the detached mole in Gibraltar on the 15th August and as the only surviving, serviceable carrier, she prepared to return to the United Kingdom. She embarked 45 officers and 446 ratings as survivors from the sunken carrier *Eagle,* the cruiser *Manchester,* the torpedoed destroyer *Foresight* and ten officers from the damaged *Indomitable,* before setting out for Rosyth and a month's refit the next day. After a slight brush with the carrier *Furious,* which damaged her bows as she cast off, *Victorious* arrived in Scapa on 21st September and until the end of October spent the intervening six weeks carrying out more Seafire flying and the initial deck landing trials of the new Fairey Barracuda. Designed to replace the Swordfish and the Albacore, the Barracuda was designed to specification S24/37 and took six years to get from the drawing board into service. If a really worthwhile aircraft had eventually materialised, the long delay would have been acceptable, but when the 'Thing' appeared it looked exactly what it turned out to be – a triumph of misplaced ingenuity. The classic remark was made by a US Navy Lieutenant when the aircraft first landed aboard USS *Saratoga*: 'Jesus Christ! – the Limeys'll be building airplanes next!' 'No aircraft which looks like that could possibly be a good aircraft', was another opinion, equally apt, expressed by a well-known British Admiral.

In spite of all, however, the Barracuda was to have her moments of glory as we shall see later, but she was never really liked by her aircrews. Irreverently called the 'Barraweewee', she had the nasty habit of plunging into the sea out of control and this endearing feature, together with numerous other un-explained and equally fatal accidents, tended to send her to the bottom of the popularity charts.

Chapter VI

THE INVASION OF NORTH AFRICA
(OPERATION TORCH)

Victorious was next to see action as one of the force of British carriers covering the invasion of North Africa, scheduled to take place on the 30th October 1942. A great combined force of British and American troops was to land in Morocco and Algeria and seize the key ports of Algiers, Oran and Casablanca. Timed to coincide with Montgomery's advance from El Alamein towards Tobruk, it signalled the start of offensive moves which, if successful, would bring ultimate victory to the Allied cause in the Middle East.

On 16th June 1940, all military resistance came to an end on the continent of Europe, leaving Britain to stand alone to face the Germans across the Channel. With the capitulation of France, the powerful French Fleet based mainly in the Mediterranean and on the west coast of Africa would fall into German and Italian hands. If nothing were done to prevent this catastrophe, then the whole balance of sea power would be shifted out of our favour – creating a situation of the direst consequence for Great Britain. Our very lifeline was in danger and British survival and continuation in the war depended on our maintaining control of the sea lanes. In 1940, our maritime supremacy was slender and being seriously challenged by the German Navy. As far as we were concerned, the situation was balanced on a knife-edge.

The German terms of surrender signed by France on the 22nd June 1940 laid down that the French Fleet was to be 'collected in ports to be specified, demobilised and disarmed under German and Italian control.' If the French fleet were allowed to go over to German control, the whole balance of power would shift and there would be no question of a knife-edge parity, for the Germans would gain the upper hand in one fell swoop. The British Government reacted swiftly and naval forces were dispatched at once to the French ports of Dakar and Oran. Their mission was to try to persuade the French Naval Commanders to join the side of the British, to join the fight with the Free French under the leadership of General de Gaulle – or, if they refused, to neutralise the ships to prevent them falling into German hands.

The story of the tragic operations against both Dakar and Oran is well known – the talking, persuasion, cajoling and threats all failed and so, reluctantly, Force H under Admiral Somerville and the ships of the French Navy clashed at Oran. The fiasco at Dakar was considerably less bloody but at both ports subsequent events caused a needless loss of life and provoked incidents, unhappy memories of which exist to this day.

Now two years later, America was in the war as Britain's ally. For some months past there had been talk of a Second Front, but the main question had been – where? The Russians had been pressing for months to get an Allied invasion of Europe to relieve the German pressure on their Russian front. The Americans had also favoured an Allied assault in Europe and it seemed that only Britain argued for the attack in North Africa. After weeks of strong argument and fiery debate, the differences of opinion were resolved and now a combined British and American force sat poised to invade the shores of Morocco and Algeria. Both ex-French Colonial Territories were occupied in the name of Germany by the Vichy Government of France and had been chosen because, in spite of 1940, it was hoped that sympathies would still lie with the Allies, thus simplifying the task of the invaders. In Winston Churchill's eyes, the operation was of paramount importance for, if successful, this great enterprise involving over 400 ships and 70,000 men would rank as one of the major strategic strokes of the war, and would give the Allies control of North West Africa and secure the vital Mediterranean route.

In spite of some early difficulties, the first week of the Seafire and Barracuda deck landing and flying trials had gone well. They had started on 23rd September and, if progress continued at its present rate, *Victorious* would be able to complete the trials, sail to Greenock to embark her squadrons, and still have time in hand for a short work up, before leaving to arrive for 'Torch' on 30th October.

On 26th September 1942, however, one of those Hollywood-type, stranger than fiction incidents took place that was to have a dramatic effect on the whole operation. Paymaster Lieutenant J.H. Turner was a passenger in Catalina flying-boat FP 119 en route back to Gibraltar with some vital, top secret documents, when the aircraft was reported overdue and thought to have crashed. An unsuccessful air search was finally abandoned, but a day or two later the body of a man was washed ashore near Cadiz with a letter on it addressed to the Governor of Gibraltar from Major General Clark, US Army. The body was identified as that of Lieutenant Turner and was accordingly handed over by the Spaniards to the British Consular Authorities in Cadiz. Although the letter did not appear to have been tampered with, it gave the Target Date for Operation 'Torch' and, furthermore, stated that the Allied Commander-in-Chief General Eisenhower would reach Gibraltar on D minus 2 or 3. Addressed to Turner's Superior Officer Commodore W.E. Parry, a second letter had been opened, although apparently by the action of sea-water, and no chances could be taken. As more articles were being washed ashore from the ill-fated aircraft, the Governor considered that other valuable and compromising documents would be discovered and that they would find their way into the hands of the Spanish authorities and thus inevitably – of the Germans. His warning reached the War Office on the 28th September and must have caused quite a stir; as a result the date of the operation was postponed until 8th November.

The second week of October was crowded with incident for *Victorious*. She finished the Barracuda and Seafire trials on the 14th October and to liven things up had three Seafire crashes during the last three days, plus a visit from the Prime Minister Mr Winston Churchill and the Lord Privy Seal, Sir Stafford Cripps. She sailed for Greenock on the 16th and after embarking her aircraft, continued to work up her Squadrons. 809 Squadron in particular, received a good deal of training in the Tactical

Reconnaissance and Army Co-operation roles. 882 Squadron under the command of Lieutenant Commander H.J.F. Lane had been reconstituted from the nucleus of 806 Squadron, recently returned home from 'Pedestal' in the *Indomitable*. They retrained hard as they worked up with an assortment of Martlet Is, IIs, and IIIs, but finally embarked with their full complement of 12 Martlet IVs together with 6 Seafires of 884 Squadron, under the command of Lieutenant Commander N.G. Hallett. Again 832 Squadron re-embarked in *Victorious* for the forthcoming Mediterranean operation, but this time they left 'A' Sub-Flight ashore at Manston to work with Coastal Command for mine-laying duties and anti-shipping strikes. To complete the Air Group, 817 Squadron of 9 Albacores flew on board and, led by Lieutenant G.R. Beer, they prepared themselves for yet another round against the enemy.

Victorious finally left Greenock on the 30th October 1942 as one of seven aircraft carriers to be employed in the operation by the Royal Navy, including three of the new and latest escort carriers recently received from the United States under the Lease Lend Agreement. Four of the carriers including *Victorious* had embarked the new Seafires, a navalised version of the famous Spitfire and armed with 20 mm cannon, while others carried Sea Hurricanes which had first made their appearance at sea on the Kirkenes and Petsamo raid a year earlier. Discounting the initial deck landing trials, it is of interest to note that the 6 Seafires of 884 Squadron embarked in *Victorious* for 'Torch' would be the first, last and only time that she would operate Seafires in her whole career. Another interesting point was that with the two types of aircraft already mentioned, together with the Swordfish, Albacores, Fulmars and Martlets carried in the carriers, plus the Walrus aircraft in the capital ships and cruisers, every type of naval aircraft in current operational service with the Fleet was to take part in 'Torch'.

As already stated, the overall command of the operation rested with Lieutenant General Dwight D. Eisenhower of the United States Army, while Admiral Sir Andrew Cunningham was the overall Commander-in-Chief of the Naval Forces. These were divided into three groups: the Western Naval Task Force consisted entirely of American ships and aircraft carriers and their object was Casablanca; the Central Naval Task Force was a British responsibility under the command of Commodore T.H. Troubridge – consisting of the carrier *Furious* and the escort carriers *Biter* and *Dasher,* this force was to provide support for the landings at Oran; finally, there was the Eastern Naval Task Force – again British and commanded by Rear Admiral Sir Harold Burrough, this force comprising the two escort carriers, *Argus* and *Avenger,* was to tackle the port of Algiers. *Victorious,* flying the flag of Rear Admiral A.L. St. G. Lyster, and the other fleet carrier, *Formidable,* were the two carriers comprising Force H; together they were to form part of the covering force for the assault on Algiers and Oran, and to protect the Central and Eastern Task Forces from interference by either the French or Italian Fleets. Provided that his first duty of protecting the assault forces against attack by heavy surface ships permitted, Admiral Syfret was to bring his Force H to within 20 miles of Algiers by daylight on D Day. Here he would rendezvous with Force O and Rear Admiral Lyster would then assume operation control of the carriers of both forces, to give air support to the Algiers landings.

It was the 6th November or D minus two as the enormous gathering of some 400 ships passed slowly through the Straits of Gibraltar, line after line of merchant ships, majestically cutting through the water and disappearing towards the eastern horizon. To the watchers ashore on the nearby coast of Spain it was certainly an impressive sight, but where was it heading? – another massive convoy to the beleaguered garrison at Malta? Gibraltar's North Front Airfield was bulging at the seams with aircraft, for in addition to the RAF and Fleet Air Arm Squadrons currently resident to provide the anti-submarine protection for shipping using the Straits, there were 30 Squadrons of RAF and USAAF Spitfires parked there in transit. To the eye of the casual observer and the ear of the German informer, they were yet more reinforcement for Malta. In fact, the aircraft were waiting until the airfields of North Africa had been secured by the invasion forces, but until that time the responsibility for the air defence of the Fleet and the close support for the Army, would rest entirely with the aircraft from the seven British carriers.

With the Hudsons and Sunderlands from Gibraltar flying round and round the force to provide the necessary anti-submarine protection, the great Allied Expeditionary Force continued on its way eastward into the Mediterranean. Another day had passed quietly and it seemed that nothing could spoil the pleasant warmth of this 'Mediterranean cruise'. It was now the 7th November and with less than twenty-four hours to go to D Day and Zero Hour for the landings, the first incident occurred. All through the 7th, the carriers had been sending up defensive fighter patrols – or, CAPs – over the convoy and Force H. At 1600 in the afternoon the force had its first visit by an enemy aircraft – an Italian Potez 63 reconnaissance plane. Lieutenant Jerome was flying CAP from the *Formidable* and was ordered to intercept. The enemy aircraft was flying at 10,000 feet and after a brisk but short engagement, the enemy aircraft was shot down. Later that night at 2130 torpedo tracks were sighted on the starboard side of *Victorious,* but whoever fired them had missed and the ships steamed on their way uninterrupted.

We now know that the intended ruse worked exactly according to plan and that, in fact, the Germans and Italians were completely deceived. They had been led to believe that this was another large convoy en route for Malta, but at the appointed time during the night of the 7th, all the ships turned ninety degrees to starboard towards the coast of North Africa, the force split up to make for their objectives and the assault was on. Zero hour was timed for 0100 on the morning of the 8th and while the smaller carriers *Furious, Argus, Biter, Dasher* and *Avenger* proceeded close inshore, to fly off their fighters at first light and give cover to the transports unloading and patrol the assault beaches, Force H with *Victorious* and *Formidable* would remain in the background, keeping some 80 miles from the coast, and provide the distant cover.

Shortly after midnight, the RAF aircraft began taking off from North Front at Gibraltar to give added weight to the A/S protection of the landing area. As the assault forces made their final run in, all was quiet and they met with no opposition. However, some three hours after the start of the landings enemy aircraft were detected to seaward of the assault force. Although they flew around and dropped flares for about an hour, by some strange coincidence no detection seemed to have been made and no attack developed. Throughout the planning and execution of this operation, everything possible was done to foster the impression that it was an American and not a British undertaking. With memories of Dakar and Oran still fresh in the mind, the planners felt that the French would be less inclined to oppose an American landing and to this end the British aircraft even carried American markings; in any case, the French roundels were the reverse of the British and, in combat, it would be difficult to distinguish the difference.

As dawn approached, the carriers made ready to fly off their first sorties. *Argus* and *Avenger* were off Algiers, *Furious*, *Biter* and *Dasher* off the beaches of Oran and *Victorious* and *Formidable* in 'deep cover' some 80 miles off shore. At five o'clock first reports began to come in of the successful landings by the invasion troops. Half an hour later it was light enough to start flying and *Victorious* launched her first two Albacores. They were to fly anti-submarine patrols round Force H and were quickly followed by three more. These were ordered to fly inshore to prevent enemy ships from leaving the harbour, and to look for U-boats in the vicinity of the stationary transports.

At 0545 four Martlets of 882 Squadron were launched from *Victorious* with orders to patrol over the French military airfield at Blida, roughly 30 miles to the south-west of Algiers. Fifteen minutes later, fighter aircraft from both *Victorious* and *Formidable* were over the air bases of Maison Blanche and Blida, with orders to prevent any French aircraft from leaving the ground and to attack any that tried to do so. When they reached Blida, they saw two aircraft preparing to get airborne and one was already moving, but after a quick burst of machine gun fire both aircraft were destroyed and all movement ceased. Apart from some light anti-aircraft fire, there was no other opposition and after two hours they returned to *Victorious* to land on at 0800.

Another section of four Martlets was flown off to continue the patrol and again headed for Blida. This time the section was led by Lieutenant (A) B.H.C. Nation and as they circled the airfield, he noticed a group of people waving what appeared to be white flags. After a discussion over the air with the Staff in *Victorious* he was eventually given permission to land and accept the surrender of Blida. Leaving the other three Martlets of 882 Squadron orbiting overhead in case of trouble, Lieutenant Nation landed his aircraft without mishap and taxied towards the group of French officers. The Commandant stepped forward and handed the British pilot a piece of paper on which was written the words: '*La base de Blida est disponible pour l'atterrissage des armees allies. Blida, 8 Nov 1942*': a courteous though formal surrender, signed by the Commandant. Somewhat embarrassed by having a large airfield on his charge, he merely took what he considered to be the best course of action under the circumstances, and waited! Later that morning a group of Commandos arrived on the scene and after handing over 'his' airfield to their care, he flew back to *Victorious*. It was the first time that the Fleet Air Arm captured an airfield, but not the last: Sembawang Airfield on Singapore Island was formally surrendered by the Japanese in September 1945, to Lieutenant Commander Douglas, DSC, RNR, Commander (Flying) of the escort carrier *Attacker*.

The Albacore squadrons also had their share of the fun for, apart from the routine and rather dull anti-submarine patrols, they were invited to co-operate with the army ashore and to help secure Algiers harbour. The capture of this important harbour intact was vital to the success of the operation and, accordingly, two destroyers were ordered to crash through the defence boom, to stop sabotage in the harbour and prevent any scuttling to block the port. After great difficulty, one of the destroyers managed to force an entrance, but met with considerable opposition from the forts guarding the approaches – particularly one situated on the Jetée du Nord.

At 1100, six Albacores of 832 Squadron took off to silence the fort which was situated on the northern breakwater of Algiers harbour. Each carried six 250-pound semi-armour-piercing bombs as they climbed steadily to 7,000 feet. After flying a few miles to the north of Algiers Bay, the leader decided that he would bring the aircraft in to attack from south to north, flying across the breakwater. This would give the aircraft a good run in and reduce the possibility of bombs overshooting the target and falling on the town, or worse, hitting friendly shipping in the harbour. The aircraft had so far met no opposition, but during the final approach, the high angle guns opened up and slightly damaged one of the Albacores. As the bombs dropped, hits were obtained on the fort, which put the guns out of action and partially destroyed the fort itself.

Before the aircraft returned to *Victorious,* another request was received to silence Fort Dupere. This fort was situated on an escarpment to the north-west of Algiers and held a commanding position overlooking the sea. It was proving very troublesome to the attacking troops and putting up a stiff fight; once again the Fleet Air Arm was invited to 'soften up the resistance'. A second striking force of 8 Albacores was ready and waiting on the flight deck of *Victorious* and at 1300 they were launched together with an escort of 2 Fulmars from 809 Squadron. As before, each Albacore carried a load of six 250-pound SAP bombs and the formation consisting of 6 aircraft from 817 Squadron and 2 more from 832 climbed away towards their target. This time there was a layer of nearly solid strato-cumulus cloud at 2,500 feet, but climbing as high and as near up-sun as the clouds would allow, the formation circled the fort to confirm identification, before diving to attack from the south-west. With no opposition and each aircraft carrying out deliberate bombing at one minute intervals, all the bombs fell within the fort area. A large number of the fort's buildings were destroyed and the guns probably put out of action by blast from two salvoes which detonated about 50 yards away; a large explosion was seen 50 yards to the south-east of the gun emplacement. The only damage to the attacking aircraft occurred when one enthusiastic Albacore made a very low pass and sustained slight damage from his own bomb shrapnel. The raid was an obvious success, for shortly after the raid the white flags came out and the fort surrendered to the advancing troops. All the fun did not go exclusively to *Victorious,* for at about the same time Albacores from 820 Squadron in *Formidable* were dealing with an equally troublesome battery at Fort Matifu, an outpost manned by units of the French Navy on Cape Matifu at the eastern end of Algiers Bay.

Towards evening the escort carriers *Argus* and *Avenger* off

Algiers moved inshore to within four miles of the coast. About 5 pm, as dusk was approaching, *Argus* scrambled a patrol of three Seafires. While they were still climbing they sighted 15 Ju 88s, flying at 9,000 feet, but before the Seafires could gain sufficient height to intercept the enemy, they dived to attack *Argus*. Another three Seafires were ranged and ready on the flight-deck with the pilots sitting helplessly in the cockpits, but when the attack came the carrier had not yet turned into wind, so that they could not be flown off and just had to sit there. The Junkers roared in and, coming down to 500 feet, they bombed the ship for four minutes. There were several near misses and the last bomb hit the port quarter, blowing the tail off a Seafire ranged on the port side of the flight-deck and damaging the others with blast. Fortunately the pilots were unhurt but, because of the mess on the flight-deck, the three Seafires who were still in the air were invited to land at Maison Blanche and returned to the carrier on the following day.

A formation of Ju 88s also attacked Force H at dusk on 8th November, but it was a very half-hearted attempt and caused no damage, although one of the Ju 88s managed to slip in undetected and only just missed *Victorious*. Indeed, throughout the operation there was no sign of the heavy air assaults upon the fleet, which had been so characteristic of previous operations in the Mediterranean. The enemy Ju 88s were based a long way away in Sicily and Sardinia, and with over 1,000 miles to fly, enemy air activity near Force H usually took the form of an armed reconnaissance twice daily by Ju 88s, flying singly or in pairs at a great height and carrying only one bomb. On the approach of the defending fighters, the attackers would hastily drop their bomb and make off at full throttle in headlong flight, before the fighters could intercept. According to German sources, the opposition from the carriers' aircraft and ships' anti-aircraft fire was so devastating that they were unable to mount effective air attacks.

809 Squadron Fulmars in *Victorious* supported the army during the first day and carried out seven tactical reconnaissance flights over the Algiers area. Early on the morning of the 8th, they were ordered to gather intelligence on the movements of all French forces within the area 60 to 100 miles from Algiers,

contact our forward patrols and give them the latest and most up to date information. To prevent embarrassing mistakes, they had to identify our forward patrols and establish their requirements before taking any positive action. In other words, they were not to shoot first and ask afterwards. Two aircraft were hit by light flak during the sorties and one aircraft ditched near *Victorious,* but the crew were rescued unharmed and the army's needs were more than satisfied.

On the 9th, the fighters of 882 Squadron again flew some 60 patrolling flights over the Force. Very little enemy activity occurred during the actual period, but interest was kept alive by the periodic visits of German shadowers and the occasional attempted strike. At a quarter past one on the afternoon of the 9th, two Martlets of 882 Squadron intercepted and shot down a German He 111 in flames. At the same time two other Martlets on Combat Air Patrol from the same squadron, caught a Ju 88 trying to sneak in a quick bombing raid against the carriers. Although they only managed to damage him, the aircraft was successfully diverted from his intentions and, jettisoning his bombs, made good a hasty escape. Towards evening, the Ju 88s made another attempt to approach the force; again they were intercepted and a Martlet of 882 succeeded in damaging one.

809 Squadron continued in their role of army support throughout the 9th and although there was again no action, they did drop food to two forward patrols at the airfield at Maison Blanche. Carrier flying operations continued throughout D plus one and, to add to the aerial support, reinforcements arrived from Gibraltar. By D plus two, Allied air superiority was unchallenged for the French had lost some 70 aircraft destroyed and German interference was still very non-effective.

Oran surrendered on 10th November and with the major airfields captured and intact the work of the carriers was over.

The operations of the aircraft carriers went according to plan [wrote Rear Admiral Lyster afterwards]. After such great effort to re-equip nearly all the Naval Squadrons with modern fighters in time for this operation, disappointment has been expressed that the enemy were not sufficiently attentive to Force H.

Victorious' partner in the Pacific in 1943—USS *Saratoga*. The two ships operated in company for three months and cross-operated each others aircraft.

Members of *Victorious'* 832 Squadron loaned to the 'Dry Ship' USS *Saratoga* for a month in June 1943. Some of the squadron members can be seen wearing US Navy clothing.

Victorious has just joined Admiral Halsey USN, Commander-in-Chief of the US Third Fleet. She is preparing to refuel from the US oiler *Cimarron* and, on deck, her Martlet fighters and Avenger TBM aircraft are wearing their new American markings. The white patch was painted on the deck to represent a dummy lift in an effort to fool Jap Kamikaze pilots.

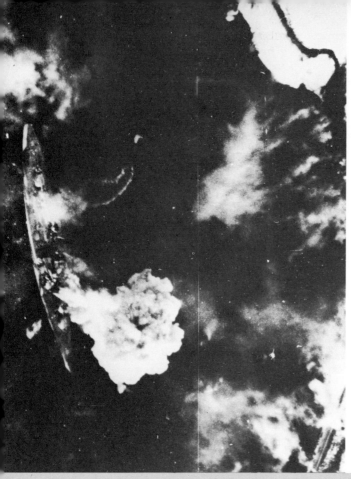

The attack on *Tirpitz*, in Alten Fiord, April 1944: the first wave has just gone in; a large column of smoke and flame is rising from a direct hit on or near 'B' turret. A total of fourteen hits were obtained on the *Tirpitz* during the two attacks.

Barracuda aircraft approaching Alten Fiord and some fifteen miles from the *Tirpitz*.

The losses in aircrew had been small, but apart from the five Albacores and one Seafire lost on the La Senia attack, no less than 25 other aircraft had been lost from other causes. The Hurricanes, and more particularly the Seafires, were prone to mishap on the deck. It was to prove time and time again, that this thoroughbred and essentially land-based aeroplane was often more of a liability than an asset when operating from a carrier's deck. As one pilot remarked after crashing his Seafire on deck: 'I shot one down, sir.' 'That's one all, then,' said the Captain eyeing the wreckage on his flight deck.

With the success of the invasion assured and the land based air forces firmly in command ashore, Force H could now withdraw. There was deemed to be little risk of interference by the Italian fleet and, accordingly, Admiral Syfret headed *Victorious* and *Formidable* back towards Gibraltar. The escort carriers remained to shepherd the returning convoys and it was during this period that *Avenger* was sunk. Hit by only one torpedo from *U155,* she blew up and sank with only 17 survivors.

Notwithstanding this loss, 'Torch' had been an outstanding success. The invasion had achieved complete suprise and the Fleet Air Arm had proved itself capable of defending the assault forces against opposition, as well as giving close support to the army ashore. It is true that in general the fighter pilots were disappointed in the lack of opposition, for some did not even fire their guns in anger, but the overall picture emphasised a significant development in the capabilities of our carriers and their better aircraft. If the lessons were learned from this operation, it augured well for the future.

During the time that 'Torch' was in progress the German submarine command rallied their U-boats in anticipation of a killing as the forces withdrew. Both *Victorious* and *Formidable* flew anti-submarine patrols day and night as they headed back to the safety of Gibraltar. Submarine scares were very frequent and, for added protection, many alterations of course and speed were ordered as the carriers returned. At 0530 on the morning of the 13th, the U-boats claimed their first success and torpedoed the Netherlands destroyer *Isaac Sweers.* The next evening, the scores were nearly evened when an Albacore from *Victorious* caught and damaged a U-boat on the surface.

At twenty-five minutes to seven on 14th November a small blip showed on the aircraft's ASV radar at a range of five miles. The night was dark and although there was a quarter moon on the horizon to the south-east, visibility was no more than a quarter of a mile down moon. Thin wisps of cloud raced past at 1,500 feet and at 1839, the blip on the screen had closed to a range of 1½ miles. The Albacore from 817 Squadron adjusted his course slightly and descended to 800 feet. Tense with excitement, the pilot released a flare three quarters of a mile from the target, turned to starboard to avoid the glare, then resumed course to try to identify the radar contact. As he peered forward into the flickering light of the flare, he could see the sleek outline of a U-boat on the surface. Caught on the surface and bathed in a bright light, the U-boat immediately crash-dived in an effort to escape. The Albacore was only a quarter of a mile away now at 600 feet with the enemy U-boat fine on his starboard bow. He roared on in; aiming at the fast disappearing conning tower, he dropped both depth charges together and they exploded some ten feet from the stern of the submarine. Although the aircraft circled the area and dropped a flame float to mark the position, nothing more was seen. This 'near miss' was converted into a success some three days later on 17th November, when an A/S patrol from *Formidable* sighted *U331* off the Algerian Coast. The submarine which had been damaged by attacks from a Naval Walrus and RAF Hudsons, was finally sunk by a torpedo from an Albacore of 820 Squadron.

It is a statistical fact that for every U-boat sinking achieved by aircraft in World War II, many hundreds of hours of tedious search and patrol had to be flown. It is amazing, therefore, that within seven days, a second chance was to fall into the lap of 817 Squadron and *Victorious*. En route from Gibraltar and two days out from Greenock, an A/S patrol aircraft reported that he had damaged a U-boat off the Bay of Biscay. At twenty minutes to eleven on 21st November, two Albacores from *Victorious* and the escort *Opportune* were sent immediately to the position. A successful attack by the Albacores sent *U517* to the bottom and *Opportune* rejoined some two hours later with 51 survivors.

Chapter VII

PACIFIC INTERLUDE

Victorious spent nearly a month in harbour after her return from the successful North African landings. Her Squadrons had disembarked ashore, Captain L.D. Mackintosh, DSO, DSC, joined as the new Commanding Officer on the 25th November and Captain Bovell left the ship just after lunch on the 28th. All was now bustle and activity as the carrier prepared for a voyage to a secret destination.

At long last she was leaving the Home Fleet and rumour was rife when *Victorious* sailed from Greenock on 20th December. But it was not until the air group had landed aboard in the afternoon, that the new Commanding Officer, Captain Mackintosh, broadcast to the ship's company that their immediate destination was Bermuda. The met forecast was gloomy and the Captain said that the ship was in for a rough crossing. Two days later a force nine gale hit the ship and his forecast proved to be extremely, uncomfortably accurate. As one 'green-faced' airman so aptly put it:

> Rough, why on that trip even the rats got sick . . . On the second day out water started coming over the flight deck and down into the hangar deck, it was inches deep at times and splashed from side to side with every roll of the ship.

At the end of 1942, our American allies were in a difficult position. The third major attempt by the Japanese to re-take Guadalcanal had resulted in the loss of the carrier *Hornet*, while the *Enterprise* had been reduced to fifty per cent operating efficiency through battle damage. This left the Americans with only one Pacific Fleet carrier, the *Saratoga*, and she was not expected to complete her repairs until the latter half of

November 1942. The urgent plea to the British by the Americans for carrier reinforcement meant that *Victorious* had had to be withdrawn from the Home Fleet and was now on her way via Bermuda to Norfolk, Virginia.

During the trip across, Captain Mackintosh took the opportunity to talk to the pilots and observers in the Wardroom. He had been trained as an observer himself and among other matters he spoke of the peril of mixing alcohol with flying. To illustrate his talk he gave his usual salutary warning: 'I once had a flight with a pilot who had been drinking. When I came out of hospital . . .' These informative chats helped to pass the time, but on Boxing Day in mid-Atlantic, the weather kindly abated and *Victorious* prepared to continue flying anti-submarine patrols. As if there wasn't enough excitement in landing on a crazy-pitching deck, another hazard was added. On the morning of 27th December an attempt was made to refuel HMS *Redoubt,* one of the escorting destroyers. With great caution *Redoubt* made her approach, but for a long time kept too far away for a line to be passed. Eventually she got in closer and the fun started as attempts were made to pass a pipe line. The rough sea took charge and the two ships met in a minor collision, resulting in some damage to the carrier's radio masts. These masts normally stand vertically on either side of the ship and are lowered to the horizontal position during flying. After a few agonising moments, the destroyer disentangled herself from the carrier's side and, to everyone's relief, the fuelling attempt was cancelled. When it came to landing the aircraft on, however, it was found that masts would not lower and from the pilot's point of view – with the masts still in the vertical position – the land-on was an experience similar to flying through a forest and hoping to miss the trees!

Victorious eventually arrived and anchored a mile off shore to the north of Bermuda. The sight of this strange, new carrier just off-shore was too much for some of the local US Servicemen, and curious American pilots would fly out to look at the odd 'Limey flat top'. The land planes would make low, slow passes, while the float planes would land in the water alongside, then taxi slowly round the ship carrying out a detailed, quizzical inspection.

Eight hours later the carrier was on her way again and the Captain broke the news that the ship would be going to Norfolk Navy Yard in Virginia and, from there, to join the American Fleet. *Victorious* carried 882 and 896 Squadrons of 12 Martlets each – COs Lieutenant Commander F.A. Shaw and Lieutenant I.L.F. Lowe and 832 Squadron of Albacores under the Command of Lieutenant Commander W.J. Lucas. On arrival in America, the British carrier would be modified to carry American weapons and the Albacores would be replaced by US Navy Avengers.

The 1st January 1943 heralded a new start for 832 Squadron as they took off and headed for the States. To cries of 'America, here we come', they made cautious, wide circuits of the airfield before landing at Norfolk Naval Air Station. The slow, old fashioned bi-planes created a minor sensation for some of the Americans and to them it was as if Time Travellers from the First World War had suddenly materialised. It was a pity, perhaps, that the bizzare appearance of the Albacore had not been accentuated on this occasion by bicycles strapped to the wing struts: it was common practice to carry one's own transport when flying from ship to shore in home waters. As many as eight cycles had been carried on one Albacore and, after landing, the crew and passengers pedalled away from the aircraft in search of other entertainment.

For the British airmen, the days that followed were crowded with activity: learning their way around the new station, adjusting to American habits and customs, adapting to the new way of doing things and carrying out their first familiarisation flights in the Avenger aircraft. It became policy to call US Navy aircraft by their American name and, to avoid confusion, American names are used throughout this book.

Familiarisation flights continued as the aircrew members swelled and the squadron increased to twenty-one aircraft, to become the largest Fleet Air Arm front-line squadron at the time. Aircrew received lectures on the American deck landing system which was difficult to execute and required constant practice, particularly for the last stage of the approach when a tricky piece of handling had to be carried out. Basically, the signals from the batsman, who stood on the deck and controlled the approach, were really quite sensible. Unfortunately, however, the important signals were the complete opposite of the British ones. For example, with the British system both arms raised from the side and outstretched 45 degrees above the horizontal meant 'Go higher', but in the American case 'You are too high'. In other words the British signals were an instruction of what to do, whereas the American signals were mirror signals advising the pilot of the position of the aircraft in relation to the correct approach path.

Again, the Americans' procedure consisted of a flat approach towards an imaginary point in space, anything up to fifty feet above the stern of the ship. When the aircraft reached this imaginary point over the stern, a cut signal would be given by the batsman, the pilot would close his throttle and then drop, like the proverbial brick. So far so good, but there was fifty feet of space between the aircraft and the deck and, usually, the plane was in a nose-high condition. To prevent a spine-jarring arrival on the deck and damage to the aircraft, the stick had to be eased forward quickly – which naturally made the aircraft drop even more rapidly – and then eased back to cushion the landing. All this would take place in a few seconds of time and, discounting luck, to make a good touch-down required consider-able skill, acquired and maintained by practice.

By contrast, the British method consisted of a nose-high descending approach, keeping the aircraft at about 10 knots above stalling speed; in other words, the same procedure as would be adopted when making a precautionary approach or a landing into a small area. The aircraft was held in this attitude until just prior to touching the deck, then the throttle would be closed and the touch-down made. The arrivals were somewhat more gentle using the British system, which is perhaps just as well, since the delicate undercarriage of the British designed aircraft could not have stood the strain.

Flying training continued with the emphasis now on what the Royal Navy called Aerodrome Dummy Deck Landings (ADDLS for short and pronounced *Addles*). After considerable practice at these, the aircrews were permitted to carry out landings on a carrier, the USS *Charger*. As well as the Avengers, the fighters had problems and tragedy struck *Victorious* during the first week in January 1943, when one flight of four Martlets had a very bad day. One aircraft spun into the deck and the pilot was killed; another aircraft went over the side still attached to the arrester wire, though happily the pilot was recovered somewhat shaken but uninjured; while a third aircraft did not arrive and the pilot's body was washed ashore several days later.

The accidents seemed to pile up one on top of the other, for the new deck landing techniques were proving difficult to master. During some local trials off Cuba, two more Martlets were lost. One piloted by Sub Lieutenant Farthing dropped into the water on take-off due to a faulty engine, but he was picked up by a US destroyer unhurt. The second accident was caused by the pilot coming in too fast on his approach. When the main wheels hit the deck the tail went down and the aircraft became airborne again — sailed over the first safety barrier and went into the second, but this was strong enough to prevent the aircraft hitting the aircraft parked forward and avoided a really nasty accident. It is worth mentioning that an accident of this sort would not happen in today's aircraft carriers, for safety barriers are no longer necessary with modern angled decks. If the last stage of approach is faulty the pilot needs only to increase engine thrust and overshoot.

Finally *Victorious* was ready to leave the Navy Yard, so embarking her squadrons and 898 Squadron, who had formed up with 12 Wildcats in Norfolk in October under the Command of Lieutenant I.L.F. Lowe, RN, she set sail for the Panama Canal on 3rd February. The carrier reached San Christobal at mid-day on the 10th and prepared to pass through the Panama Canal. As she passed the USS *Stalker,* she intercepted a signal from the USS *Massachusetts* which read 'What's the Limey flat top?' Although the reply was not decoded, for the purpose of security *Victorious* was generally referred to as the USS *Robin* — with a sense of humour and a knowledge of ornithology, there was scope for some interesting signals.

At San Christobal the ship spent two days in removing guns and other protuberances from the sides of the ship to enable her to pass through the Panama Canal. *Victorious* left dock on the 13th January in the early afternoon and headed for the Gatun Locks, the first of the three sets of locks which lead up to the lakes of Panama. Except for the men driving the little trams which towed the ship through the locks, everyone could see that it was going to be a tight squeeze to slip *Victorious* through. With seemingly reckless abandon they pressed on and the inevitable happened, the ship was allowed to go too far to port and hit the lock entrance, knocking off the port submarine lookout's position. With a cheery: 'Ah well, Senor, if I knock it off, you can always put it back on' from the foreman, the ship continued its hazardous passage. Fortunately this was the only damage done and the ship continued on with two feet to spare on either side. At last, after nearly four hours to get through the three locks, the ship was free to swing at anchor instead of being restricted to mere inches of latitude.

The anchor was pulled up early next day and a start was made through the middle Pedro Miguel locks. It was 10.15 in the morning, a lovely day and a Sunday. True to tradition prayers were held on the flight deck, but everyone was too hot to sing. To detract from the decorum of the service, the local foreman and his team of tractor-drivers struggled to pull a ship with a beam of nearly 96 feet, through a gap that looked about 90 feet wide. And, as before, the ship scraped and jarred her way along the walls of the lock to the anguished, frantic, excitable Latin American cries of 'Get her over.' Throughout the performance the congregation watched with interest and amusement and after the Hymn; 'Oh God our help in ages past' it seemed another miracle had been performed and *Victorious* was safely through. After the Pacific locks and a short stay anchored off Panama City, the carrier headed for Pearl Harbour. She joined company with her American escort of three destroyers and, conducting flying exercises en route, she headed for Hawaii and the war.

With the modicum of experience that had now been acquired, the Aviation Department realised that in its present condition, the ship was not really suitable for landing Avengers safely. These were, after all, the largest and heaviest aircraft ever landed on a British deck and the arrester gear could not really cope. Even with a maximum setting on the arrester wire hydraulic system, the wires would still pull out for a considerable way and this meant that if an aircraft caught any wire forward of the fourth, it would go into the safety barriers. This was a costly performance and hard on the nerves, so as an interim measure the flight deck personnel lowered the barriers as soon as an aircraft had caught an arrester wire. The batsman Lieutenant (JG) Tommy Thompson USN brought the aircraft in on a lower approach in an attempt to prevent them landing too far up the deck, but these makeshift arrangements were certainly not the answer and something had to be done. A number of aircraft were saved from damage by these measures, but to a certain extent it was a fool's paradise, to think that with the combined skills of the batsman, pilots and barrier operators everything would be all right until the ship reached Pearl, where suitable modifications could be carried out to the ship. As if to emphasize the point, Avenger 4X came in to land, caught the first wire and continued to roll towards the port side of the ship. The port wheel went over the edge and cut a pipe supplying petrol to the flight deck, igniting the fuel.

The fire that followed was drawn into ventilators and smoke started to appear in various parts of the ship. The blaze spread, the boat deck started to burn, the admiral's barge and a cutter were destroyed and then some stored timber caught alight. The fire raged and it was a full hour before it was brought under control. Fortunately for all concerned, the depth charges on the aeroplane just melted and were ditched over the side, thus preventing what might have been a very tragic incident though unhappily all three aircrew died later of their injuries.

Two days later, on the 27th February, a Martlet crashed on landing and caught fire. This time the aircraft's petrol tank was ripped open and again fuel gushed out over the flight deck and ignited. The enthusiastic firefighters tackled the blaze quickly, but the water from their hoses spread the flames and for a time, it looked as though another tragedy would occur. Fortunately Commander Flying shouted to the fire party to use foam and the fire was quickly extinguished, and disaster averted.

It was now nearly the end of February and in a broadcast the Captain told the ship's company among other items of interest that the ship had steamed 100,000 miles since her launching. She would sail for many thousands of miles in the vastness of the Pacific Ocean, but that was in the future. For now, she had the prospects of a refit, repairs to her flight deck and the re-equipping of her squadrons with American aircraft. *Victorious* arrived at Hawaii on the 4th March and after disembarking her aircraft to Ford Island for an intensive work up ashore, she moved into the American dockyard. Men swarmed aboard to carry out the repairs, to put in more guns, and above all, to modify the arrester gear so that the heavier Avenger aircraft could land safely. The flight deck aft had been altered in Norfolk and the round down replaced by a typical American flush-deck, so this allowed for more wires to be fitted aft of the original number one arrester wire, in addition to the modification to increase the arresting or 'braking' effect of the existing wires. One other important, morale-boosting innovation was introduced at this time. The red circle in the centre of the roundels on the British aircraft could be mistaken for Japanese markings and so, to prevent misunderstandings with trigger-happy American gunners, all the squadrons adopted American markings on their aircraft.

Finally, as the time came for the ship to leave Hawaii, the aircrew were given a short survival course in Honolulu. The aim of the course was to teach aircrew how to survive and live off the land (or sea), if they were unfortunate enough to get shot down. They were taught what fish and fruits to eat and that all shell-fish were edible. Then the marvels of the coconut trees were explained. The instructor went into great detail and some felt that given luck, wire and a suitable tree, they could almost make a radio out of it. Inevitably the keener members paid great attention to the coconut and while its edible contents were discussed, they considered how to distil alcohol from the milk. The conclusion of the survival course was a brief talk about the dreaded shark and as an airman explained:

> We were informed that sharks were more frightened of us than we were of them (except one kind of shark); and that one way of scaring them was to put one's head under the water and stare at them. We hoped that all sharks had been briefed with this bit of information!

Though they were to change their minds as the war progressed, the US Navy found much to criticise in the design of the British carrier. Most of it stemmed from our adherence to the armoured design concept, but the Fighter Direction system was much admired and formed the basis for later US Navy CIC[1] design and operation. Because of this advantage and the obvious superiority over American carriers, and because of the continued incompatibility between the Avenger and the *Victorious* arrester wires, Commander Samuel Mitchell, the USN liaison officer, recommended that *Victorious* should be employed as a fighter carrier during subsequent operations with the US Fleet.

On 7th May 1943, the aircraft were loaded on to *Victorious* from the dockside and early next morning, under a cloudless sky – the ship headed out to the wide South West Pacific in company with the battleship *North Carolina* and three destroyers. The ship carried 16 Avengers of 832 Squadron and three fighter squadrons consisting of 882, 896 and 898 with a total of 36 Martlet IVs (F4F-4B); the fighter complement should have been 42, but *Vic* was already crowded and, in any case, there were only 47 Martlets altogether on the West Coast and a proportion of these were needed for advanced pilot training. Aircrews also were in short supply in the States – only two pilots and four observers were immediately available, with another nine pilots allocated but still undergoing training. After a short stop at Noumea in the New Hebrides on 17th May, *Victorious* and the American carrier USS *Saratoga* put to sea for a sweep to the north of the Solomon Islands. Apparently the Japanese Fleet had sailed northwards from Truk, but could present a threat if they turned south and into the Coral Sea area.

Watched intently by *Victorious*, the *Saratoga* landed on sixty aircraft in forty-five minutes and on completion of the land on, the force headed for the Coral sea. After *Saratoga's* performance it was the turn of *Victorious*, who launched nine aircraft on anti-submarine patrols. This was the first time British aircraft had operated and carried out landings in full view of the *Saratoga* and all were anxious to see how they would go.

[1] Combat Information Centre – in British ships, the Operations Room.

I watched from the goofer's platform [John Fay explained] and was in mental agony when the deck was clear and the ship into the wind, before the aircraft were in position to land on. But every aircraft landed well and we had them all aboard in seven minutes which compared well with the Americans. Later that day I was watching some of our Martlets landing on; there was a misunderstanding when one of them wanted an emergency landing and the others did not realise it, but all was well until . . . it happened. A Martlet landed and as it touched down its guns went off. It was thought at first that the shots had gone into the sea without doing any damage, but in fact it quickly transpired that three people were hit, including the Navigating Officer. Apparently the bullets had ricocheted round Commander Flying's platform before hitting him, but he was not badly hurt.

In the event, the Japanese fleet did not turn south and so the task force headed back once more for Noumea. *Victorious* was at sea again between 1st and 3rd June on exercises and this time she carried Rear Admiral Ramsey USN, Commander of the Carrier Forces in the South-West Pacific and Captain Mulliner, Captain of *Saratoga*. The two officers wanted to see how a British carrier operated and, some days later, Captain Mackintosh returned the call and spent four days aboard *Saratoga* exercising off New Caledonia. For the last round of exercises, both carriers put to sea on 16th June for four days. On the final day out, the carriers cross-operated each other's aircraft. 6 Avengers and 12 Martlets from *Victorious* were exchanged for 8 Avengers, 6 Dauntlesses and 12 Wildcats from *Saratoga*. No difficulty was experienced with the landings in either carrier nor with the US Navy system.

For the next operational sortie, as part of the American Fleet, *Victorious* transferred her 15 Avengers of 832 Squadron to the USS *Saratoga* – the first and one of the few occasions on which British aircraft operated from a United States aircraft carrier. The Task Group was ordered to sail and act as the cover for an American landing in New Georgia in the Solomons. This meant that the force would be on hand in the Coral Sea in case the Japanese Fleet put to sea and attempted to interfere with the landings. Task Group 36.3, consisting of *Victorious, Saratoga* (Rear Admiral Ramsey), *Indiana, North Carolina,* with screening AA cruisers and destroyers, sailed from Noumea to cover the New Georgia landings on 27th June 1943. Rendova Island was assaulted on 30th June, but the carriers, stationed between 250 and 350 miles to the south, took no part in the actual invasion, their role being to guard against any possible interference by the still-powerful Japanese Fleet. The Task Group remained on station for 28 days in all, returning to Noumea on 25th July and without firing a shot in anger.

One of the 832 Squadron Avengers on loan to *Saratoga* had a deck-landing accident during a wave-off and went over the side, but the British aircrew were rescued by a US destroyer and returned to the *Sara.* The exchange was affected by means of the breeches buoy, but only after 25 pounds of ice cream had been sent across to the destroyer by way of payment – as was the custom. An ironical twist was given to the story, when another British crew from the *Saratoga* were rescued from their crashed aircraft by the same destroyer, and had the pleasure of eating some of the ice cream.

After three weeks in the same area with no action, it seemed that the ships were running on rails, but at last the enemy appeared. One of the American Dauntless pilots spotted a solitary Japanese 'Betty' about 50 miles from the Fleet. He dived on it, firing his front guns, but apparently did not hit it. *Victorious* had operated as a fighter carrier throughout the period at sea, with 60 F4F variants embarked – 36 of her own Martlets, and 24 F4F-4s of VF-3 from *Saratoga.* The American carrier retained 12 Wildcats, primarily because *Vic* could take no more, and in addition to her own 36 Dauntless and 20 TBFs, she had the 15 TBFs of 832 Squadron embarked. This was the only prolonged operational deployment of RN aircraft to an American carrier throughout the war, although several other units did embark for passage aboard US Navy ships.

A total of 614 sorties was flown by *Victorious* during this long stint and the ship herself was refuelled twice, by *Cimarron* and *Kaskaskia.* In addition to the 3,270 tons of fuel oil and 30,000 gallons of aviation spirit, the RN carrier was grateful to receive 20 gallons of ice cream. Another shortage – that of potatoes — was relieved by *Saratoga,* which sent over 800 pounds of de-hydrated potato in the bomb-bay of a TBF Avenger, on which was painted the name *Spud Express.* Rum had also run short, but this was a commodity which even the US Navy could not supply, and here the Royal Australian Navy came to the rescue. Thus ended the action in the Coral Sea and with the landings proceeding satisfactorily, the force headed back to Noumea. *Saratoga* transferred 832 Squadron back to *Victorious,* where after being in a 'dry ship' for four weeks, severe inroads were made into the bar stocks and the aircrew threw an impromptu party.

By the end of July 1943, the new 'Essex' and 'Independence' classes of carrier were finishing their work-up periods and were preparing for their first operations in the Central Pacific. With New Georgia firmly held by the Allies, *Victorious* was released from South West Pacific Fleet and on 31st July, after turning over five of her eleven remaining TBFs to Air Group 12 at Tontouna, she set sail once more for Pearl Harbour in company with *Indiana, Converse, Boyd* and *Halford.* The ships of Task Unit 34.5.1 arrived at Pearl Harbour on 9th August 1943, and *Victorious* left for the last time on 12th bound for San Diego, with 52 aircrew from *Saratoga* aboard as passengers. The task was done and the ship on the first leg of its journey back to Britain. Avengers from the *Saratoga's* squadrons came along to 'beat up' the ship as she departed, but their show was rather marred by the fact that two of the aircraft collided! Fortunately it was only a case of the propeller of one aircraft taking bits off the tail of another, and bits of metal fluttered down round the ship. Then the fighters came in and gave an impressive, if nail-biting, display.

In addition to the American passengers, there were two Japanese prisoners of war on board: an ironic touch, that after the immense effort that went into transferring a British carrier to the Pacific, the only enemy with whom contact was made were prisoners of war. In strategy however, mere presence and availability can achieve much. The *Victorious* had been part of the US Fleet during the vital interval that occurred just before the new US carriers were entering the Pacific to replace ones that had either sunk or were badly overdue for a refit. It is doubtful whether the landings in the Solomons could have taken place without the covering force, of which the *Victorious* was a vital part. Alternatively, operations elsewhere might have been curtailed or postponed as other units of the fleet were stretched to fill the gap.

Victorious finally left the Pacific on 25th August 1943, when she began the east-bound transit of the Panama Canal. She took with her the congratulations of Admirals Nimitz and Towers, both of whom regretted the lack of action, but hoped that their next meeting would prove to be more active. She arrived at Liverpool and entered the Gladstone Lock for a refit that was to last until 4th March 1944. In the intervening period, she said goodbye to Captain Mackintosh and welcomed her new Commanding Officer, Captain Denny. Prior to her departure for the Pacific the *Victorious* had crossed swords with the enemy in other oceans. After the refit and on her second trip to the Far East she was to see much action. In the interim, 1943 had been a quiet year and she had steamed from Britain to the Coral Sea and back without sighting the enemy, so this time for her it was truly a Pacific Interlude.

Chapter VIII

OPERATION TUNGSTEN

Next to the famous attack on the Italian Fleet at Taranto by the Fleet Air Arm in 1940, Operation 'Tungsten' — the attack on the German battleship *Admiral von Tirpitz* in Alten Fiord — rates probably as one of the most brilliantly conceived, planned and executed Fleet Air Arm actions in World War II. Monday 3rd of April 1944 was the day and *Victorious* one of the ships taking part.

The *Tirpitz* was the most powerful enemy ship afloat with the exception of the Japanese battleships *Yamata* and *Musashi*, the former was sunk in October 1944 and the latter in April 1945. Launched at Wilhelmshaven on 1st April 1939, this 56,000-ton giant was declared unsinkable. An armoured belt some fifteen inches thick and six feet wide ran along the water-line, from forward of the forward turret to abaft the after one. Her vital compartments and machinery spaces were protected by armour plate from five to ten inches thick and, below decks, the ship was a veritable honeycomb of small water-tight compartments.

Her armament was equally impressive and consisted of eight 15-inch guns in four turrets: Anton(A) and Bruno(B) turrets forward; Cesar(C) and Dora(D) turrets aft. Either side of the ship were six twin 5.9-inch turrets making a total of twelve guns. Finally, the very considerable anti-aircraft armament of eighteen 4.1-inch guns in twin mountings, sixteen 37-millimetre and fifty 20-millimetre machine guns completed her formidable arsenal of weapons.

As described earlier in the book, *Tirpitz* had already met *Victorious* — or rather her aircraft — and but for some bad luck and a thirty—foot miss with an air-dropped torpedo, her first sortie out into the Atlantic to attack convoy PQ12 on March

5th could have ended in another *Bismarck* episode. Luck was on her side on that occasion, but thereafter she became the target for many and varied attacks by Allied seaborne and airborne forces. The seaborne forces had the first try and in Operation 'Title', the Norwegian Cutter *Arthur*, laden with mines, got within ten miles of its target only to be defeated by the weather and rough seas. Twelve months later in September 1943, the submariners tried their hand and in a daring attack by midget submarines came within an ace of sinking her and succeeded in severely damaging the battleship. As early as January 1942, Winston Churchill had given orders to sink the *Tirpitz*, stating that: 'the whole strategy of the war turns at this point on this ship' but it was to be nearly three years before a successful RAF attack finally sealed the fate of *Tirpitz* at Tromso.

Anchored as she was in her Norewegian Fiord, the *Tirpitz* presented a difficult target and, in military parlance, remained a constant threat in being. Even damaged – by the earlier midget submarine attack – she was more than just a potential menace and kept a disproportionate amount of Allied effort tied up in keeping an eye on her. The Admiralty were very concerned with the progress of her repairs and, accordingly, regular reconnaissance flights were flown over her anchorage by Spitfires operating out of Veanga. Working day and night, it had taken about six months to repair the damage and although not one hundred per cent completed, intelligence and some excellent aerial photographs indicated that she was just about ready to sail. If this assessment was correct then, once more, she constituted a very real danger to the ships on the North Russian convoy run and something would have to be done about it.

The operation to neutralise the *Tirpitz* was to be the task of the Fleet Air Arm and should have taken place between the 7th and 16th March, but *Victorious* was delayed in dockyard hands during her refit in Liverpool, so it had to be postponed by about a fortnight. During this time, *Victorious* carried out her post-refit trials in the Greenock and Irish Sea areas, while her air group flew as much as possible to train for the forthcoming operation. A dummy range was built at Loch Eriboll to represent *Tirpitz* at anchor in Kaa Fiord, at the far end of the Alten Fiord. This Loch in Caithness on the northern coast of

Scotland had a remarkable similarity to Alten Fiord, and the aircrews spent many hours co-ordinating the method of attack and perfecting their dive-bombing. The strikes were planned in great detail and the dummy range provided invaluable training, for in the case of the newly formed *Victorious* squadrons, there was little enough time. Rehearsal followed rehearsal and after a final practice off Scapa on 28th March, all was ready for the Barracudas of No. 8 Bomber Torpedo Reconnaissance Wing of *Furious* and No. 52 TBR Wing of *Victorious* to try their skill!

Kaa Fiord was a natural defensive anchorage at the extreme end of Alten Fiord; with its steep 3,000 foot mountain sides sloping down to the narrow slit of water some three quarters of a mile wide, it presented a protective shield and a formidable obstacle to would-be aerial attackers. Defended by anti-submarine and anti-torpedo nets, a host of AA guns, flak ships and radar, she would provide a difficult target, but to add to the problems smoke generating apparatus on shore could reduce visibility in a matter of minutes, throwing a protective blanket over the great ship and hiding her in an impenetrable smoke screen. As a further deterrent to seaborne attack, five 'Narvik' Class destroyers were stationed at Alten Fiord in addition to a number of submarines – normally employed to counter the North Russian convoys. Units of the German air force based in the area were small, but they could be reinforced rapidly in an emergency and, in any case, they flew three routine recon-naissance flights in and around the area almost daily. Surprise would be a key factor in the success of this venture and great secrecy attended every stage in the vital planning and training.

On 27th March, Convoy JW 58 consisting of forty-nine ships sailed from Loch Ewe for the Kola Inlet and under cover of this convoy, the attacking force of carriers and escorts commenced their 1,200 mile passage towards Norway. Admiral Sir Bruce Fraser, the C-in-C Home Fleet had entrusted the preparations for the *Tirpitz* attack to his Second in Command; Vice Admiral Sir Henry Moore flying his flag in the battleship *Anson*. On the morning of 30th March, Admiral Fraser sailed from Scapa with Force 1 consisting of *Victorious,* the battleships *Duke of York* and *Anson,* the cruiser *Belfast* and six destroyers. After a calibration shoot by the battleships and live bombing practice by aircraft from *Victorious,* the force then headed for the rendezvous some 250 miles north-west of Alten Fiord, scheduled to take place on the evening of the 3rd April. Initially, Force 1 was to provide heavy cover to the convoy should *Tirpitz* attempt to leave the fiord, while Force 2 under the Command of Rear Admiral Bisset consisting of the fleet carrier *Furious* and the escort carriers *Emperor, Searcher, Pursuer* and *Fencer,* three cruisers, two oilers and ten destroyers sailed for the launch position direct.

With the intelligence information available, it was just possible that *Tirpitz* would venture out and attack any Allied shipping on the Russian Convoy route and for this reason, the C-in-C and his strong force would remain near the convoy. If however the *Tirpitz* remained in the protected anchorage then he would leave the convoy as soon as possible, and continue with his original intention to go for the battleship in Alten Fiord. As convoy JW 58 steamed on towards its destination, a breakout by *Tirpitz* seemed less and less likely and though shadowed intermittently by enemy aircraft, the convoy and its close escort was making good progress and seemed well able to take care of itself. Accordingly Admiral Fraser ordered the attack to be advanced twenty-four hours and headed his force for the rendezvous. Admiral Bisset and his escort carriers of Force 2 increased to their maximum speed of 17 knots, and the two forces met about 220 miles to the north-west of Alten Fiord, on the afternoon of the 2nd April. Admiral Moore took his attacking force of carriers towards their launch position, while the C-in-C in the *Duke of York* escorted by two destroyers, cruised some 200 miles to the north until the attack was completed.

It was a splendid dawn that morning over Norway with an almost perfect visibility. The few wisps of cloud that clung to the mountain tops soon dispersed to leave them sharply defined against the back drop of a clear sky. On the bridge of *Tirpitz,* the Captain was well pleased as he watched the bustle of activity to get his ship to sea. The full power trials on the 15th March had gone well and she had been all set to sail again yesterday. Unfortunately bad weather had caused Captain Meyer to delay his sailing for 24 hours, but today, 3rd April 1944, two tugs stood by to help the great ship clear the anchorage, to clear her torpedo nets and proceed for extended sea trials. *Tirpitz* was secured to the shore. The first anchor was weighed, the stern lines slipped, then the second anchor was weighed and slowly the ship was edged clear.

Meanwhile, aboard the carriers, the final preparations had been in progress since the previous evening. The attack was to consist of two strikes, with the first wave of twenty-one Barracudas from *Victorious* and *Furious,* escorted by a fighter umbrella of forty-five Corsairs, Hellcats and Wildcats, followed some sixty minutes later by a second strike of another twenty-one Barracudas again escorted by some forty-five fighters. In order that the wings which had so carefully rehearsed together at Loch Eriboll should strike together, *Victorious* and *Furious* had each exchanged one Barracuda Squadron before the Force sailed.

In *Victorious,* the flying programme was complicated by the fact that she was carrying far more aircraft than she had been designed to operate. Her hangar and flight deck were crowded with no less than 49 aircraft. She carried 14 Corsairs of 1834 Squadron, 14 Corsairs of 1836 Squadron, 12 Barracudas of 827 and 9 more Barracudas of 829 Squadrons, but by 1700 on the evening of the 2nd April all the aircraft were fuelled, serviceable and waiting to be 'bombed up'. With a crowded ship involving as it did a permanent deck park of aircraft, there was a certain amount of anxiety felt about the serviceability of those aircraft necessarily parked on deck. For the exposed aeroplanes, a day or two of North Sea winter conditions could be disastrous and as Captain Denny of *Victorious* said: '*Victorious*' flight deck is very wet in any weather, and the spray and sleet were freezing on deck.' In the event, the risk in carrying additional aircraft, was more than justified by the increase in striking power, for as it turned out, only one Barracuda was unserviceable on the day of the attack. To improve matters however, the aircraft on deck were all allocated to the second strike and after engine runs during the night of the 2nd/3rd, they were struck down into the comparative warmth of the hangar, while the aircraft already in the hangar were being ranged on deck for the first strike.

To add to the problems, considerable difficulties arose

because the aircraft had to be loaded with no less than four different types of bombs in mixed loads. Changes in the elaborate bombing-up procedure due to last minute and unforseen servicing requirements, resulted in a fairly hectic time for the armourers. In many cases, they had to search for their aircraft, chasing it through the hangar, up one lift and along the flight deck and having found it – bomb it up with either 1,600-pound armour piercing bombs, two types of 500-pound bombs or the new 600-pound A/S bomb. By 6 o'clock that night the trials and tribulations of the armourers, flight deck handlers and maintenance men were overcome and the aircraft were ready and waiting.

In *Victorious*, selected officers had been briefed for the intended operation some days earlier, under conditions of the strictest secrecy. The mass of intelligence data had been assimilated and during the days immediately preceding, the attack, most detailed squadron briefings had been given. At 0130 on the morning of the 3rd, the aircrews filed into the briefing rooms for their final full briefing and last minute instructions – Army Liaison Officers, Intelligence Officers and Air Staff Officers all contributed their valuable information and by 0400 – all was ready.

Action stations sounded in *Victorious* at 0345 that morning and as the aircrews manned their aircraft, they could see that flying conditions were superb. There was no swell, a light off-shore wind of 12 to 14 knots from the southward and excellent visibility. Zero hour for the launch was 0415 and by five past four all the aircraft were ready – engines warmed up and a noisy, throbbing roar on deck. Every aircraft had started and there was not a single failure in any carrier, which was a fine tribute to the hard work and thoroughness of the maintenance personnel and aircraft handling parties. The bows of *Victorious* came round to the south-east and the revolutions built up until she was shuddering along at 28 knots. The wind over the deck was now sufficient and the first aircraft taxied clear of the deck-park, wound on full throttle and waited for his 'GO'.

At exactly sixteen minutes past four the first of the ten escorting Corsairs left the deck of *Victorious*, followed eight

minutes later by the twenty-one Barracudas from her and
Furious, while the escort carriers launched the remaining fighter
escort. The departure point for the strikes was fixed as four
miles from the Fleet carriers in the direction of the escort
carrier force.

> It was a grand sight with the sun just risen [Rear Admiral
> Bisset said later], to see this well balanced striking force of
> about 20 Barracudas and 45 fighters departing at very low
> level between the two forces of surface ships, and good to
> know that a similar sized force would be leaving in about
> an hour's time. It was especially heartening to an ex-carrier
> Captain accustomed for several years, to be very short of
> aircraft (especially fighters), and made one wonder 'what
> might have been', if the Fleet Air Arm had been adequately
> supplied with aircraft in the early days of the War!

For twenty minutes the strike led by Lieutenant Commander
R. Baker-Faulkner, and the escorting fighters led by Lieutenant
Commander F.R.A. Turnbull and Lieutenant Commander J.W.
Sleigh, DSC, flew low over the water, then some 25 miles from
the Norwegian coast, the force commenced their climb to
10,000 feet. They crossed the coast about 50 minutes after take
off, passing near the head of Alta and Lang Fiords, where the
fighters jettisoned their long range tanks, before heading eastward down the valley towards Kaa Fiord and the *Tirpitz*. The
Corsair pilots flew north to the small port of Narvik on Alten
Fiord, turned south again towards the *Tirpitz*; their mission was
to range out over the fiords, to intercept any enemy fighter
opposition from Bardufoss and protect the heavily laden
Barracudas. All was quiet, the enemy were unsuspecting and
even the roar of the Hellcat Squadron, as it flew over a
destroyer and a large merchantman in Lang Fiord, failed to
produce any opposition or prompt any sign of life. For good
measure, the fighters engaged a flak ship, a destroyer and two
armed trawlers on the way to the target and left the latter on
fire.

As the third shackle of the second anchor was heaved in, the
Captain heard the first report of enemy aircraft approaching.
The smoke generators were started ashore and at 0528, the

alarm rattlers sounded in *Tirpitz* and the men raced to their
action stations. AA guns swung round and pointed to the sky
seeking out the attackers, while the shore batteries also joined in
and opened fire. The short warning interval meant that men
were still closing water-tight doors and hatches when the attack
started, so they were not at their proper action stations and not
all the guns crews were closed up. The Captain estimated he was
only 80 per cent shut down for action and, helplessly, he
watched the next few minutes of devastation rain down on his
ship from the sky. Unable to use the ship's speed to avoid the
deluge of bombs for fear of running aground – he had to rely
on his anti-aircraft fire and trust to luck. This time, however, his
luck ran out!

The attack was carried out exactly as planned, and it was
soon clear that the enemy had been caught napping. No hostile
aircraft were seen, nor was there any interference from flak till
the strike was within 3 miles of the target area. By then it was
almost too late. The Barracudas deployed and began their dive
from 8,000 feet; at the same time high angle batteries at the
head of the fiord and elsewhere opened a heavy but inaccurate
fire, and the *Tirpitz* was sighted in the expected position. Diving
to keep hill cover and hedge-hopping over the hills, Lieutenant
Commander Baker-Faulkner sent all Hellcats and Wildcats down
to beat up the flak positions and strafe the target, which they
did most effectively and 'undoubtedly spoilt the *Tirpitz*
gunnery', while the Corsairs as a defence umbrella patrolled over
the whole area at about 10,000 feet. The smoke generators,
started as soon as the aircraft were sighted, were now going all
round the fiord, but it was too late. The smoke screen was very
thin and only partially hid the ship, with the foretop remaining
completely uncovered. For some of the first aircraft to go in,
the target was completely clear and with perfect precision and a
good aiming point, the bombers dived to the attack, releasing
their bombs from heights of between 3,000 and 1,200 feet. Hits
were scored immediately, causing heavy explosions and flames,
and it was evident that the *Tirpitz* was severely damaged.

Sub Lieutenant David Clarabut, RNVR, from Rochester,
Kent, describing his experience, said:

As I was about to bomb, a great sheet of flame shot up from the *Tirpitz*. Billowing clouds of smoke came up to a considerable height. Then I dropped my own bomb through the smoke and immediately the whole 'kite' seemed to lift in the air.

Twenty-four-year-old Lieutenant Commander Kevin Gibney, DSC, an Irishman from near Dublin, was the observer in the third plane, which got a direct hit with a 1,600-pound armour piercing bomb.

We picked up our target well [he said] and saw a great black swastika painted on the fore-castle of the *Tirpitz*. We had one of the big 'cookies' [1,600-lb armour piercing high-explosive bombs] aboard, and our wings lifted as it went down. I watched it hurtling down towards the *Tirpitz*. I couldn't see it hit, but the tail gunner of the following plane said it exploded in a cloud of smoke and flame.

Another Barracuda pilot, twenty-two-year-old Sub Lieutenant Clifford Montague Lock, RNVR, from Bournemouth, should not have been in the raid at all. While flying off Scotland just a week earlier, a gull flew through his windscreen and smashed it into a thousand pieces cutting his head. But by persistent pressure on the ship's doctor, he had obtained permission to fly only that morning. At the subsequent de-brief of the aircrews he reported:

We picked up the *Tirpitz* about four miles away, standing out clearly. There were about six Barracudas going in ahead of me, and quite a lot of flak about. The Huns were putting up a box barrage. The *Tirpitz* didn't seem to be camouflaged, but the Germans started laying smoke as we turned away from the attack and made for the open sea again.

In vain the *Tirpitz* attempted to evade and to manoeuvre slowly, but the bombs continued to hit the upper decks — piercing the light armour, smashing, twisting, shattering and killing. Everywhere men lay wounded and killed in pools of blood — machine gun bullets ripped into the gun positions, splintering decks and killing off the exposed men. One after another the aircraft came in; many were too low for AA fire to be effective or to hit them. The Captain of *Tirpitz* complained that with the great number of fighters coming in at the ship from so many directions, it was impossible to co-ordinate his AA defences. In any case, the main flak battery and both forward flak fire controls had already been put out of action by the fighter gunfire. One of the first hits smashed most of the communications so that neither damage nor casualty reports could get through to the bridge and, to add to the confusion, the Captain himself was wounded by splinters and had to turn over the ship to his Second-in-Command.

All the time the Barracudas were attacking, the fighters were spraying bullets into the German anti-aircraft battery posts and roaring to and fro across the battle area waiting for the German fighters which never came up. Friendly air activity was hectic — at sea over the carriers, Swordfish carried out A/S patrols while Seafires patrolled the air overhead in case of enemy intervention. The air over the target was thick with aircraft as the escorting Wildcats shot up anti-aircraft guns, destroyers, tankers and tugs; Hellcats patrolled at medium height while the Corsairs formed the top layer, both waiting and watching for the approach of enemy fighters. Still they did not come and amidst the flock of carrier aircraft, the ungainly, ugly Barracudas dived towards their target — straight through everyone and everything.

A Corsair pilot, Sub Lieutenant Don Sheppard, RCNVR, from Toronto, Canada, recalled:

The first strike caught the Germans with their trousers down. We stooged around in high cover at 12,000 feet. I counted hit after hit, a dozen perhaps, or more. The *Tirpitz?* It was smoking, and burning . . . just taking it.

Exactly 60 seconds after the first bomb had fallen, the attack was over and, leaving the enemy on fire in several places, the exultant aircraft headed to the north-west for Silden Island and home to the carriers. No difficulty was experienced on the return passage and the carriers were sighted at a distance of 40

miles. The attack had been a great success and only one
Barracuda was lost. Aircraft M of 830 Squadron and flown by
Sub Lieutenant Bell, RNVR, was last seen after the attack in a
controlled glide with his engine stopped. The aircraft was then
at 1,000 feet proceeding up the fiord and was thought to have
force landed. The remainder, to quote from the *Victorious*
report, 'returned in flight formation with an unanimous broad
grin', landing thankfully back on board without incident at half
past six.

One Hellcat flown by Sub Lieutenant Hoare, RNZNVR,
returned to the carrier with a hook damaged by enemy flak.
Admiral Bisset decided that it was too risky to attempt to land
it back on either of the fleet carriers, because it would
inevitably crash into the barriers, thus fouling up the deck while
the wreck was cleared. As there were a lot of other aircraft in
the sky waiting to land on, he ordered the pilot to ditch
alongside and he was later recovered cold, wet but unhurt by
the destroyer, HMCS *Algonquin*.

Meanwhile, at 0525 – just as the first strike was attacking –
the second strike commenced flying off the carriers. One
Barracuda failed to start and, to save precious time, it was
pushed over the side. Another, Aircraft Q of 829 Squadron
piloted by Sub Lieutenant Bowles, RNVR, failed to gain height,
crashed into the sea and was lost with its crew, while one
Wildcat had to return to *Pursuer* with engine trouble. Nevertheless, the remaining 19 Barracudas and their escort of 40 odd
fighters got airborne in only nine minutes, formed up at
between 50 and 200 feet and took departure for yet another
onslaught against the enemy. This time, the strike was commanded by Lieutenant Commander V. Rance of the *Victorious*,
with Lieutenant Commander M.F. Fell of the *Searcher* as senior
officer of the close escort fighters.

After crossing the coast at 10,000 feet, height was slowly
reduced so that the aircraft would be between 7,500 and 7,000
feet, when they commenced their final dive to attack. By now
the generators were fully effective and the blanket of the smoke
screen was visible from 40 miles away. Lieutenant Commander
Rance leading the Barracudas in said:

The smoke did not interfere with the bombing, but must have hampered the close range weapons considerably.

The aircraft approached from the port side of the target, building up to an attacking speed of some 210 knots. The fighters went in first to deal with the flak positions and try to silence the *Tirpitz's* guns and then, for the second time, the Barracudas screamed down on to a smoke covered and battered *Tirpitz*. She appeared to be on an even keel with a normal trim and draught, despite the successful attacks by the first strike; but she had changed her berth and was now swung across the fiord with her stern nearly aground, and she appeared to be drifting.

In fact, we now know that *Tirpitz* was expecting another attack and her acting Captain was desperately trying to manoeuvre his ship back into the safety of her net-defence enclosure. A difficult task without the aid of tugs, which with discretion as the better part of valour had departed to safer parts of the fiord! She was half in and half out of her defensive anchorage when the planes struck, and through the flames and smoke her anti-aircraft gunners tried desparately to fend off this new threat.

Again the Barracudas dive-bombed in rapid succession — one after another they roared down steeply from between 45 and 60 degree dives. The pilots sweated as they fought to hold the planes on the target, buffeting and juddering as the speed built up, they released their bombs at about 3,000 feet and then hauled back on the 'pole' to pull out and make their getaway. With the element of surprise completely gone for the second attack, there was considerable close range flak to contend with, and Barracuda M of 829 Squadron was hit during the dive. Although the pilot bravely completed his attack and pulled out of the dive, the aircraft was mortally wounded and was last seen diving vertically in flames on to the mountain side.

As with the first attack, the second strike lasted just one minute and by the time the last aircraft dived, *Tirpitz* had stopped firing her guns and was burning with a fierce glow amidships. Sub Lieutenant George Burford, from London, who was in one of the last Barracudas to attack, said in his debrief:

The *Tirpitz* was apparently still on an even keel when we went in. I saw a great flame from one explosion – it came up possibly to 500 feet and just spread right across the ship. Our own middle bomb hit her too.

The bombers and escorting fighters weaved and twisted their way clear of the smoke and death in Kaa Fiord, triumphantly heading for Lang Fiord, the carriers and safety. Behind them lay *Tirpitz,* shrouded in pillars of smoke, terribly damaged and temporarily out of control. On the way back, the fighters took the opportunity to engage any and every target that came their way. A 5,000 ton merchant ship in Lang Fiord was left smoking, another of 3,000 tons received the same treatment in Oks Fiord and finally, a wireless receiving station was strafed and damaged.

The strike was now over and one by one the aircraft circled their parent carrier and landed on. A minor excitement was caused when a Barracuda landed on *Victorious* with a 600-pound bomb still in place. In spite of all his efforts, the pilot had been unable to jettison the weapon owing to an electrical fault. Hastily the flight deck was cleared in case of mishap and then last of all, it landed on – safely! It was now two minutes to eight, all the aircraft were home and with a sigh of relief and full of elation, the force headed to the north-west and cleared the area.

Admiral Moore had intended to launch more attacks the next day, but decided to cancel it because he believed the *Tirpitz* to be seriously damaged and also because of the 'fatigue of the aircrews and their natural reaction after completing a dangerous operation successfully' – a factor frequently mentioned by the US Navy after operations in the Pacific and believed to have caused a number of accidents. Accordingly, he ordered all the forces to return to base and after an uneventful passage *Victorious* reached Scapa Flow on the afternoon of the 6th April.

As the attackers withdrew, the Germans in *Tirpitz* began to take stock of the situation. The ship was in a shambles around the upper deck, and although the bombs had not penetrated the heavy armour, she had sustained no less than fourteen direct hits. Her light armour and upper deck had taken a terrible pounding and exposed personnel had suffered dreadful casualties. After the first attack there were 108 killed and 248 wounded, but after the second onslaught the figures had risen to 112 killed and 316 wounded — many very seriously. Working night and day, it was to be nearly three months before *Tirpitz* would be fit for sea again and the Fleet Air Arm had ensured the temporary safety of the vital Arctic convoys, as well as releasing many of our valuable warships for service in other theatres of war.

The proficiency and competence of the young aircrew was both significant and gratifying for, as already stated, no operation since the successful Taranto strike in November 1940 had been so carefully planned, so rehearsed and the results so decisive. In this operation, there were 201 aircrew taking part of which no less than 149 were reserve officers from five different countries, plus 14 regular Royal Navy Officers and 41 rating aircrew Air Gunners — most of them seeing action for the very first time.

Down below in the carriers, reports were being drafted and pictures of the attack developed. They were to show that the victory was one of the smoothest and greatest of the war — a very unpublicised achievement that did great credit to all concerned. Even today, little has been published about the Fleet Air Arm's success against *Tirpitz,* but when the force came back to their base it was to one of the greatest welcomes of the war. The tremendous and moving reception accorded to the *Tirpitz* striking force when it returned to harbour was aptly described by Desmond Tighe, Reuter's special correspondent, who accompanied the expedition in *Victorious.*

> The flagship and other ships of the Home Fleet [wrote Tighe] cleared the lower decks, and gave three rousing cheers as the fleet carrier force that smashed the *Tirpitz* steamed line ahead into port. The carriers were welcomed home with full honours. As we passed each ship the officers and ratings lining the quarter-decks took off their caps and cheered, the sound reverberating across the blue waters. It was an inspiring sight, and, standing on the

Admiral's bridge of the carrier, I felt very proud of being in such a ship.

The sleek, green Barracudas that had done the job were lined up astern of the flight deck and up forward, and the blue uniformed pilots, observers and gunners stood in line. The Fleet Air Arm boys are happy to-night and they deserve to be. Congratulations to the Fleet Air Arm in general and to the Barracuda crews in particular on the success of the attack on the German battleship *Tirpitz* in Alten Fiord, and in those congratulations should be joined the Fairey Aviation Company Limited as designers and builders of the Barracuda.

Perhaps his praise of the 'Barraweewee' as the Barracuda was derisively called was not entirely justified, nor shared by the aircrew. But there is no doubt that in the *Tirpitz* raid, the Barracuda had its hour of Glory.

With the ships anchored in Scapa Flow, the flood of congratulatory messages started to pour in. One from His Majesty, King George VI and relayed via the Admiralty read:

IMPORTANT

HM The King wishes the following message to be passed to those who took part in yesterday's attack Begins:— Hearty congratulations on your gallant and successful operation yesterday.

George R.I.   Ends

and another from the Prime Minister, Winston Churchill:

Pray congratulate the pilots and aircrews concerned on this most brilliant feat of arms so satisfactory to RN and to whole world cause.

Ends

Victorious was planned to take part in four more attacks on *Tirpitz* in Kaa Fiord during April and May, but unkindly, the weather intervened and they had to be cancelled. However, whenever conditions moderated sufficiently, she was sent off to her old happy hunting grounds, to attack enemy shipping off the coast of North Norway. The first two of these under the codenames of 'Ridge Able' and 'Ridge Baker' were scheduled for the 26th April. *Victorious, Furious* and the four escort carriers, *Searcher, Pursuer, Emperor* and *Striker* were sailed to attack enemy shipping in and around Bodo and Narvik. There was some confusion in the orders for these operations and to add to the problems, the weather rapidly deteriorated. A feature of her next few trips was to be the number of mines encountered, but this hazard enlivened the proceedings more than somewhat and when one passed within 200 yards of the ship on 15th May – it caused a mild stir on the bridge. Off the Norwegian coast, gale force winds whipped up the seas, causing the flight decks to pitch up and down very violently. So bad was the movement, that a Hellcat on *Emperor's* deck broke loose and caused some damage as she smashed into other aircraft parked nearby. Nevertheless, in spite of the deck movement, frequent snow storms and a freezing level of only 500 feet, 27 Barracudas escorted by 56 Wildcats, Hellcats and Corsairs took off.

A German convoy of five ships and its escorts were sighted off Bodo and although conditions for bombing were not good, with a cloud base of a little over 2,000 feet and frequent snow showers and storms, three ships totalling some 15,000 tons were sunk. During the attacks, another ship of 800 tons was severely damaged and an escort destroyer hit. All for the loss of one Hellcat, two Corsairs and one Barracuda.

Later on the afternoon of the 26th, *Victorious* launched a further six Corsairs of 1834 Squadron to carry out an armed reconnaissance of the beaches and landing grounds in the Narvik area. The somewhat doubtful aim was to try to convince the enemy that they could expect an Allied landing in Norway in the immediate future, but the weather was so bad, with low cloud, poor visibility and heavy seas, that the aircraft could do little except risk themselves. With no improvement in the weather conditions forecast, the force returned to Scapa as soon as the aircraft landed on – a very frustrating experience after the success of the *Tirpitz* raids.

The last anti-shipping strike occurred on the 1st June, when under the Code name of Operation 'Lombard', *Victorious* and *Furious* were ordered to attack shipping in the Aalesund area — halfway between Bergen and Trondheim. This time the weather was kinder, with a calm sea, only 3/10 cloud cover and almost unlimited visibility. Again dodging mines, she arrived off Stadtlandet in south-west Norway and commenced launching aircraft. Sixteen Barracudas armed with three 500-pound bombs each took off from the two carriers, escorted by 22 Corsairs as middle and top cover and 12 Seafires as close escort. As they approached Kram Island, the striking force sighted and attacked a small convoy of enemy ships, escorted by destroyers and flak ships. The fighters immediately went in to strafe the flak ships and convoy escorts to minimise the AA fire, while the Barracudas commenced to bomb the merchantmen. For the loss of only one Corsair and one Seafire, the bombers remained unscathed and managed to sink the *Leonhardt* of 4,000 tons and the 2,300-ton *Sperrbrecher 181* and damaged two others. One ship, the 5,500-ton SS *Florida* was so badly hit that she had to be beached. The attack over, the aircraft headed back again to the carriers and the force returned once more to Scapa.

That really ended the story of *Victorious'* part in the *Tirpitz* raids and her spell in home waters. Soon she was to be on her way to the Far East, to join the British Pacific Fleet and take part in the war against Japan. As it turned out, *Tirpitz* was able to effect repairs by 1st July, but she was never again to put to sea to attack Allied shipping or menace our convoy routes. After several more air attacks while she was at anchor, the mighty *Tirpitz* was finally destroyed at Tromso by Lancasters of Numbers 9 and 617 Squadrons of RAF Bomber Command on 12th November 1944, using 12,000-pound 'Tallboy' bombs.

Chapter IX

THE EASTERN FLEET

Just after lunch on the 12th June 1944, *Victorious* slipped quietly out of Greenock for the last time and set course for yet another part of the world. Her Corsair and Barracuda squadrons were ranged on the flight deck and she made an impressive picture as she said goodbye to the Home Fleet and the port she knew so well, the port that together with Scapa had been home since March 1941 – for nearly three and a half years. One week later she met her sister ship *Indomitable* off Algiers and together, they sliced through the calm, blue waters of the Mediterranean as they headed for the Canal, the Red Sea, India and the future. At long last *Victorious* had departed from her battleground, the cold, inhospitable waters of the Northern Seas. From now until the end of the war, she would steam in the warm, humid waters of the tropics and range across the vastness of the Pacific Ocean. Her new base would be Trincomalee and from there she would fight against the Japanese as a member of the Eastern Fleet. This carrier would form part of an ever-growing British contribution to the war in the Pacific, and for *Victorious*, the symbol of the swastika was replaced by the scourge of the Rising Sun.

From March 1942 and throughout 1943, Admiral Sir James Somerville had been commanding the British Eastern Fleet. It was very much a Cinderella force, for with the attention firmly focused on events in Europe and the Mediterranean, not only had he been forgotten, but he had been left virtually without ships. The higher priorities accorded to the struggle against Hitler and the Italians, meant that few ships were available to wage naval warfare in his area of the Indian Ocean and beyond. At last events in the Pacific were turning in favour of the Allies, for after a long series of disasters inflicted by a seemingly invincible enemy, the Japanese Fleet received two severe defeats at the hands of American carrier-based aircraft. The first occurred at the Battle of Midway on 4th June 1942 when, in one incredible stroke, the US Navy carriers halted Japanese expansion, sank four enemy fast carriers and, for the loss of the *Yorktown,* exploded the myth of Imperial Japanese naval supremacy. A stalemate settled over the Pacific for a time but exactly two years later at the Battle of the Philippine Sea the Japanese lost three more of their precious carriers. On paper her fleet still looked formidable, but shortage of aircraft, trained and experienced pilots, aviation fuel, escorts and the serviceability of her vital eleven remaining aircraft carriers were causing grave concern – since only four were operational and events were rapidly developing towards a final showdown. 'I will return!' – vowed General Douglas MacArthur to the people of the Philippines in March 1942, and two years and seven months later that promise was fulfilled after the biggest carrier battle of the war. The tangled, confused and bloody action off Leyte Gulf was to end, for all time, the effectiveness of Japanese naval power at sea.

In September 1943 the surrender of the Italian Fleet released a number of ships from the Mediterranean and the escort carrier *Battler* was sent out to Trincomalee, but until *Illustrious* joined in January 1944, she was the only carrier east of Suez. As early as 1943, the Combined Chiefs of Staff had been pressing to send out units of the Royal Navy to fight alongside their American Allies. Winston Churchill was also keen that the Royal Navy should play a full and active part in the war against Japan, and now that ships could be spared, he offered a token force to be sent at once.

In spite of American reluctance – mainly due to the fact that unless self-supporting, our ships would place an extra supply and maintenance burden on the already stretched United States Navy resources, they finally agreed to the addition of British effort. At the second Quebec Conference on 13th September 1944, Mr Churchill offered the British Fleet to the Americans and President Roosevelt's reply came back: 'No sooner offered than accepted.' The British Pacific Fleet was formed officially on 22nd November 1944.

Early in 1944, the Admiralty began preparations to send a fleet to the Pacific later in the year. This Pacific Force would be formed from the nucleus of the existing British Eastern Fleet, suitably re-inforced by ships sent out from other theatres. The aim was to develop a powerful British Pacific striking force based round aircraft carriers, whilst leaving sufficient ships in the Indian Ocean to protect the important Bombay Aden convoy route and when possible to carry out independent minor operations against the Japanese in south-east Asia.

Illustrious joined the Fleet in January 1944 and was shortly followed by the aircraft repair ship *Unicorn*, temporarily used as an aircraft carrier due to the shortage of available carriers in the area. By April the overall situation was looking better for Admiral Somerville's Fleet, it was further reinforced by the escort carriers *Shah* and *Begum* and temporarily by the American carrier *Saratoga*. Together with two British and three American destroyers, and with the French battleship *Richelieu*, at long last he was now in a position to strike effectively at the enemy.

The fleet carriers *Victorious* and *Indomitable* arrived at Colombo from the Mediterranean on the 5th July. *Victorious* had come straight from the successful *Tirpitz* strike and, as we have seen, she was no stranger to the Pacific, having already served with the US Fleet in the area in 1942. Now she was to join her sister ship *Illustrious* in the first of a series of strikes against the Japanese. Under the codename 'Crimson', the two carriers were to neutralise the enemy airfields near Sabang, just off the northern tip of Sumatra; to provide spotting aircraft whilst the Fleet carried out a bombardment; and, additionally, to provide the air defence of the force and fly photo-reconnaissance sorties to assess the results of the bombardment.

Force 62 sailed under the flag of the Commander-in-Chief, Eastern Fleet, Admiral Somerville on 22nd July from Trincomalee. Comprising two carriers; four battleships, *Queen Elizabeth* (Flag), *Valiant*, *Renown* and *Richelieu*; seven cruisers, *Nigeria*, *Kenya*, *Gambia*, *Ceylon*, *Cumberland*, *Phoebe* and *Tromp;* plus ten destroyers, the force made their final approach to the area two nights later. The two carriers were detached and, escorted by the *Phoebe* and two destroyers, made for the launch

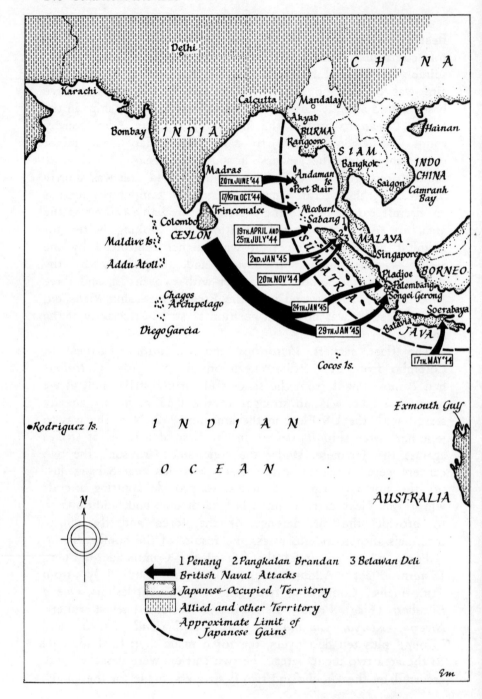

1 *Penang* 2 *Pangkalan Brandan* 3 *Belawan Deli*
British Naval Attacks
Japanese Occupied Territory
Allied and other Territory
Approximate Limit of
    Japanese Gains

area some 35 miles to the west-north-west of Sabang, while two submarines, *Templar* and *Tantalus,* were stationed for air/sea rescue duties between the carriers and the target.

'Crimson' was the first really serious attempt by the British forces to strike at the Japanese and to get valuable experience for the future; the aircrews were briefed to attack Lho Nga and Kotaraja airfields and to attack any aircraft or targets of opportunity found there. In addition, they were to strike at any shipping in Sabang Harbour and at port installations, as well as bombing the oil storage tanks burned out and heavily damaged by a strike in the previous May, but since repaired.

The initial launch had been ordered to take place 33 minutes before sunrise, but was delayed for five minutes because of an unusually dark morning. Even with the delay in the fly-off, it was still too early and in consequence, the aircraft had great difficulty in forming up.[1] The darkness made the join up by the aircraft slow and ragged and this in turn delayed the departure of the strike.

On arrival over their airfield targets, the Corsairs found that it was still too dark to accurately machine gun or even see their targets very clearly. The enemy was alerted and waiting and opened up with anti-aircraft guns as soon as the first aircraft came within range. The close proximity of the jungle, poor light and very effective camouflage added to their problems; as a pilot stated in his subsequent debrief: 'At 400 knots and with flak opposition, a camouflaged aircraft in a revetment is not a very conspicuous target.' In spite of this, however, the attacking fighters managed to dispose of two enemy fighters.

The Barracudas did not find much to interest them either. There was little or no shipping in the harbour, although they did manage to attack and sink two small ships totalling some 1,500

1 Victorious — 1834 Squadron, 14 Corsairs; 1836 Squadron, 14 Corsairs and 21 Barracudas of 831 Squadron. 831 Squadron were veterans from the *Tirpitz* raid in the carrier *Furious,* but had transferred to *Victorious* on the 11th May for further operations against German shipping off Norway, before sailing with her to join the Eastern Fleet on the 12th June. *Illustrious* disembarked her Barracudas for this strike and took on board an extra squadron of 14 Corsairs from 1837 Squadron. Together with 14 Corsairs each from 1830 and 1833 Squadrons, she carried a total of 42 Corsairs for this particular mission.

tons. Instead they concentrated in bombing the harbour buildings and damaging the oil storage tanks yet again, before returning to *Victorious* without loss.

The bombarding force reached their allotted position at 0640 and while the battleships concentrated on the harbour and the military barracks of Sabang with spotting provided by aircraft from *Illustrious,* the cruisers engaged the W/T station on the Island of Pulo We and silenced enemy shore batteries. The destroyer force split into two groups and while one group shelled a radar station, the other force of four ships, led with verve and dash by Captain (D) 4th Destroyer Flotilla, Captain R.G. Onslow, went to shell the harbour installations at very close range. Although three ships were engaged and hit by Japanese shore batteries, casualties were not heavy and after an exciting gun duel and firing their torpedoes into the harbour, the destroyers retired.

During the Fleet's withdrawal from the area, the enemy started to take an interest and two Jap reconnaissance aircraft were shot down. The position of the fleet had obviously been reported, or the enemy had made a good estimate of their probable position, for later that afternoon a group of about nine Mitsubishi Zero-Sen Navy single-seat fighters were detected approaching the force. It looked as though the enemy intended to retaliate, but they were engaged by 13 Corsairs from the two carriers and in the ensuing battle, they managed to shoot down two, damage two more and drive the remainder off without loss. Sub Lieutenant Heffer, RNZNVR, of 1836 Squadron was flying CAP in Corsair 7H and got one of the enemy:

I was directed towards the enemy at 1645 and sighted about five enemy aircraft There was a large weather storm astern of the Fleet, but *Victorious* managed to direct me onto them. One of the enemy aircraft dived past me and after a short burst, I followed him down, hitting him on the port quarter with a long burst of fire. He was weaving, but flames were coming from his port wing. He disappeared into cloud and, following him, I came out dead on his tail at a range of about one hundred yards. After another long burst he went up in a sheet of flame.

After the unhappy experience at Petsamo and Kirkenes in 1941, *Victorious* had been accustomed to good intelligence material being available in the European theatre before undertaking any action against the enemy. Now she was out in the Far East, it looked as though things were back to square one and the intelligence organisation needed a thorough overhaul. After the 'Crimson' attack her captain ruefully reported:

Intelligence was such as to make it impossible to obtain good targets, without breaking the element of surprise.

For *Victorious* this lesson had been learnt the hard way and at great cost; they were not prepared to forget experience gained in operations against the Germans. The first sortie of 1836 Squadron Corsairs made a bad landfall and approach to their airfield target, but in this they had the excuse that no landfall photographs were available, and that the maps with which they had been supplied only showed the barest of detail; next time things would improve.

The attack on Sabang was the last for Admiral Somerville, who relinquished command of the Eastern Fleet to Admiral Sir Bruce Fraser on 23rd August, and *Illustrious* departed for South Africa and a much needed refit – her first for over a year. To compensate somewhat for this loss, the battleship *Howe* arrived at Columbo on the 3rd August to augment the ever-growing strength of the Royal Navy in the Far East, but in the event she was a timely replacement for *Valiant*. The unfortunate battleship *Valiant* was in the floating dock (*AFD23*) at Trincomalee, when it collapsed and so much damage was caused that she had to be sent back to England for repairs.

The new commander was keen to keep up the pressure, so Force 64 sailed again on the 19th August for operation 'Banquet' under the command of Rear Admiral Clement Moody, Rear Admiral Aircraft Carriers, Eastern Fleet. As before, the force was ordered to strike at Sumatran targets, principally the importance was placed on the destruction of the cement works, as it was the only plant of its kind in the Dutch East Indies and practically the only source available to the Japanese for the construction of the vital airfields and defence works in South-East Asia.

Intelligence reports, admittedly some four months old, suggested that the Japanese Navy did not make use of Emmahaven harbour for the Netherlands submarine *K14* had carried out a reconnaissance in April, but had seen neither ships nor any signs of activity at either Emmahaven or Padang. She reported that the harbour installations seemed perfectly intact, but the port cranes were not in use and the warehouses were shut up.

The weather conditions for the strike were perfect, with good visibility and little or no cloud, and at 0550 on the morning of the 25th, both carriers commenced to fly off their aircraft.[1] To improve matters still further, there was almost a complete absence of enemy opposition. Although light flak brought down one Corsair fighter over the target and killed the pilot, Sub Lieutenant T.A. Cutter, of 1834 Squadron, the attacking Barracudas remained untouched and managed to achieve a high standard of bombing accuracy. A large number of hits were obtained on the cement works, which was left in a blanket cloud of smoke and flames rising to between 800 and 1,000 feet and succeeded in reducing the output for several months. One pilot remarked after the attack:

> I suspect the only cement produced at Padang in the next two or three months will be that SWEPT off the surrounding countryside.

Another Sub Lieutenant observer said that after they had dropped their bombs, 'we were busy avoiding the cement'.

---

[1] *Victorious* carried the same three squadrons as for 'Crimson', while *Indomitable* carried two squadrons of ten Hellcats each from 1839 and 1844 Squadrons, together with 24 Barracudas from 815 and 817 Squadrons. The first strike consisted of ten Barracudas each armed with 500-pound bombs from the two ships and escorted by 12 Corsairs from *Victorious*. One hour and twenty minutes later, the second strike of nine Barracudas from *Indomitable* and three Barracudas from *Victorious* took off armed with 500-pound bombs and were escorted by 12 Corsairs from *Victorious*. The fighter protection of the carrier force was provided by a CAP of Hellcats from *Indomitable*.

In Emmahaven they had less success and only two merchant-men were damaged in the harbour which was empty of shipping. Nevertheless, one merchant ship of about 3,500 tons received four direct hits with 500-pound bombs and another smaller one of 2,500 tons, two hits; both ships were left on fire and burning furiously as the bombers turned their attentions to other targets. Wharves, warehouses, a coaling jetty and a railway yard received numerous hits and were heavily damaged. Petty Officer Leslie Gurden recalls the attack on the port: 'We dived to attack two small ships which were oiling alongside a jetty. One bomb hit the nearby wharf and caused a terrific flame and oily black smoke.' The Corsair fighters concentrated their efforts on the airfield at Padang, as well as strafing the harbour to reduce flak interference and to keep the enemy's heads down. The aircrew considered it extraordinary that although a few enemy aircraft were in the air at the time of the attacks, no serious attempt was made by the Japs to interfere with our air striking forces. Commander Ronnie Hay says that after the attack, 'the fighters roamed the area looking for the most impressive buildings in the area. These would then be machine gunned in the hopes that the Japanese overlords were in residence.'

The object of this second British operation was to pin down enemy air and naval forces and so divert Japanese attention, while General MacArthur developed his own US Army operations against New Guinea. It was not really successful in that the Japanese did not react as expected and paid our forces virtually no attention, except in their usual propaganda radio broadcast. Picked up by the battleship *Howe* at noon on 25th August, the following Japanese news broadcast in English was relayed to an interested Fleet: 'Our forces in Western Sumatra yesterday beat off and inflicted severe casualties on two air strikes attempting to attack the installations there'.

In spite of Japanese claims to the contrary, opposition was very light and for the aircrews taking part, the value of the operation was somewhat reduced by the lack of enemy reaction. One cannot help wondering what the outcome would have been if the Japanese had counter-attacked. *Indomitable*'s squadrons had been in the ship for a total of only three weeks, and in both carriers the majority of aircrews were young, untried and inexperienced. 'Banquet' could have misfired, or proved an ideal opportunity for training and experience under valuable battle conditions, but in the event it went off like a damp squib.

Two other points of interest arose from Operation 'Banquet' and are worth recording. The first was that a fully trained and equipped photographic unit had operated from a British carrier and, as the results more than justified the effort, they were henceforth to be a regular feature in our front-line operational carriers in the Pacific. The second one was somewhat more sinister in its implication. The capacity to replace aviation petrol and fuel oil for the carriers was very limited and in this operation *Victorious* had used over 12,000 gallons of aviation fuel. This represented about a quarter of her total capacity and prompted considerable thought for the future. It was obvious that the Fleet Train of replenishment ships would have its work cut out to keep the carriers supplied in the future if they operated for long periods away from base and flew continuous air operations.

Under the codename Operation 'Light A' the next venture for *Victorious* and *Indomitable* was to fly a fighter sweep over Japanese airfields in the Medan and Belawan Deli areas, as well as a photographic reconnaissance to the south and east of Pangkalan Soe Soe in Aru Bay. Again escorted by the battleship *Howe*, the cruisers *Cumberland, Kenya* and seven destroyers, the two carriers sailed from Trincomalee at 1200 on 14th September. They reached the area at first light on the 17th, but the weather conditions were so bad that the operation had to be cancelled, and the carriers continued with Operation 'Light B' scheduled for the next day. 'Light B' involved an air strike against the Japanese railway repair and maintenance yards at Sigli in Sumatra, and by 0600 the two carriers had reached their launch position. By this time the weather had moderated and with a light wind of 10 knots, low sea state, virtually no cloud and excellent visibility, *Victorious* flew off ten Barracudas each armed with 500-pound bombs followed by 16 Corsairs. For this operation she had embarked another Squadron of 21 Barracudas of 822 Squadron under the command of Lieutenant Commander Watson. This exchange was to give 831 Squadron a break from operations and allowed them a few days ashore in Trincomalee.

Indomitable also launched her force of ten Barracudas followed by eight Hellcats, but the take off, form up and departure were very slow and took 40 minutes to achieve. Part of the trouble was because several of *Indomitable*'s aircraft went unserviceable at the last minute on deck – probably due to bad weather during the previous two days, but to add to the problems, one of her Barracudas ditched on take off, and three of *Victorious*' Corsairs went unserviceable in the air before departure and had to return back on board.

At last the aircraft were formed up and on their way, but as the aircraft headed for the target the weather steadily got worse until over Sigli itself they met shifting winds, low cloud with heavy rain and poor visibility. In spite of the fact that there was no air opposition and negligible flak, from this point on things seemed to go from bad to worse; and shocking R/T discipline, confusion and a poor standard of bombing made the results of this attack most disappointing. All the Barracudas except three reached the target and completed their bombing in 60 seconds, but unlike the speed of the bombing in the *Tirpitz* attack, the accuracy of this performance left a lot to be desired. Although some damage was done, many other targets escaped unscathed and neither Admiral Moody nor Admiral Fraser were impressed by the effectiveness of their air striking power. If they couldn't hit the targets when there was no opposition, what would it be like when the enemy resisted in force? Two other incidents dampened the spirits still further. In the first case one Hellcat and one Barracuda from *Indomitable* fired by mistake on the surfaced submarine *Spirit,* while she was busily rescuing the crew of a ditched Barracuda. Fortunately no damage or casualties were caused though somewhat understandably, the submarine Commanding Officer's comments on the affair are unprintable. In the second incident, an enemy aircraft was reported by *Howe* later that afternoon and Corsairs were sent out to intercept by *Victorious.* Regrettably another silly mistake was highlighted when they had to be recalled in the middle of the interception as someone had forgotten to fit the long-range tanks; they would have run out of fuel and been forced to ditch if allowed to complete the action. Admiral Moody decided that as the result of this operation he would embark on an intensive training programme to raise the standard of proficiency in the carriers. They were engaged in a battle against a formidable, experienced, cunning and totally ruthless enemy; there would be no room for mistakes and no second chance.

By the autumn of 1944, the point had been reached where the Americans were ready to begin the reconquest of the Philippines. The long-awaited landings at Leyte Gulf were due to take place on 20th October, and the Eastern Fleet were to create a diversionary feint, with the intention of damaging Japanese naval and air forces and to lure the enemy into suspecting an invasion. The area selected for the diversionary attack was the Nicobar Islands and on the morning of 15th October, *Victorious, Indomitable, Renown,* four cruisers and eleven destroyers sailed from Trincomalee for Operation 'Millet'. Two days later at 0600 and in position some 30 miles to the east of Batti Malv Island, the two carriers broke away from the main force and headed north-east to their launch positions.[1]

Four minutes after half-past-six, *Victorious* launched 19 Barracudas armed with 500-pound bombs to attack the airfields, escorted by 8 Corsairs as cover, while *Indomitable* flew off ten more Barracudas and eight Hellcats for a strike on Nancowry harbour. In fine weather, the enemy were caught completely by surprise and for several minutes, the attackers had no opposition whatsoever. This time the bombing was accurate and though targets were few and far between, the attacking aircraft gave a good account of themselves. After the initial lull, the enemy responded in a very aggressive manner and the flak was heavier at Nancowry than had been expected. It proved very troublesome below about 3,000 feet, but for the loss of only one Barracuda which failed to pull out of its dive, many small ships were sunk including the *Ishikari Maru* of 830 tons. There was some opposition to the Corsairs over the enemy airfields and two crashed just north of Malacca, but again, the fighters and

[1] *Victorious* carried her usual complement of 21 Barracudas from 831 Squadron, but the two Corsair squadrons had been increased from 14 to 18 aircraft each, while *Indomitable* had also increased her outfit of aircraft. She was now carrying 12 Barracudas each from 815 and 817 Squadrons, as well as 14 Hellcats from 1839 and another 14 from 1844 Squadron.

bombers succeeded in damaging enemy targets before returning to their respective carriers.

The carriers and their escorts cruised off the area to seaward and, as planned, the strikes went on for a total of three days from the 17th to the 19th October. For the very first time, a British carrier force remained in the battle area for more than a few hours and by proving that it could be done, set the pattern for future operations and tested the logistic support of the Fleet Train. The next day *Victorious* launched an attack of 14 Corsairs to strafe shipping in Nancowry and though they caused little damage, four aircraft were hit but returned safely to the carrier. *Indomitable* also flew off eight Hellcats and nine Barracudas armed with 500-pound bombs for another unsuccessful strike at shipping at Nancowry. One Barracuda stalled with engine failure and crashed into the sea on take off, but the crew were rescued unhurt as were two pilots from *Victorious,* who went over the side when trying to land their damaged Corsairs on the carrier.

As before, the Japanese paid virtually no interest in our limited attempts at a diversion. Though irritated by our pin--pricks on their flanks, they were fighting a bloody battle against the massive American assault in the Philippines some two thousand miles to the east, and the first reaction occurred on the last day. At 0840, a twin-engined aircraft avoided our attempts to intercept and reported the presence of the British force. It didn't seem very significant but about an hour later, nine Oscars (Japanese Army fighter aircraft) were detected approaching at 7,000 feet, with a top cover of three more Oscars at 16,000 feet. The two carriers scrambled their defensive fighters to intercept and although the raid was missed by *Indomitable's* aircraft, the enemy flew headlong into the Corsairs from *Victorious*. After a very fierce dogfight between the Oscars and Corsairs, the enemy were driven off some 12 miles to the north-east of the carrier force. The air fighting continued for over 40 minutes, by which time four Oscars had been knocked out and others damaged for the loss of two Corsairs and one Hellcat. Meanwhile *Indomitable's* fighters which had been recalled were despatched to take care of the top cover of three Oscars who had broken clear and were some twenty miles away. After a spirited chase and a short scrap, all three Oscars were accounted for without loss.

This ended the first of the real air battles in which our squadrons had taken part and, for the total loss of six aircrew, the Fleet Air Arm had had a good crack at the enemy. The aircrew had proved for the first time that our American-built fighters were a match for the latest Japanese army fighters and that in spite of irritating equipment defects and snags – morale was good. As Commander Hay commented:

> The US Navy Corsair was just the right aircraft for that war. It was certainly better than anything we had and an improvement on the Hellcat. It was more robust and faster and although the Japs could out-turn us in combat, we could out-climb, out-dive and out-gun him. By far the most healthy improvement was its endurance, with about five hours worth of fuel in your tanks, you didn't have the agony of wondering whether or not you would make it back to the carrier.

From Japenese records we now know that the enemy were fully committed in their desperate struggle against the Americans. Short of an all-out attack or invasion of Singapore, nothing would have caused him to redeploy his hard-pressed air and naval forces. From the British point of view, the operations of 1944 were of a tip and run nature and though they provided good training, they were as one correspondent stated:

> Little more than banging at the back door of the Japs and running away before the door was opened.

Perhaps it is just as well that the enemy did not react to our harassing efforts, for our few ships, limited support and lack of experience would have put us at a grave disadvantage. We had gained time and learned a few lessons and by the beginning of 1945, more and more, the British Fleet were equipped to take the offensive; *Victorious* would be there to play her part, a small but active part that would help speed the course of the war of Japan's now setting sun.

Chapter X

THE BRITISH PACIFIC FLEET

In October of 1944, Admiral Fraser went to London to discuss the formation of a new British Fleet that he would command in the Pacific. At long last ships were available and the all-important aircraft carriers were being sent to the Far East to form the teeth of a new powerful fleet. By American standards it was a very small fleet, but with the arrival of the large and most modern British carriers, morale was on the up-swing and there was a sense of real purpose in the air. After years of waiting, a strong and mobile British Task Force was assembling and soon would put to sea and fight alongside the Americans in what had been up to now a strictly American War.

The great sea battles between the Japanese and American carrier fleets had been fought at long range with carrier-based aircraft slogging it out against each other's naval forces, and because of the vast distances involved in the Pacific theatre, these forces had spent weeks at sea and many hundreds of miles from their bases. This factor alone had created enormous logistic and support problems, but the Americans had had three years of experience in the Pacific on which to build their enormous Task Forces and solve the even more complex logistic and support organisations. On the other hand, the British Pacific Fleet had little experience, fewer ships, less resources and far less time. To enable the carriers to remain at sea and be supplied with regular replacements and a host of stores, fuels and armaments, an efficient Fleet Train of supporting ships was a vital link in the chain.

Admiral Fraser had some formidable problems to overcome. For a start there were only forty-four ships available to form a Fleet Train to support a fleet of two battleships, four carriers, five cruisers and three flotillas of destroyers. To be effective, they would have to operate for long periods at great distances from the nearest support base. To add yet further to his problems, there was a critical shortage of supply ships, stores and armament supply ships, repairs ships and tankers, and the forty-four ships represented the entire logistic availability with little hope of an increase for some time to come. With inadequate resources Admiral Fraser would be forced to compromise, adapt and solve the seemingly insurmountable difficulties, but at all events the BPF would not be deflected into the role of a secondary or supporting force undertaking minor operations. In spite of American doubts, the Admiral was determined to achieve success and to emulate the Americans by keeping his force at sea in the battle area.

The new Commander-in-Chief returned to Colombo in November and as we have said, on the 22nd November the British Pacific Fleet was officially formed. Comprising the battleships *King George V* and *Howe,* the four fleet carriers *Victorious, Indefatigable, Illustrious* and *Indomitable,* five cruisers and supporting destroyers, Admiral Fraser prepared to take command and hoisted his flag in the battleship *Howe,* while Vice Admiral Sir Bernard Rawlings became his Second-in-Command and hoisted his flag in the battleship *King George V.* The remaining ships formed the East Indies Fleet under the command of Admiral Sir Arthur John Power and consisted of three capital ships *Queen Elizabeth, Valiant* and *Renown,* the 5th Cruiser Squadron, eight escort carriers and thirty-four destroyers. Thus the stage was set for the British naval forces to take the offensive and to hit at the enemy as often and as hard as possible – the chance that Admiral Somerville had waited so patiently for during the previous three long years.

As the BPF became a reality, the Americans had just fought and won the battle of Leyte Gulf and, in four days of bloody and bitter fighting, destroyed four Japanese carriers, three battleships, ten cruisers and nine destroyers, as well as damaging a substantial number of other vessels. This very decisive engagement against the Imperial Japanese Navy was the real turning point of the war, for her Navy never again seriously challenged the Allied fleets. The future battles in the Pacific were fought

Late afternoon, 2nd April 1944: the escort carriers *Emperor*, *Pursuer*, *Searcher* and *Fencer*, or Rear Admiral Bisset's Force II, head for the rendezvous, to join *Victorious* and *Furious* in the first strike against *Tirpitz* next morning.

A small price to pay: one of the returning Barracudas crashes into the barrier on its return from the strike. The crew were unhurt and the wreckage is soon cleared.

Barracudas of 822 Squadron (*Victorious*) and 815/817 Squadrons (*Indomitable*) head for the target at Sigli with a naval 'Blockbuster' under the wing of the Barracuda taking the picture.

The results of the successful strike by 43 Avenger and 12 Fireflies from *Victorious*, *Indomitable*, *Illustrious* and *Indefatigable* on the Pladjoe refinery around Palembang in Sumatra on 24th January 1945. Escorted by over 50 fighters, the Avengers dropped 172,500 pounds of bombs.

against the Japanese shore-based Army and Navy Air Forces, and
the new sinister and devastating weapon – the Kamikaze: the
manned suicide aircraft that had made its first appearance in
force at the battle of Leyte Gulf, a last desperate gamble that
the Japs hoped would counter the overwhelming superiority of
the Allies and bring them ultimate victory.

The Japanese were by this time critically short of oil and
particularly of aviation spirit. The exact position was not
known, but the American onslaught against enemy tankers was
making the losses unacceptably high and was fast becoming too
costly to be borne. In the last quarter of 1944, the tonnage of
tankers importing petroleum products into Japan reached a
staggering peak of two millions, but sinkings and other delays
reduced the amount reaching their destination to a mere
217,000 tons; little more than ten per cent of the tanker
tonnage employed. Before leaving for Australia to discuss the
setting up of bases for the support of his new fleet, Admiral
Fraser arranged that Admiral Power should use the ships of the
new British Pacific Fleet, to carry out a series of operations to
hit the enemy where it hurt most – at his vital petroleum
supplies. The Australian Government had been assured that the
BPF would be in the area of the Pacific before the end of 1944,
but this date could not be kept if the fleet attacked the
Japanese oil targets and, in any case, if the promise was to be
honoured then the carriers could only reach Australia in an
unworked up and non-operational state. The problem had been
aggravated by the fact that some carrier squadrons had changed
over from their British Barracuda aircraft to the new American
Avenger bombers, and this in turn had meant that the aircrews
needed an intensive training period on their new aeroplanes.

The decision having been made, the choice of a suitable target
was obvious. Palembang was the centre of the most important of
the Japanese oil supplies and was situated in south-east Sumatra,
about 55 miles from the mouth of the Musi River and 150 miles
inland from the nearest point on the coast of the Indian Ocean,
the western side. The oil field consisted of two principal
refineries known as Pladjoe – owned by Royal Dutch Shell and
the largest and most important refinery in the Far East – and
Soengei Gerong – owned by Standard Oil, second only to

Pladjoe in importance and one of the largest producers of aviation spirit. Vital to the Japanese war effort, they were very heavily defended by a ring of fighter airfields and anti-aircraft defences and Admiral Fraser decided that he would attack these two plants with the maximum carrier effort available, before the force left the Indian Ocean for the Pacific. Palembang would be a hard nut to crack for experienced and battle-seasoned veterans let alone the new and untried BPF, so before attacking Palembang, the Admiral decided that his aircrews should benefit from the experience and training of a dress rehearsal. He intended that they should carry out one or more attacks on the Pangkalan Brandan refineries in northern Sumatra as a prelude to the main operation; and this operation together with the main strike on Palembang was given the codename of 'Outflank'.

Victorious arrived back at Trincomalee from Operation 'Millet', the attack on the Nicobar Islands, on the 21st October, and for the second time in two months she had to make the trip to Alexandria Dock in Bombay with aggravating steering and engine defects. Her centre engine and rudder had caused trouble on the way out to the Pacific and she had been forced to go into dry dock for repairs on the 30th September for five days. In addition, she had had considerable problems with a leaking gland on the centre propeller shaft and the Captain had been forced to stop the centre of his three engines. All had seemed well after the shaft refit but once again the faults with her steering gear had recurred and she had to make yet another docking. She arrived in Bombay on the 16th November and after nearly a month finally departed for steering trials once more on the 14th December, but too late to join the BPF on the first of their rehearsal attacks on the Japanese oil fields. The refinery was situated about 50 miles north of Medan and 250 miles south-east of Sabang. Crude oil was piped to the refinery from the oilfields and the refined products exported from Pangkalan Soe Soe, a port about eight miles north of the refinery and connected to it by pipelines. There was tankage for something like 30 million gallons at Pangkalan Soe Soe, but because the major installations were destroyed by the Dutch in 1942 and there was insufficient water for large tankers to top up to full capacity, the Japs were reported to have laid a pipeline from the refinery to Belawan Deli, the port of Medan.

The carriers *Illustrious* and *Indomitable* sailed for the first of the 'Outflank' series of strikes against the Japanese oilfield Pangkalan Brandan on the 20th December. Codenamed Operation 'Robson' it was frustrated by bad weather and the aircraft had to go for the secondary target – the port instal-lations of Belawan Deli. After an attack in which the results were largely unobserved, the force returned to Ceylon and prepared for a second attempt early in the New Year.

By the time *Victorious* arrived in Trincomalee on 29th December, two months had elapsed since she had seen action against the Japanese. During her period of inactivity away from the fleet, her air group undertook intensive weapon training and 831 Barracuda Squadron were replaced by 849 Squadron with 21 Avengers. This change-over gave her better aircraft and, under the command of Lieutenant Commander D.R. Foster, the newly formed squadron were ready to meet the Japs.

Operation 'Lentil' was the second and last rehearsal before the big strike on Palembang; in high hopes, the force sailed from Trincomalee at 1030 on New Year's Day 1945. Escorted by four cruisers and eight destroyers, *Indomitable* – Flag ship of Admiral Vian (AC1) – *Victorious* and the newly arrived carrier *Indefatigable* headed once more for Pangkalan Brandan. The force carrying 96 fighters, 63 bombers and 12 fighter/bombers[1] reached the flying-off position just to the north-east of Simalur Island early on the morning of the 4th, and in perfect weather with a visibility of nearly 50 miles the carriers commenced to launch. The intention was to fly off a fighter sweep to attack the airfields near the refinery, before sending in the main attacking force of bombers. Accordingly at 0610 eight Corsairs from *Victorious* and eight Hellcats from *Indomitable* were launched. The selected launch position on the western side of Sumatra meant that the aircraft would have a more difficult

[1] *Indomitable* carried 28 Hellcats from 1839 and 1844 Squadrons and 21 Avengers from 857 Squadron. *Indefatigable* carried a Photographic Reconnaissance detachment of 8 Hellcats from 888 Squadron, 32 Seafire 111s from 887 and 894 Squadrons, 12 Fireflies of 1770 Squadron and, finally, 21 Avengers from 820 Squadron. *Victorious* carried her usual 28 Corsairs from 1834 and 1836 Squadrons as well as the 21 Avengers from the newly formed 849 Squadron.

passage over the mountains to the target, but it did mean that the force could keep out of the narrow, vulnerable and restricted confines of the Malacca Straits. If the Japanese counter-attacked from the air, the carriers would have plenty of sea room to manoeuvre and they could spend more time in the area if necessary. As the planned strike involved a force of forty-four bombers escorted by thirty-two fighters as well as the fighter 'Ramrod'[1] sweep of sixteen aircraft, the take off and form up was a matter requiring detailed planning and organization.

The main strike took off one and a half hours after the fighter Ramrods and though they met no opposition en route, there was heavy and accurate flak on the final approach at Pangkalan Soe Soe. About 12 miles from the target the 12 Fireflies from *Indefatigable* were detached to rocket and strafe the harbour and town of Pangkalan Soe Soe. In the face of accurate enemy fire, they managed to hit and set a small enemy tanker on fire.

Each armed with 500-pound bombs, the remaining 16 Avengers of the main strike from *Victorious* and *Indomitable* proceeded to their own targets, escorted by 16 Hellcats from the *Indomitable* and 16 Corsairs from *Victorious*. As the Avengers prepared to bomb, the Japs closed in and the fighter escort was engaged by up to twelve enemy fighters. In one group of enemy aircraft reported to the east of the target and engaged by the escorting Corsairs, no less than five Oscars (Japanese Army Fighters) were shot down. Sub Lieutenant D. Sheppard was one of those pilots flying a Corsair from *Victorious* as bomber escort and at 0850, he sighted an Oscar at 7,600 feet and just below him. As he closed to attack, the Jap pilot went into a steep spiral dive and then, pulling out, desperately tried to out-turn the Corsair:

> The Jap's cockpit seemed to glow as I hit him with a long burst and I could see the bullets hitting the engine and cockpit. He levelled out at 300 feet and then went into a

[1] Codename for offensive fighter sweeps against airfields, shipping, AA concentrations or other specific targets.

climbing right hand turn. I fired again and the pilot baled out as the aircraft rolled over and went into the sea. I watched the pilot land in the water, but he appeared to be dead.

So excited were the fighter pilots by the appearance of real Jap opposition and their first chance of combat with enemy aircraft in the Far East, that they broke away from their escort duties to join in the fun. Forgetting their charges they took on anything and everything that looked like a Jap plane. Meanwhile, the unprotected Avengers went on in to bomb the oil refinery in the face of light and inaccurate AA fire. In spite of the fact that the target was soon obscured by flames and thick black smoke, the bombing was accurate and they managed to inflict considerable damage, but with their fighter escort otherwise engaged, the Avengers offered easy-meat to enemy fighters and it could have proved disastrous. Fortunately their luck held as they came out of the attack and the enemy, otherwise engaged, did not appear. The losses were remarkably light; only one Avenger was damaged by an enemy fighter as it approached the target, and a second one ditched with engine failure some 12 miles off the coast, but the crew were rescued.

The fighters carrying out the Ramrod strike on the airfields of Medan and Tanjong Poera had a field day. They caught the enemy completely by surprise and destroyed seven out of the 25 aircraft on the ground as well as shooting down a Dinah (Twin-engined Mitsubishi Army Reconnaissance bomber) and a Sally (Mitsubishi Japanese Army bomber). Lieutenant Durno was over Medan airfield in one of 1834 Squadron's Corsairs, when he saw a Dinah in the landing circuit at 500 feet with its wheels and flaps down. Accompanied by his number two, Sub Lieutenant J.H. Richards, he roared in to attack this sitting duck. As they climbed up from zero feet Richards fired the first burst which damaged the enemy, while Durno coming in from astern gave a five-second burst from a range of only 50 yards. The Dinah staggered for a second or two and then blew up with an enormous explosion and crashed in bits on the edge of the airfield. Lieutenant Durno nearly did the same because he was so close to his victim that he flew on through the explosion and the bits of falling wreckage. His luck held and it turned out to be his day, for a few minutes later he caught another Jap Sally closing the airfield. Opening up with an eight-second burst — about 80 rounds from each of his six 0.5-inch calibre machine guns — from a range of 200 yards, he hit the engine and fuselage and set the plane on fire. As he watched, the plane seemed to lurch, the rudder broke off, then the port wing and the aircraft plunged finally out of control, to smash itself up in the jungle. In those last seconds as he watched the death throes of the Jap plane, he could see the pilot and co-pilot fighting each other in the cockpit to get out of the stricken plane, but neither of them made it. For them the war was over, their rising sun had set. With the attack over, the aircraft returned to the carriers. A Firefly ran out of fuel as he reached the force and had to ditch near *Indefatigable,* but the remaining planes landed safely and the force withdrew, arriving at Trincomalee on the 7th.

As one can imagine, the debrief of this operation was somewhat heated and produced the complaint from the bombers that they had been deserted and left unprotected and very vulnerable during the attack. As soon as they had arrived in the target area, the escorting fighters had gone off to strafe ground targets or join in dogfights, leaving the Avengers to fend for themselves. The appearance of Japanese fighters had drawn our own fighters like magnets, and the urge to have a go was too strong. 'By attacking the enemy, we were defending the bombers. And, anyway,' said an escorting fighter pilot, 'the Avengers were busily bombing,' As Commander Hay recalled:

It is a fairly natural reaction for any bomber pilot to feel that he is the only aircraft in the sky — seldom can you fly in neat, regular formations with the escort flying on your wingtip as a morale booster.

The sky is never so empty as when you're flying and you appear to be all on your own with the enemy. The more so, if some of the escorting fighter COs are inexperienced.

Lieutenant J.B. Edmundson of *Victorious'* 1836 Squadron who found himself in charge of the escort when his leader had to return with R/T trouble defended the actions of the fighters:

What always seems to happen is that someone sees a
'bogey', makes a hasty report, and chases off, followed by
everyone else who is anywhere near. The fault is, actually,
that it's not every month of the year that you see a Zero
in the Fleet Air Arm, so you can hardly blame a fighter
pilot for making the most of his opportunities. [The heat
was taken out of the discussion when he added, encourag-
ingly:] I think Avengers are a pleasure to escort, and the
more we do it, the better protection they will get.[1]

That really ended the debrief, but obviously the point had got
home and everyone would try a little harder at Palembang.

On the credit side, 1834 and 1836 Squadrons from *Victorious*
received well-deserved praise after 'Lentil' when the Director of
Naval Air Warfare later commented:

These two squadrons have rendered most satisfactory
combat reports displaying good tactics and good shooting.
It is most encouraging to see an almost complete lack of
mechanical failures which points to good maintenance.

The small scale attacks on the two oil refineries in Operations
'Robson' and 'Lentil' provided the aircrews with some very
useful experience, but were they ready to turn their attentions
to bigger game and go for the large refineries at Palembang?
Admiral Vian obviously thought so, but to test the carrier
organisation he ordered one more full scale practice at sea off
Ceylon. He wanted to iron out all the snags and perfect the
complex organisation necessary to get all the aircraft airborne
and on to the right target at the right time, and in view of the
recent debrief comments, to see that the bomber was properly
escorted and protected. The enemy was sure to defend his vital
oil to the utmost of his resources and there would be no room
for mistakes. The British carriers and Admiral Vian intended to
see that there weren't any.

[1] John Winton's *The Forgotten Fleet* (Michael Joseph 1969).

Chapter XI

PALEMBANG

Operations 'Meridian One' and 'Two' were the last planned strikes in the 'Outflank' series against the Japanese oil refineries at Pladjoe and Soengei Gerong near Palembang. By far the most difficult yet attempted, the outcome was to rank as one of the most rewarding achievements by British carrier-borne aircraft. The Palembang raids were a formidable undertaking for any seasoned fighting force, let alone the relatively inexperienced and untried British Pacific Fleet. Intelligence suggested that any attack would meet with the most determined enemy opposition, for if the Allies appreciated the importance of these fields to the Japanese war effort, then the point was hardly likely to have escaped the Japanese themselves. The flight path to the target involved a long overland crossing of 150 miles and then the attacking aircraft would have to face a very strong defensive ring formed by the enemy airfields of Palembang, Lembak, Talangbetoetoe and Mana, as well as large concentrations of both heavy and light anti-aircraft batteries. There were misgivings in certain quarters about the wisdom of undertaking such an ambitious venture at this early stage. Critics argued that heavy bombers would achieve more than the carrier aircraft, though in fact the B29 Super Fortresses had already attempted to bomb the refinery from high level with little or no success. It was further argued that if we went ahead with the attack, the the aircrew losses would be very high and this in turn would have an adverse effect on morale, and lastly the Fleet would be late arriving in the Pacific. Admiral Fraser successfully countered the arguments and although he may not have convinced all the critics and pessimists, Force 63 sailed from Trincomalee for the last time on the afternoon of the 16th January 1945.

Force 63 was under the command of Admiral Vian, the man who had won fame and much publicity when as Captain of the destroyer *Cossack* he snatched some 300 British Merchant Navy prisoners of war from their prison ship the German *Altmark* on 16th February 1940. He was an aggressive fighter who lived for action and was just the type of leader to inspire and weld the newly formed BPF into an efficient fighting force. There was a degree of apprehension in the aircrew that he might not take account of the opinions and experience of his aviators, but this fear was soon dispelled for, as Ronnie Hay said, 'he turned out to be most sympathetic and willing to listen — he was a breath of fresh air.' As the ten destroyers, four cruisers, his flagship *Indomitable* with three other carriers *Victorious, Illustrious, Indefatigable* and the battleship *King George V* steamed towards the east and their first real taste of combat, there could be few who doubted that if anyone could prove the worth of the British Pacific Fleet, then that man was Rear Admiral Sir Philip Vian.

The four aircraft carriers of Force 63 carried the largest complement of aircraft yet embarked by the Fleet Air Arm at sea and amounted to a grand total of 244 aeroplanes.

	Avengers	Fireflies	Corsairs	Hellcats	Seafires	Walrus	Total
Indomitable (Flag)	21 + 4*	–	6**	29	–		60
Victorious	19	–	34	–	–	2	55
Illustrious	18	–	36	–	–	–	56
Indefatigable	21	12	–	–	40	–	73

* 4 spare Avengers from *Illustrious*   ** 6 spare Corsairs from *Victorious*

After meeting the oiling force escorted by the cruiser *Ceylon* and one destroyer *Urchin* on the 20th, the ships refuelled that day and then proceeded to the launch area, some 35 miles off the west coast of Sumatra towards Enggano Island. Bad weather and a gloomy forecast delayed the operation for two days but on the night of the 24th/25th conditions had improved sufficiently for Admiral Vian to decide to launch his attack the next morning.

Victorious carried her usual group of three squadrons of aircraft, but like the other carriers her flight deck was crowded and created its own particularly irritating problems. The continual rain storms, spray and generally humid conditions

prevalent at that time of the year played havoc with the
serviceability of aircraft parked on the exposed flight deck. As
Captain Denny reported, 'the fact that *Victorious* was carrying
four Corsairs and one Avenger over her normal complement
necessitated a deck park and – as with her previous experiences
in the North Atlantic – this contributed to a high unserviceability rate.'

At 0615 the next morning the strike was launched, but not
without incident and mishap. In *Victorious,* one of the Avengers
on deck failed to start, one more got airborne but had to make
a hurried and undignified return with an emergency, and three
more returned before reaching the target. Other ships had their
problems too, and *Indomitable* lost a couple of its Avengers in
the first launch. One enthusiast 'gunned' his throttle and the
aircraft rolled forward to collide with another aircraft waiting to
go. It was not an auspicious start to the operation, and other
things were to go wrong as well.

The form up took quite a long time to complete and
finally, at four minutes past seven, just over 110 aircraft started
on their long journey to Palembang. Weather conditions were
excellent as the aircraft struggled with their loads to climb over
the mountains that separated them from their target. Fourteen
minutes later they crossed the coast and the thin wispy low-level
stratus clouds soon dispersed overland leaving a 10/10ths layer at
about 20,000 feet, helping the fighter pilots to look directly
into the sun. At 12,000 feet the strike levelled out and in a
visibility of 60 miles, they could see the sweep of the lush rich
Sumatran countryside rolling away beneath them to the horizon.
It was a quiet, peaceful scene as the aircraft continued their
uninterrupted passage but, with something like twenty miles to
go, the pilots noticed an unexpected hazard in front of them.
The Japs were flying anti-aircraft barrage balloons as a protective
measure over the target, and this added problem gave an
indication of the importance that they attached to their refineries. The Fireflies who had taken off in the second range
from *Indefatigable* and had now caught up with the main strike
were invited to shoot up the balloons and dispose of the
unwelcome menace, but because of poor communications, the
message did not get through.

ORDER OF BATTLE
FOR THE ATTACK ON
PALEMBANG AND TALANGBETOETOE
25th January 1945

1. First strike of No 1 and No 2 Bomber Wings were composed of 47 Avengers each armed with four 500-pound MC bombs and were ordered to bomb the refinery at Pladjoe:
   a. 12 Avengers (849 Squadron) from *Victorious*
   b. 12 Avengers (820 Squadron) from *Indefatigable*
   c. 12 Avengers (854 Squadron) from *Illustrious*
   d. 11 Avengers (857 Squadron) from *Indomitable*

The strike was to be given four groups of escorting fighters plus the Air Co-ordinator and his flight of four Corsairs to control the strike from *Victorious*.

2.   a. Top Cover — 11 Corsairs (1834, 1836 Squadrons) from *Victorious*

    b. Strike and bow close escort — 12 Fireflies (1770 Squadron) from *Illustrious*. Armed with cannon and eight 60-pound rockets

    c. Stern close escort — 8 Corsairs (1833 Squadron) from *Illustrious*

    d. Middle Cover — 8 Corsairs (1830 Squadron) from *Illustrious*

3.   A minor strike on the airfield at Mana was composed of:
4 Avengers (857 Squadron) from *Indomitable*

with an escort of — 4 Hellcats (1839, 1844 Squadrons) from *Indomitable*

4.   Ramrod Airfield sweeps — 12 Corsairs (1834, 1836 Squadrons) from *Victorious*
12 Corsairs (1830, 1833 Squadrons) from *Illustrious*

Note: Major R.C. Hay, RM, who became a Commander, RN, after the war, was the Air Co-ordinator for the BPF and the name is self explanatory. On 19th February 1945 the title was changed to Air Group Leader.

The incoming strike had been detected as it crossed the coast and soon the enemy sirens were wailing out their warning. Major Hideaki Inayama of the 87th Air Regiment led his Tojo army fighters into the air in an effort to intercept the carrier strike and at 0808, the Japanese ground batteries opened up. The Jap fighters clawed their way into the sky to gain precious height and as the British aircraft approached their target, about 25 Tojos screamed down on the force. They concentrated on the lumbering bombers and entered the battle with determination and enthusiasm. The Avengers were already going into their circular bombing orbit and as they commenced their 35-degree glide attacks, the fighter defence took on the attackers.

A fierce dogfight followed and one of the first successes went to Major R.C. Hay, Royal Marines from *Victorious,* who was the Air Co-ordinator for the whole strike. He was in Tardjoengradi area and at about ten minutes after the start of the action, he saw a Tojo diving out of the sun from above and followed him down: 'It was 0825 and after a five minute chase I caught him at 0 feet at 250 knots. Then I gave him a stern shot of about two seconds which hit his tail and engine and he crashed and broke up but did not burn.' After the attack, his advice to the other younger and less experienced pilots was that, 'providing you can get on his tail without him seeing you, he's easy meat. Therefore use your excess speed to keep out of sight behind him, dictate the terms of combat and stay alive.' After the raid was over, Hay went up to 10,000 feet with his three consorts to take photographs of the attack. As they commenced the photographic runs a couple more Tojos jumped them and paid the price: 'they went down in flames into the "ulu" ' [jungle] said Hay.

The 7th Area Air Army were taught to fly in the Palembang area and a number of the air bases were used specifically for that purpose. Although there were student pilots in the air that day, the opposition met quite a few of the Japanese experts In marked contrast to many of the easy turkey-shoot type of encounters, some of the Jap pilots were obviously the flying instructors and veritable aerobatic aces. Sub Lieutenant Griffin of *Victorious* was unlucky and must have met one during the attack that day, for he reported: 'I was flying over Pladjoe at

300 feet just as the raid started and found myself below and
behind a Tojo, who was quietly minding his own business and
stooging along at 500 feet.' Griffin closed from astern and fired
a five second burst from a range of 200 yards, before his guns
jammed. The effect was electric, for the Jap pilot weaved,
twisted and turned and then, at 400 feet, he flicked onto his
back and pulled down in a terrifying low half hoop, to pull out
at tree-top level and get the hell out of it and escape.

A less spectacular and more conventional method of escape
occurred when Sub Lieutenant Chute of 1836 Squadron from
Victorious intercepted a Tojo in his Corsair at 11,000 feet. The
Jap pilot immediately went into a half roll followed by a steep
left hand spiral dive in a frantic effort to escape, but Chute
followed him down firing as he went. Bullets were seen hitting
the cockpit and forward part of the engine and finally the Tojo
started to burn. This was the time for the enemy to evacuate
and he stood up in his cockpit and Sub Lieutenant Forsyth who
was following down as the number two, saw a parachute billow
out and drag the Jap from his cockpit.

A total of four Avengers, two Fireflies and one Corsair had
fallen by the wayside through unserviceability before the strike
had reached its objective. In spite of the fact that the Fireflies
did not get the order to shoot up the barrage balloons, the
Avengers pressed home their attack. The barrage balloons were
extremely difficult targets to hit and knock out of the sky and
on this occasion, the attack seemed even more of a hazardous
undertaking for as one pilot of the Avengers explained:

The Japs were very cunning in their use of the balloon
barrage. It was not floating at a set height, but they waited
until we were committed to our attack and then allowed
the balloons to come up. The balloons came up quite fast
to meet you and in my opinion this was deliberate Japanese
policy and not because they were caught by suprise. It is
impossible, of course, for the pilot to see the cables, but
one can see the balloons and one knows that the cables are
below but not where. If one hit a cable very much
outboard on the wing, you might survive; but one could
only afford to lose about two feet of the wing tip; striking

anywhere else inboard of that towards the wing root and that was the finish. The whole wing would go, and the plane would spin crazily into the ground. From a pilot point of view, it is an unpleasant experience to be formating one moment with an aircraft flying alongside you — and then suddenly a wing goes and the other plane spins down.[1]

To reduce the risk of striking a barrage balloon cable, the pilots had been told that they could release their bombs above the height of the balloons. The attack started at 0814 and the Avengers dived down through enemy fighters and fairly intense flak with great bravery and determination, while a few even braved the balloon cables to bomb from lower down and try for greater accuracy.

One of the early lessons learnt was that the fighter cover was inadequate to meet and counter the Jap onslaught. The fighter defence of the striking bombers was provided by both a high cover to intercept the enemy attacks, and a close cover to take care of any Japanese aircraft that got through the outer defences of the high cover. Additionally, the fighter Ramrod sweeps were supposed to hit the enemy airfields before the main strike arrived over their targets, and thereby prevent the Jap fighters from getting airborne. Because of the crowded decks on the four British carriers, it had been necessary to fly off the strike in two separate ranges and, unfortunately, the 24 Corsairs detailed for the airfield sweeps had been in this second range. The direct result of this was that the bombers had arrived over the target before the carrier fighters could prevent the enemy fighters from getting airborne to intercept the strike.

One after another the Avengers followed in succession to plant their bombs on the refinery and the storage tanks and soon thick oily smoke and flames were blanketing the target area so that it was more difficult for the aircraft at the tail end of the attack to get a good aiming point. Nevertheless the bombing was extremely accurate as action photographic evidence from Major Hay and the dive-bomber pilots was to show.

---

[1] Quoted from Peter Smith's *Task Force 57* (William Kimber, 1969).

Admiral Vian was more than pleased with his first attack and in his report he stated:

> Crude distilleries and run down tanks: hits. Reforming unit, redistillation unit, cracking unit and distillation units: hits in area — probably about 30 per cent destroyed. Main boiler and electric power house: probably one hit and two transformers destroyed.

In eight minutes the attack was over and, freed at last from the added weight of some two tons of high explosive the Avenger pilots headed at top speed for their rendezvous about fifteen miles west of Palembang. It was during the flight from the target to the rendezvous that the bombers ran into most of their trouble and, in the words of one of the pilots, 'The cards were stacked against us from the start of that nightmare trip'. Inevitably the Avengers came out in a long follow-my-leader procession and into the arms of the waiting Japanese fighters. To add to their problems their escorting fighters were mostly engaged in running battles miles away from the rendezvous and, to cap it all, the route to the rendezvous was north of target and straight over a large concentration of flak positions, where they encountered a very heavy and accurate anti-aircraft barrage.

The Japanese fighter pilots had been briefed to go for the bombers and this they did. Although they did not achieve much success during the early stages of the attack, some of the more cunning enemy pilots waited until the attacking Avengers had completed their bombing run and were straggling towards the rendezvous. There were two flights of Corsairs and another of Hellcats patrolling the rendezvous position, while the Fireflies flew up and down the line of Avengers as they left the target and headed for the join up position and the protection of the friendly fighter escort, but they offered a realatively easy target to the waiting Jap planes. Major Hideaki Inayama was one of those pilots who waited for the Avengers leaving the target area and describes his attack:

> At 1500 feet two Avengers were flying southwards, their leader trailing smoke. Sitting ducks. I carefully turned in

behind them concentrating on the damaged Avenger which still had its bomb door open. Probably its hydraulics had been damaged. Six hundred yards, five hundred yards. Suddenly its ball-turret gunner opened fire. Red tracer slipped past my Shoki [Japanese name for the Tojo – meaning Demon], but I held my fire. Two hundred yards. I could clearly see the gunner in the ball-turret. Now I was flying in the wash of my quarry and my aircraft was bouncing around like a mad thing. Steadying up the Shoki I fired at point blank distance. The bullets from my four 13-mm guns ripped into the Avenger, its green-house canopy bursting into fragments, like leaves in a gale. Flames seared back from the port wing roots and the Avenger rolled on to its back and fell away into the jungle below.[1]

The enemy fighters did not have it all their own way for Sub Lieutenant Richards, RNZNVR, caught a Tojo just after he had made an attacking pass at an Avenger: 'he was in a steep crossing turn to the right and in spite of a difficult deflection shot, I gave him a long burst and the enemy flopped on his back and the pilot baled out'. The Japanese had shot down one Avenger and damaged many others, but decided to call it a day after losing at least eleven of their number. They broke off their attacks at 0825 to allow the strike to return to their carriers without further incident.

The airfield Ramrod strikes also had their troubles and the large numbers of enemy aircraft in the air lent proof to the fact that they had not been entirely successful in their mission. The Avengers from *Indomitable* dropped their bombs on Mana airfield and the fighters had strafed and destroyed 34 enemy aircraft on the ground, but they encountered intense and accurate anti-aircraft fire and the raid had cost us five Corsairs lost. Sub Lieutenant A.H. Brown of 1830 Squadron was hit and lost during the attack on Lembak airfield and Lieutenant A.W. Sutton, his Senior Pilot, went missing after the attack on Talangbetoetoe. So intense and accurate was the airfield anti-aircraft fire that yet another Corsair was hit over

[1] Major Hideaki Inayama; *Royal Air Force Flying Review,* Vol XV, No. 8.

A tall column of smoke rises into the air from the refinery at Pangkalan Barndan, heavily damaged by aircraft from *Victorious*, *Indomitable* and *Indefatigable*.

Avengers of *Indomitable*'s 857 Squadron about to dive on to the Pangkalan Brandan refinery.

Top left: a Mitsubishi Zeke 52 Kamikaze plane taken from the bridge of *Victorious* a second before it hit the carrier.

Damage was not heavy—a small hole was made in the deck and the catapult and forward lift were put out of action.

Top right: the first Kamikaze to 'miss' *Victorious*—it exploded 80 feet clear of the port side, 1st April 1945.

Victorious after her second Kamikaze attack on 9th May 1945.

Although hit and set on fire, the aircraft hit the port quarter, skittered across the flight deck, wrecked four Corsairs and finally plunged over the side.

The British Pacific Fleet under heavy Kamikaze attack off Sumatra, 29th January 1945.

Two Sallies burn on the water after being shot down by Seafires and AA fire. A third bomber can be seen to the right, just below the horizon, while a Seafire (right) and a Hellcat (centre) pull up above the Air Defence Zone.

Talangbetoetoe, but the pilot, Sub Lieutenant E.J. Baxter, was seen to bale out safely and was captured. The Japanese pilots were not particularly keen to get caught up in the hail of lead flying up from their own AA guns and were happy to let the airfields look after themselves. In addition to danger from flak, the general melee over the enemy airfields was to produce yet another hazard. Sub Lieutenant I.L. Grave of 1834 Squadron from *Victorious* had a mid-air collision and his aircraft went down in flames. Lieutenant Commander R.D.B. Hopkins was 'Yoke' leader for the Ramrod of 1834 and 1836 Squadrons from *Victorious,* and strafed the airfield at Talangbetoetoe against very intense medium and light flak. After the attack he said: 'I found it difficult to silence the guns of light calibre or to wipe out groups of Japs when running'.

However, the fighter Ramrods did manage to prevent sustained attacks by enemy aircraft on the main strike or any counter-attack on the fleet, and returned to their carriers to land on at 1015. They were followed by the PR Hellcats who returned to *Indomitable* at 1130. These aircraft had covered large strips of the Malayan coast with their cameras, and the photographs were to yield much valuable information.

When the final count was taken, it was found that we had lost six Corsairs, two Avengers and one Hellcat in action, plus one Corsair pilot and one Seafire pilot who had had to bale out in the vicinity of the fleet, but had been picked up uninjured. Against this, the enemy had lost eleven aircraft shot down and up to 34 destroyed or damaged on the ground. The refinery had been well and truly hit and, as later Japanese records were to show, the production of the important Pladjoe plant was reduced by a half.

With the land on completed, Force 63 made to the south-westward at 22 knots and, though the odd enemy 'bogey' showed up on the radar screens, they quickly faded and the airborne CAP was unable to make contact. As ever, the fuel situation was to be the predominant factor and after fuelling the force on the 26th and 27th, there was only enough left for one more strike on Palembang. The debrief was both exhaustive and comprehensive, for with another strike to be undertaken, it was imperative that the same mistakes were not made twice.

As only one of the plants had been attacked, it was reasonable to suppose that the enemy would be expecting another attack. The Admiral was under no illusions about the Japanese methods of extracting information from our captured aircrew, for they had repeatedly broadcast their intentions to kill any captured pilots and thus the problems of making them talk was unlikely to present any major difficulty. Nevertheless, strict wireless security was maintained by the force to keep the enemy guessing about its position, future movements and – more important – the launch area. The destroyer *Ursa* was detached to the Cocos Islands with the urgent dispatches for transmission and, her task completed, she rejoined while the fleet was refuelling on 27th January.

The Seafires which had been used exclusively for the defence of the force on CAP duties during the strike, had had a quiet though disastrous war: low wind speed over the deck caused problems for *Indefatigable* resulting in very slow operation as well as a series of unfortunate deck accidents, which again highlighted the inherent weaknesses of the Seafire as a fleet fighter. This time the CAP would be augmented by four fighters, each from the three remaining carriers – a decision taken by Admiral Vian and prompted no doubt by the possibility of an enemy counter-attack on the carrier force itself.

For the next attack, the fighter sweeps would be flown in two parts timed to arrive over the main enemy airfields of Lembak and Talangbetoetoe simultaneously. They would try to prevent any enemy aircraft from getting airborne and then establish a patrol over the enemy airfields in an effort to keep them there. To help protect the bombers of the main strike, it was decided to provide a Firefly close escort throughout the raid and after the attack. On completion of the bombing, the Avengers were briefed to head southabout from the target to the rendezvous and thus avoid the heavy concentration of flak which they had encountered to the north of Palembang when leaving the oilfields after the last strike. These measures, together with others taken to deal with the barrage balloons and reduce the R/T chatter and general lack of radio discipline would, it was hoped, remedy some of the more obvious mistakes of the earlier attack.

The codename given to this next and last operation was 'Meridian Two' and Force 63 arrived in the flying off position at six o'clock on the morning of the 29th. Two days earlier *Victorious* refuelled from the tanker *Echodale* and topped up her reserves of aviation petrol and fuel oil, but because of parted hoses and lack of practice it had taken a long time to fuel all the ships. More serious was the overall fuel reserve left in the tankers after the ships had had their fill, for even steaming at the relatively slow speed of 22 knots the fuel consumption of the force had been considerable. With no more tankers available, Admiral Vian realised that the fuel oil reserve would allow for just one more strike, so they had better make the most of it.

The launch position was some 30 miles from land and although the coast of Sumatra seemed to be enjoying reasonably clear weather, the force was sitting under a very heavy belt of rain and low cloud. Admiral Vian decided to delay the fly-off and it was not until forty minutes later, in a clear period between the rain storms, that the leading aircraft got airborne and headed for the second of the refineries at Soengei Gerong.[1] It took time to get all the aircraft off the carriers and the weather deteriorated again. With low cloud and driving rain storms, at times the visibility was reduced to less than half a mile. One doesn't need to be an airman to imagine the frightening and dangerous situation created by over 100 aircraft flying under those

---

[1] 'Meridian Two' aircraft were assigned to their missions as follows:
Air Co-ordinator for the strike – Major R.C. Hay and 4 Corsairs from *Victorious;* Soengei Gerong strike – 12 Avengers (849 Squadron) from *Victorious,* 10 Avengers (820 Squadron) from *Indefatigable,* 12 Avengers (854 Squadron) from *Illustrious,* 12 Avengers (857 Squadron) from *Indomitable,* Strike leader Commander W. Stuart (RNVR); Close escort – 12 Corsairs (1836 Squadron) from *Victorious* led by Lt Cdr C.C. Tomkinson, 9 Fireflies (1770 Squadron) from *Indefatigable;* Mid cover – 16 Hellcats (1839, 1844 Squadrons) from *Indomitable* led by Lt Cdr T.W. Harrington; Top cover – 12 Corsairs (1830, 1833 Squadrons) from *Illustrious* led by Lieutenant P.S. Cole; Ramrod airfield sweeps – 13 Corsairs (1834 Squadron) from *Victorious* to attack Lembak and led by Commander R.D.B. Hopkins (Force Yoke), 12 Corsairs (1830, 1833 Squadrons) from *Illustrious.* (Force X-ray) to attack Talangbetoetoe and led by Lieutenant Commander A.M. Tritton; Mana armed reconnaissance – 2 Fireflies (1770 Squadron) from *Indefatigable.*

Note: Armament for the strike was the same as for 'Meridian One' strike on Pladjoe.

conditions in complete radio silence. In the words of Lieutenant Commander C.C. Tomkinson of *Victorious,* 'the form up was something of a nightmare'. The Air Co-ordinator Major Hay was more than a little irritated as the aircraft milled around the carriers, searching for their strike leaders and trying to get into the correct formations before setting off for their targets. Eventually the situation was sorted out when the flagship itself broke radio silence and ordered the strike to depart at 0735 – to everyone's surprise only four minutes late.

The first clash occurred some five miles from the target, when several Japanese fighters launched an attack at the rear of the Avenger strike and succeeded in damaging a few aircraft. In spite of the enemy fighter attacks, and intense box barrage of anti-aircraft fire and the barrage balloons, the Avengers deployed into their bombing pattern at 0845 and began their dives from 7,500 feet. This time more aircraft elected to release their bombs below the balloons which were going down in flames and two Avengers had wings ripped away. Lieutenant Commander W.J. Mainprice, Commanding Officer of 854 Squadron and his wingman, Sub Lieutenant R.S. Armstrong, both hit cables and were lost with their complete crews.

The bombing was more accurate than in the previous attack on Pladjoe, though inevitably the smoke from the burning oil tanks again made it difficult to see the target. When each aeroplane completed the dive and dropped its bombs, it turned to the south of Palembang to avoid the flak concentrations to the north and headed for the same rendezvous – an island in the Musi River some fifteen miles to the west of Palembang. As before, the aircraft came out in ones and twos and were pounced on by the waiting Tojos. In all, seven Avengers were surprised by up to nine enemy fighters and all received damage.

One of the Avengers from *Victorious* was under heavy attack from a couple of Tojos and was saved by another Avenger flown by Lieutenant G.J. Connolly of 854 Squadron. With great dash and showing a complete disregard for his own skin, Connolly waded into the attack shooting down one Tojo and shaking off the other. He then escorted the damaged Avenger to safety.

Lack of adequate fighter protection and force of circumstances made many of the pilots fly their bombers like fighters.

They displayed great courage and skill as they literally threw their cumbersome machines at the attacking Jap fighters. Sub Lieutenant W. Coster and Lieutenant Jones of 820 Squadron had a most exciting encounter with a Tojo who finally ran out of ammunition and patience. At the end of a long engagement during which the Jap pilot emptied his guns and failed to secure a kill, the frustrated enemy pilot broke away in front of Coster and got the full benefit from the forward firing guns of his Avenger. The Jap was last seen trailing flame and smoke in an involuntary aerobatic manoeuvre – upside down and a few feet above the trees.

A very amusing story concerns one Avenger flown by Sub Lieutenant (A) W.A.M. Mackie, RNVR, of 857 Squadron. As he left for the rendezvous he was pounced on by a Jap fighter and was saved by the quick thinking of his Telegraphist Air Gunner. Out of ammunition, the Air Gunner heaved packets of leaflets into the slipstream, and they flashed and scattered crazily astern of the Avenger and into the path of the attacking enemy fighter. As Lieutenant Mackie (now Surgeon Captain) said, 'it must have given the Jap pilot a nasty shock to see all this stuff pouring out of the back of our aircraft and, thinking it was some new sinister weapon, he broke away and left us alone'.

The bombers collected themselves at the rendezvous and in company with their escort, finally departed at 0901 to cross the coast at about 0945 and land on the carriers about 1100. Many of the aircraft were damaged, struggling to stay in the air, and six Avengers had to ditch near the carriers. One aircraft from *Victorious* had been hit in the attack and the observer, Sub Lieutenant M.J. Gunn of 849 Squadron was seriously wounded; in spite of every effort by the Telegraphist Air Gunner Petty Officer A.N. Taylor, he died of his injuries aboard the rescue ship *Whelp*.

The fighters from *Victorious* again had a field day and Hay's flight destroyed two Jap aircraft. The first – a Tojo – was very quickly dispatched and with barely time to draw a breath, a second one appeared seconds later. 'This inquisitive fellow was an Oscar and, obviously attracted by the smoke of the earlier victim, came to have a look'. Sub Lieutenant D. Sheppard continues the story:

Hay ordered his flight of three aircraft to climb and not engage. This we did until we had a 1,500 feet height advantage and the leader and I then attacked. It was a vigorous dogfight and, after a series of steep turns, the Jap settled down for a moment straight and level. My shells hit the pilot's cockpit which glowed with a dull red as the bullets slammed home, then he rolled over and crashed into the trees.

The Admiral thought the enemy would attempt to locate and attack the force and his suspicion was fully justified. At 0900 that morning a single enemy aircraft was detected on radar and the Seafires confirmed it as a Tojo, but before they could intercept he eluded the friendly fighters and escaped in cloud. Thereafter enemy aircraft shadowed or attempted to attack Force 63 for the next ten hours. The Seafires again intercepted a small force of enemy aircraft a few minutes after the initial contact at 0900 and this time were more lucky, for Sub Lieutenant J.H. Kenahan of 887 Squadron from *Indefatigable* shot down one Dinah (Japanese Army reconnaissance aircraft) at 0939.

A group of twelve or more enemy aircraft were detected at 1026 and again a CAP of Corsairs and Seafires were vectored out to intercept. The enemy did not attack the force, but on its return the CAP found they had lost one Corsair flown by Sub Lieutenant S.G. Maynard of 1836 Squadron from *Victorious*.

Our luck could not hold, for sooner or later the enemy were bound to make contact and attempt to strike the carriers. Shortly before noon the Japanese found our ships and at ten minutes to twelve a small raid of seven twin-engined 'Sally' aircraft was detected approaching the force. The aircraft were later identified as suicide planes of the Special Attack Corps and although broken up by the CAP, most of the Jap planes succeeded in reaching the carriers. They kept very low on the water and, when within visual range, could be seen making straight for *Illustrious* and *Indefatigable*.

By US Navy standards our ships did not have nearly enough of the heavier calibre close-range anti-aircraft fire power. American experience showed that guns of less than 40-mm

calibre were virtually useless when it came to stopping a
determined pilot, and our ships were still waiting for more
40-mm guns to be fitted. Nevertheless, the ships put up a very
considerable barrage with everything that would fire, 6-inch,
5.25s, bofors, pom-poms and Oerlikons. The CAP were having a
field day and, in some cases, followed the enemy right through
the fleet barrage on to the barrels of the guns.

Despite all that has been said about the Seafire as a deck-
landing aeroplane and its poor endurance, they were lethal when
they got into combat as the Japs found to their cost. All seven
aircraft were splashed by the Seafire CAP before they could hit
our forces, but there were some close shaves. One Sally got to
within a few hundred yards astern of *Illustrious,* a second hit
the water three hundred yards short of the beam of
Indefatigable, while a third fell close to *King George V.* As R.C.
Hay said later, 'the Seafire handled beautifully in the air and
was more than a match for any Jap aircraft in a dogfight. Even
when we practiced dogfighting with Seafires in our excellent
Corsairs, you could only hold them if you really pulled 'G'[1] and
got your eyeballs down by your boots.'

On this occasion the enemy attack had been frustrated before
it could do any harm, but the Fleet had suffered some
self-inflicted damage. HMS *Illustrious* had received hits by two
anti-aircraft shells from *Euryalus,* and these had struck the flight
deck and island causing casualties of 12 killed and 33 wounded.
At 1530 Admiral Vian made the signal 'Meridian completed' and
the Fleet withdrew. Although enemy aircraft continued to
shadow our forces until that evening, no more attacks developed
and the carriers started to count the cost.

When the final count was taken, it was found that we had
lost a total of 32 aircrew, but *Victorious* had been one of the
hardest hit in terms of aircrew losses. She had seen eleven of her
aircrew go down – seven of them from 849 Squadron of
Avengers. Ten of her Avengers were either missing or badly
damaged in combat, and the force as a whole had lost 16
aircraft to enemy aircraft and a further 25 from other causes.
Against this, the Japanese had been severely mauled and in the

[1] G – Force of gravity which acts on the pilot during violent manoeuvres
such as aerobatics or combat.

air had lost 30 aircraft as well as a further 38 destroyed on the ground.

Nine aircrew had survived when their aircraft were shot down and they were made prisoners by the Japanese. Subsequent information shows that these officers were later murdered by their captors after the surrender of Japan. They were all beheaded by three junior Japanese officers and their bodies dumped in the sea. Although there was insufficient evidence to implicate any senior officer, the three culprits anticipated their fate and committed suicide. This incident shows why both British and American forces went to such lengths to provide efficient air/sea rescue services, which on occasions went beyond the bounds of reason and put the rescuers at greater risk than those they were trying to save, for as Admiral Vian stated, 'it remained ever a problem of where to draw the line.'

It is worth recording that *Vic*'s Walrus rescue amphibian wanted to fly inland to a lake in Sumatra where a crashed Avenger had been sighted, but Admiral Vian refused permission on the grounds that he had insufficient fighters for CAP and to accompany the SAR aircraft. Nevertheless, he was always anxious that his aircrews should know that, when in trouble, the whole effort of the Fleet would be directed towards their recovery. On the few occasions when this could not be done, such decisions must have grieved him deeply.

The damage reports and aerial photographs showed that both refineries had been successfully attacked and many of the installations received direct hits. The strike on Soengei Gerong refinery stopped production until the end of March when both plants were able to run at one third capacity, improving to no more than half capacity three months later.

Although the aircrews and the British Pacific Fleet could be proud of the results of this their first real action – very many lessons had come out of it. Perhaps the most important one had been the question of resupply by the Fleet Train. Clearly the fuel situation would have to be improved and more tankers provided to enable the task force to remain on station. A third strike against Palembang might have put the refineries out of action completely, for all the signs indicated that the Japanese fighters were beaten by the end of the second strike and were unable to secure reinforcements. It was a cruel twist of fate that lack of oil fuel for the ships was to cause the cancellation of the vital and perhaps decisive third blow.

Again – aircraft and aircrew losses highlighted the need for a reserve carrier from which could be drawn the necessary replacements. *Victorious* and *Illustrious* had both suffered badly, but had to wait until they reached Australia to make good their losses. This was an operational limitation that demanded early attention and remedy. The first attacks by the seven aircraft of the Japanese Special Attack Corps had emphasised a very real danger, for as far as our anti-aircraft fire was concerned our ships had shown that 'they were unable to look after themselves'. It was true that the Jap suicide aircraft had been shot down to the last man, but this new form of deliberate attack emphasised the need for more of the 40-mm guns and, as the accidental damage to *Illustrious* had tragically shown, an urgent improvement in the standard of AA gunnery and control and co-ordination of weapons in the Fleet.

On the air side, the carriers had improved greatly with practice, but the large aircraft ranges on deck and the filling of each carrier to capacity created many problems and, though we were learning fast from the Americans, we still had a long way to go and such a policy threw great burdens on the Flight Deck Personnel. Lieutenant Commander Bill Sykes was Flight Deck Officer of *Victorious* and achieved the impossible by pleasing everybody for, as one of his admirers said, 'He was a genius at providing serviceable aircraft on deck for a launch at the right place and right time, and with the greatest good humour and skill.' This was indeed praise for, as anyone who has had experience will tell you, the aircraft you require on the next launch is always inaccessible in the hangar and cannot be got up in time – an almost impossible task when the ship is overcrowded with aircraft.

The aircrews had learned a lot in a very short time but they owed a great debt of gratitude to Commander Charles Owen, the Operations Officer of *Victorious* who was partly responsible. His task was the planning and briefing of all air operations and, as one airman put it, 'cheerful coaxing of the aviators into the more unpleasant operations'. Captain Denny recorded:

The Palembang attacks were of immense value in increasing the efficiency of my young pilots in *Victorious*. I was always thankful for them because of the excellent training they provided. The real object of the creation of the carrier Squadrons was for the final business of fighting the Japanese in their home waters, but it was fortunate that these earlier attacks took place when they did as the experience was something we all needed.

The enemy were not so impressed and a typical broadcast on the Japanese radio reported:

After this costly attack it will be a long time before the enemy come to a decision to carry out further attacks on Japanese held territory in South East Asia.

Again the ship's air maintainers won the praise of their masters back home at the Admiralty, for the Chief Inspector of Naval Ordnance wrote:

Generally a high standard of armament maintainance seems to obtain on this ship. This is reflected in the confidence shown by the pilots in their guns.

In fact *Vic's* fighter Squadrons had had only eight gun stoppages in the whole of the Palembang operation and only one camera gun failure. This was a very creditable performance for the aircraft were mostly old, tired and worn out Corsair Mark 2s and as the Pacific War went on, maintainence and serviceability were to create nightmare problems for the overworked aircraft maintainers.

Force 63 fuelled on the 30th, reached Fremantle on the 4th and Sydney on the 10th. The reception accorded to the British Pacific Fleet by the Australians was truly fantastic, and their generosity and hospitality provided a timely morale-booster to the new fleet. But events in the Pacific were moving towards the climax and Fraser was keen to get his fleet nearer the war zone. There was a powerful force of British ships waiting to play their part, but for the time being it would seem there was no part to play.

Chapter XII

OPERATION ICEBERG

The Okinawa Gunto comprises a number of islands situated approximately in the centre of the Nansei Shoto chain which runs for 500 miles south-west of Japan. Operation 'Iceberg' was the codename given to the assault on Okinawa and was the stepping-stone by which the Allied forces would ultimately reach the mainland of Japan. After the crushing defeat of Leyte Gulf, the Imperial Japanese Navy deployed little more than nuisance value, but as the Allies moved ever closer to the heart of the Japanese Empire, resistance was expected to stiffen and come mainly from the ground and air.

The enemy air force based in Okinawa was small but could be reinforced quickly from airfields in Formosa and Kyushu, whilst the distance of the nearest US airfields in Luzon was too great to allow close assault support by land-based fighters. This meant that, in the early stages, the military operation would have to be supported by carrier-based aircraft and at the same time, enemy reinforcement would have to be prevented.

The future role of the British Carrier Force was in some doubt, but after much argument, uncertainty and a long wait, the British Pacific Fleet was ordered to prevent Japanese air reinforcement of Okinawa through the Sakishima Gunto and Amami Gunto island chains. The Japanese had constructed a number of airfields in these island groups and could stage aircraft through from China, Formosa and the mainland of Japan to attack the Okinawa invasion forces, and the British carrier force was charged with ensuring that this did not happen.

It is worth re-emphasising that our ships were sent to Australia for political reasons before the base was sufficiently developed to maintain them. Essential support was always a little late because the rear base in the United Kingdom was 12,000 miles away from the forward base in Sydney, while the advanced base at Leyte Island – used during the first part of 'Iceberg' – was 800 miles from the combat area. At no time before the war ended was the Australian base able to supply and maintain the British Pacific Fleet completely without the help of US bases, fuelling facilities and spare parts; and it is unlikely that any of our ships would have remained operational for long without American help. As it was, the operation of the British Carrier Force in 'Iceberg' was described as a scramble.

The striking force, Task Force 113, had arrived at Sydney from the Indian Ocean and Palembang on 10th February. Its initial supplies of stores, air stores, aircraft and men were still arriving from the United Kingdom even when it sailed on the 28th for its advanced anchorage, Manus in the Admiralty Islands. The stay in Australia had been hospitable and a welcome break for the crews of the British Fleet, but as they waited and exercised at Manus, morale started to take a nose dive.

After the Australian welcome, 'We've had an American occupation and were so glad to see you Limeys', anything would be an anti-climax. It is probably easier to understand their boredom and frustration if one considers the conditions under which the men were living, for apart from the Air Group who were disembarked to Pitilu, swinging round at anchor in Manus with the bright lights of Sydney in their minds and not knowing their future employment, was not the BPF's idea of helping to win the war. The humidity and general discomfort meant that life aboard *Victorious* was not a rosy rest cure for anyone from the Captain downwards. The trying conditions were reported by one correspondent at the time who said that 'tropical Sea War is an unending Turkish bath,' and added: 'With no drying room.'

> The long flight decks of the carriers [he went on] are made of steel. They absorb the rays of the tropical sun and retain the torrid heat night and day. That heat penetrates down into the ship to meet the intense heat rising from the boiler rooms and galleys. At action stations warships are closed

up, scuttles – portholes – are shut. Watertight bulkheads, which section off the ship into bootbox compartments, are locked with great iron pins. Four-fifths of an aircraft carrier's ship's company work sandwiched between those two layers of heat – stifled, sweating, every minute of every hour of every day and night until they are back in port.

They suffer prickly heat and other skin disorders. The men of *Victorious* think of the damp when they were fighting in the icy cold of the Arctic and the North Atlantic. When it is freezing cold at sea you can, with many layers of clothing, at least get some warmth into your body; but out here you cannot get cool. Even the water you drink is as warm as that in which at home you would take a bath.

While the men sweated and waited and exercised the days dragged on. Eventually the long awaited signal was received and the Fleet moved up to Ulithi Atoll in the Caroline Islands on 18th March. It was, as an officer said, 'one of the most fantastic sights in the world with ships in every direction as far as the eye could see – ships, more ships and still more ships'. Admiral King delayed his decision to assign the British Carrier Force to Operation 'Iceberg' and Admiral Rawlings was consequently two days late in beginning operations. Moreover, after the BPF had been allocated to 'Iceberg', it needed the combined represent-ations of the Commander-in-Chief Pacific Fleet and the Commander Seventh Fleet to dissuade King from withdrawing the British Force, in order to cover the Australian landings in Borneo on 1st May for which no US carriers were available. Nevertheless Admiral Nimitz who wanted the BPF as his most flexible reserve won the day, and on 23rd March it became Task Force 57 assigned to the US Fifth Fleet.

Although they were given the status of Task Force, in terms of aircraft numbers the British carriers did not equate to a single Task Group in the American Fast Carrier Force, and there were four Task Groups forming Admiral Mitscher's Task Force 58.

The British Task Force slipped quietly out of the enormous Ulithi Atoll at 0630 on the morning of 23rd March to com-

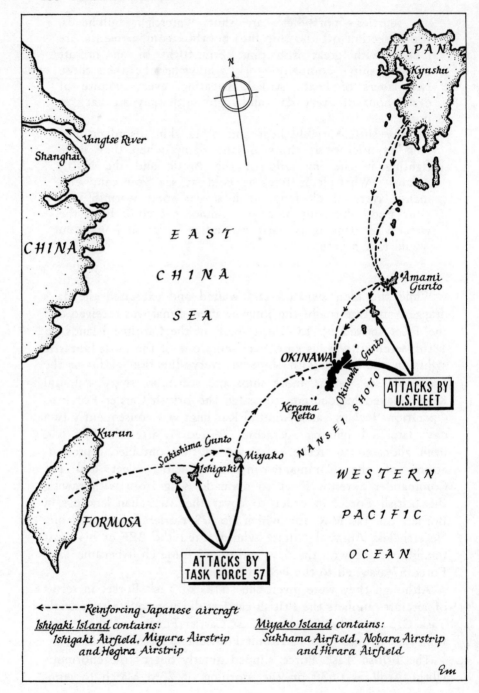

N

JAPAN
Kyushu

Yangtse River
Shanghai

CHINA

EAST

CHINA

SEA

Amami
Gunto

OKINAWA

Okinawa Gunto

ATTACKS BY
U.S. FLEET

Kerama
Retto

NANSEI SHOTO

Kurun

Sakishima Gunto

Miyako

WESTERN

Ishigaki

PACIFIC

FORMOSA

OCEAN

ATTACKS BY
TASK FORCE 57

- - - - - -Reinforcing Japanese aircraft

Ishigaki Island contains:
  Ishigaki Airfield, Miyara Airstrip
  and Hegina Airstrip

Miyako Island contains:
  Sukhama Airfield, Nobara Airstrip
  and Hirara Airfield

Em

mence the first phase of Operation 'Iceberg'. The battleship *King George V* and flagship of the Commander Task Force 57, Vice Admiral Sir Bernard Rawlings, led the fleet followed by the battleship *Howe*; the fleet carriers *Indomitable*, flagship of Admiral Vian (AC1), *Victorious, Illustrious*, and *Indefatigable*; the light cruisers *Swiftsure, Gambia, Black Prince* and *Euryalus* and the destroyers *Grenville, Ulster, Undine, Urania, Undaunted, Quickmatch, Quiberon, Queensborough, Quality, Whelp* and *Wager*.

The force headed north for their first objective in the Sakishima Gunto. En route they carried out gunnery communications exercises, before refuelling from the Replenishment Group in the early hours of the 25th. As soon as they had cleared harbour and formed up, all ships carried out anti-aircraft sleeve firings at drogue targets towed by Marauders of the US Utility Squadron based at Leyte. Due to the low cloud and communication difficulties, the carriers were unable to carry out any long range firings, but managed to account for four sleeves with their close-range armament. On completion of the serial the carrier *Indomitable* apologised to the battleship *Howe* for pom-pom shells which had been fired in error in her direction during the serial.

The scores were evened in another exercise later on when *Howe* let fly with her close-range armament and prompted the following signal from *Indomitable*:

One of my aircraft handling party was struck painlessly on the buttock by a fragment of shell during serial 5. Suggest this cancels my pom pom assault.

The point was taken by the battleship who replied:

From *Howe* to *Indomitable*
Your 0950. Please convey my regrets to the rating and ask him to turn the other cheek.

The weather conditions got steadily worse as the force steamed northwards and, by the time they met the Replenishment Group, they had to contend with strong winds and a very heavy swell. Unlike the Americans, our tankers were not able to use the present day system of fuelling from abeam. We still trailed a buoyant hose astern of the tanker to oil the big ships, and with a slow pumping capacity the whole operation was lengthy, tedious and difficult. Parted hoses forced Admiral Rawlings to cut short the fuelling and at 1530, TF 57 increased to 23½ knots to reach the launch position by the next dawn.

At 0605 on the morning of the 26th, the fleet was turned into wind to fly off the first fighter sweeps from a position 100 miles due south of the island of Miyako. Two escorts were detached to carry out the duties of radar pickets to give the fleet adequate warning of the approach of enemy aircraft, and at 0615 the first aircraft was launched. The order of battle for the carrier aircraft was as follows:

> *Indomitable;* 29 Hellcats, 15 Avengers. *Victorious:* 37 Corsairs, 14 Avengers, 2 Walrus. *Indefatigable:* 40 Seafires, 20 Avengers, 9 Fireflies. *Illustrious:* 36 Corsairs, 16 Avengers.

Six airfields had been built on the two islands of the Sakishima Gunto with the airstrips of Miyara, Hegina, and Ishigaki on Ishigaki Island, while on the other island, Miyako, the Japanese had built Nobara, Hirara and Sukhama. The aircrews of the BPF were briefed to neutralise these airfields by cratering the runways, strafing the defences and parked aircraft, and to prevent the enemy from staging in replacement or reinforcement aircraft by keeping a permanent CAP over the enemy fields.

In *Victorious* the aircrews listened as the briefing officers described the targets. Strike 'Baker' would consist of 15 Corsairs briefed to attack barracks at the northern end of Miyako Jima, a radio station south-east of Hirara town, buildings at Hirara airfield, barracks at Nobara airfield and finally a factory at Tomari. This would be followed by Strike 'Charlie' consisting of a bombing attack by 6 Avengers and 12 Corsairs on the airfields of Hirara and Ishigaki two-and-a-half hours later.

Victorious launched her first aircraft at 0615 consisting of a CAP of four Corsairs. This was followed fifteen minutes later by a launch of 15 Corsairs led by Lieutenant Commander C.C. Tomkinson, CO of 1836 Squadron to carry out Ramrod airfield sweeps over the airfields of Hirara and Nobara on the island of Miyako. He states:

> The form-up took longer than usual as the aircraft had not been ranged on deck in the correct order and several went unserviceable.

Sub Lieutenant D.T. Chute, RNVR, continues:

> A low level approach was made until nearing Miyako Jima when the sweep climbed to 8,000 feet and swept round to an up-sun position of Hirara airfield. Drop tanks were released and Green Flight followed Red Flight in a steep diving attack on the airfield from the north-east, opening fire at long range and closing to zero feet where it could be seen that the targets attacked were either dummies or damaged aircraft.

Swinging to the left, Nobara Airfield was attacked at low level, but once again with no apparent result. A certain amount of ack-ack was received from Hirara town and airfield area – 'accurate for height but not for aim', said one pilot somewhat thankfully. The first attack was carried out before the bigger guns commenced firing, but Lieutenant Commander Tomkinson was hit and forced to ditch and though the SAR Walrus carried out a thorough search of the area, no trace was found. Although he had only one kidney and had completed his tour of duty, he had elected to stay, and the current opinion among his aircrew friends was that when he ditched, this very gallant gentleman was too weak to swim and drowned. Whatever the cause Captain Denny reported that:

> The loss of Lieutenant Commander (A) Tomkinson, RNVR, is thought to have been caused by a faulty life jacket. He was observed in his life jacket in sight of land and the position was accurately fixed. Sub Lieutenant (A) Rhodes saw him in the sea and took part in the search.

He was an experienced Corsair pilot, a first class Commanding Officer and a serious loss to *Victorious*.

The first big strike of the day took off at 0920 to attack the airfields when six Avengers from *Victorious* joined with those from the other carriers to form a raid of over forty aircraft, each armed with four 500-pound MC bombs. The intention was to crater the runways, bomb and strafe any other targets of opportunity and keep up the pressure round the clock during daylight hours. Although the Japs were denied the use of the airfields by day, it is questionable whether the results justified the effort. The runways were made of crushed coral — available in unlimited quantities since the islands were themselves built of and on coral — and any damage caused could be filled in and repaired overnight. If only we had had night intruder aircraft capable of hitting the enemy during the hours of darkness the rewards might have been well worthwhile. Ronnie Hay made the point when he said: 'we would have been better off using three-cornered tin tacks instead of bombs designed to sink the *Tirpitz*; they just went in — made a small hole and the Japs filled them in again that night.' Few enemy aircraft were caught on the ground during the day strikes and our own aircraft had to face increasingly more accurate and intense anti-aircraft fire. Sub Lieutenant S. Leonard, RNVR was leading Strike 'Dog' on the second day and was briefed to attack Hirara Airfield:

> I strafed dummy aircraft and AA positions. Sub Lieutenant Spreckly from *Victorious* was flying on my port side, in line abreast, and was apparently hit by AA fire. He nosed over from 50 feet, hit the ground and exploded. After the first few days the Jap gunners stopped using tracer bullets and as we couldn't see them firing, up went our casualties.

In the first two days of the operations, four major strikes of forty aircraft each were flown daily interspersed with Corsair and Hellcat sorties to keep the enemy's heads down. These attacks claimed twelve Japanese aircraft destroyed on the ground with a further twenty-eight shot down over their airfields, for the loss of nineteen Fleet Air Arm planes.

The Jap reconnaissance planes kept up a constant vigil around the Fleet throughout the hours of darkness, and our need for a radar equipped night fighter was keenly felt. In spite of this, however, one persistent Dinah was given a nasty shock in the early hours of the 27th when Lieutenant N.G. Mitchell of 1839 Squadron was launched in the moonlight to attempt an interception. It nearly came off, but as he got his Hellcat within firing range – the moon went behind a cloud. But it did cause the enemy to think and thereafter keep at a respectful distance.

The American landings on Okinawa were scheduled for 1st April and the BPF were ordered to re-strike the airfields of Sakishima Gunto during the critical period 31st March to the 2nd April. More attacks had been planned for the 28th March, but a typhoon warning had caused Admiral Rawlings to cancel further strikes, so that his force could replenish and be back on station in good time to cover the American assault.

Task Force 57 met the replenishment force at 0730 on the 28th March and commenced to fuel, replace lost and damaged aircraft and take on stores, provisions and replacement aircrew. The strong winds and choppy seas made the RAS a lengthy and somewhat hazardous affair, which lasted until the afternoon of the 30th. Captain Denny commenting afterwards said:

> The enormous advantage possessed by ships who have the first 'rub' at the hoses was made abundantly clear when *Victorious* attempted to fuel from *San Ambrosio* as last of the party. The gear was in a shocking condition with 50 per cent of all joints leaking, hoses abraided, seizings to jackstays worn out or carried away. After some nine hours of continuous struggle 350 gallons of petrol and 623 tons of oil fuel had been embarked.

As if they hadn't had enough excitement for one day, *Victorious* had to go full speed astern to avoid a collision with the escort *Wager*. It was 2008 in the evening and the small ship thought he would get to his station more rapidly if he took a short cut – across the bows of *Victorious*. One officer humorously pointed out that the '*Wager*'s Wager' paid off and he made across the bows in spite of some jangled nerves and a few terse signals, but unhappily the signal logs do not record the dialogue that passed between the two ships *after* their near miss.

At 1430 on the 30th, the fleet proceeded to the combat area at 22 knots and flying commenced at 0600 the next morning. In order to husband the strength of Task Force 57 until the enemy showed signs of using the Sakishima Gunto airfields, the Commander decided to have two plans ready for execution. Plan 'Peter' was to be carried out if little use was being made of the island airfields; Plan 'Queen' was to be put into effect if the enemy was staging through large numbers of aircraft. Both plans started with a fighter sweep, but in Plan 'Peter' a small combat patrol was then to be maintained over each island to keep watch and only small harrassing bombing raids were to be flown. In Plan 'Queen' larger escorted bomber strikes and fighter sweeps would be sent to prevent enemy reinforcement. The Air Group Commander plus his three escorting Corsairs made a first reconnaissance of the area daily and based on their report, the command decided on a 'plan' for the rest of the day.

On 31st March the first fighter sweep of eight Hellcats and sixteen Corsairs reported no apparent change in the state of the airfields since they were there four days earlier, so Plan 'Peter' was confirmed and patrols of four fighters were flown off in succession to each island during the day. A proportion of these fighters carried bombs which were dropped on the airfields and, in addition, two small bomber strikes of eleven Avengers each were flown off at 1215 and 1515 respectively, with small fighter escorts to attack Ishigaki Airfield and the airfield installations. Intelligence suggested that Ishigaki rather than Miyako was likely to be used by the enemy. Once again there was no enemy reaction except flak, and more damage was caused to the runways and airfield buildings.

Six Avengers from 849 Squadron led by Lieutenant (A) R. Swain, RNVR, took off in the first of these strikes at 1215. They took departure at 1235 and climbing to 10,000 feet set course for Ishigaki Airfield. They carried out a good attack and hits were observed on runways and buildings as well as near misses on both the barracks and radio station. Swain reported: 'Number 6 Avenger of 849 Squadron was hit during the run in and observed to crash on the runway after making his attack.' Unfortunately Sub Lieutenant R.C. Sheard and his crew were lost in this strike.

At 0600 on the morning of Easter Sunday 1st April, the American assault on Okinawa commenced. It was preceded by an enormous bombardment from seaward and for the first few hours, the attacking US Marines had a relatively easy time. It is likely that the Allies underestimated the strength of the Japanese on Okinawa both on the ground and in the air, for in fact they had some 70,000 troops with an additional 30,000 supporting naval and garrison personnel. The air strength was considerable and consisted of nearly 6,000 aircraft of the 5th Air Fleet and 6th Air Army based on the mainland of Japan and Okinawa, and nearly two thirds of these were composed of the newly formed Special Attack Units of Kamikaze squadrons. By Day Two, the Japanese resistance had stiffened to halt the American advance and, for the first time, the enemy took retaliatory measures against the British Pacific Fleet.

The first Allied experience of a Kamikaze attack occurred on 17th May 1944 when Major Katashige Takata deliberately crashed to self-destruction on to a US destroyer off Biak, New Guinea. He was a fighter pilot in the Imperial Air Force and flying a Nakijima Ki 43 'Oscar' fighter armed with two 500-pound bombs; he successfully dived his aircraft at the unfortunate ship which sank with the loss of many lives. Major Takata had sacrificed his life in accordance with the teachings of the ancient and symbolic Bushido Code which gave the Japanese youth the inspiration to 'meet their personal sons of heaven' in a very spectacular and devastating manner.

The military impact of the Kamikaze was not lost to the Japanese for in it they saw the means of redressing the balance of the overwhelming might of the Allied Naval Forces. The advantages were obvious; the pilots would require far less training and skill for their one way mission and secondly, the terminal accuracy of the bomb would be higher than the average skilled dive-bomber pilot and, lastly, the damage inflicted would be out of all proportion to their losses in both aircraft and pilots. Kamikaze Special Attack Squads to wipe out the US carrier forces in the Pacific were initiated by 1st Air Fleet in July 1944 and recruitment began in earnest. The young men of Japan came forward in their hundreds to volunteer for the chance to fly on the 'Wings of the Divine Wind'.

By and large, the pilots were young and inexperienced and were given only a rudimentary instruction in the handling and control of their aircraft. After a short course and a few weeks of high living as heroes of the nation, they dressed in their ceremonial white belted tunics with black buttons and the special emblem of the Corps displayed on the chest – a cherry blossom with three leaves, then they tied a silk muffler inscribed with traditional poems around their throats and, clutching Samurai swords and a list of targets, they set off to meet their makers.

Later Kamikaze pilots were detailed for the task and from prisoners-of-war and diaries we now know that the one-way mission was not always regarded with enthusiasm. Some of the Kamikaze aircraft were conventional twin-engined bombers or fighters, usually loaded with bombs for the occasion, but special flying bombs were developed by the Japanese to wage this new and terrifying form of warfare. Designed by Captain Niki, the little Oka 4 (or Baka as it was called by the Japanese) was a small single seat monoplane only 15 feet in length and considerably cheaper than a conventional aeroplane. With a maximum speed of nearly 600 mph, it carried 2,000 pounds of high explosive in the nose and caused horrifying damage when it hit its target. The Baka – or Fool as it was called by the Americans – was carried into action slung under the belly of a Mitsubishi G4M (Betty) twin-engined bomber and released some distance from the target. Four rockets then propelled the missile for some 5 to 10 minutes' flight duration and the pilot selected his enemy ship and dived down. About 800 of these doodlebug-type weapons were constructed, but fortunately for us only about fifty had been launched by the time the war ended. In the latter stages, the enemy Kamikaze pilots were using anything that would fly and came in fighters, old bombers and even antiquated float-planes. The exact tally of Kamikaze planes launched will probably never be known, but by the time Okinawa fell, 2,000 and possibly as many as 4,000 suicide aircraft had been destroyed.

The British plan for the 1st April was the same as for the previous day and accordingly, at 0643, the first of the fighter Ramrods were airborne and on their way to their targets – again the airfields of Ishigaki. The escorts *Argonaut* and *Wager* were detached to take up their radar picket stations and the carriers settled down to another day of hard, but routine flying. The last of the fighters had just disappeared over the horizon when at one minute past seven, the Fleet had its first intimation of trouble. The ships' radars detected a group of aircraft some 75 miles to the westward and closing the force at 8,000 feet; and since an attack on TF57 looked imminent, the fighter Ramrods were recalled to help out and additional defensive fighters flown off. The raid split up more than forty miles from the Fleet and the strength was estimated to be fifteen plus.

The first interception was carried out by Corsairs from *Victorious* and a Zeke was shot down. Temporary Sub Lieutenants J.C. Leddy and R. Watt were on Combat Air Patrol and were vectored out to stop the enemy attack. Together they took on the Japs and after a short, spirited encounter with the Zeke, the enemy went down in flames to crash in the sea. Meanwhile Lieutenant D.T. Chute was on the recalled Ramrod sortie and reported:

> The Squadrons had reached a height of 15,000 feet heading for the islands when we were given a vector for the bogeys [unidentified aircraft presumed hostile] heading towards the Fleet. The first height given was 12,000 feet, but later changed to 19,000 feet and all squadrons climbed. The bogeys were next detected at sea level and down we went.

The British fighters waded into the enemy planes and followed them right on to the guns of the Fleet. It created a number of problems for the ships because apart from the fact that the Jap aircraft looked remarkably similar to some of our own, and thus presented a recognition problem, the gun layers and control officers did not like to fire on enemy aircraft which were being pursued by friendly fighters – mistakes are made even in the best regulated circles. At 0727, a Zeke carried out a machine gun attack on *King George V* then made a feint diving attack on the starboard side of *Indefatigable*. He was pounced on by Temporary Sub Lieutenant (A) R.H. Reynolds in a Seafire, but twisting and turning he evaded all attempts to shoot him down and dived at the carrier from the port quarter. Reynolds again attempted to intercept and only broke off when he realised that by continuing he would follow the Zeke into the deck of the carrier.

Within seconds the Zeke struck *Indefatigable* abreast the forward barrier at the junction of the flight deck and the island, and a terrific explosion from its 500-pound bomb shattered the flight deck sickbay, briefing room and both flight deck barriers. Eight men were killed outright and sixteen wounded, including Lieutenant Commander Flying, an Air Engineer Officer and half the Operations Room crew. The blast bent the flight deck armour to a depth of some three inches and splinters caused much superficial damage as well as starting a small fire in the roof of 'B' Hangar; however, the fire was put out within four minutes and at 0816, just thirty-eight-and-a-half minutes after the attack the first range of Seafires was landed on.

While the firefighters and flight deck parties were clearing up the mess on *Indefatigable*'s deck, a second Zeke scored a near miss on the destroyer *Ulster* and seriously damaged her. The escort was unable to steam and *Gambia* eventually towed her to Leyte for repairs. Thus ended for the BPF their initial taste of the Japanese suicide attack. It had obviously impressed the American liaison officers, for when one of their carriers was hit it was a matter of six months in harbour for repairs, but in the case of *Indefatigable* it had been 'Man the brooms.'

The first Kamikaze attack on *Victorious* occurred in the late afternoon at about five-thirty on the 1st April. The fleet was being manoeuvred in a succession of starboard turns when a Kamikaze aircraft hedgehopped over the destroyer escort at 500 feet, broke through the defences, climbed to get some altitude and then dived towards the carrier. The Jap pilot approached as for a deck landing from a right hand circuit and made his run in. He had been briefed to attack the British carriers and, ahead of him, he could see the slewing, oblong shape of the flight-deck which at that distance and altitude looked like a tombstone lying flat on the sea. In a few seconds he would pull up and then dive down to inscribe his own epitaph in smoke, flame and death. The ship was turning to starboard at the time and Captain Denny increased the rate of swing by using more rudder. The aircraft was believed to be a Jill or a Zeke and appeared to be doing his best to turn with the swinging ship but could not make the turn tight enough. One officer records the moment as they watched and waited for the Jap to hit them:

> *Victorious* was now swinging very fast and as we watched the aircraft banked even more steeply trying to keep on the target. He roared in and his starboard wing struck the port edge of the flight deck and caused his plane to cartwheel into the sea on the port side. The bomb detonated underwater about 80 feet clear of the ship's side and threw tons of water, a quantity of petrol and many fragments of the aircraft and pilot on to the flight deck.

As luck would have it, the carrier had her deck park of eight aircraft at the extreme forward end of the flight deck and this saved her from a successful attack. The Jap pilot had failed to smash *Victorious* and as the members of the flight deck party breathed a sigh of relief and prepared to sweep off the bits, someone noticed a small piece of paper on the flight deck and picked it up. It was the unfortunate enemy pilot's briefing instructions and target priorities and this interesting document was sent for translation to the Flag Officer Commanding Aircraft Carriers; Captain Denny was unimpressed and said afterwards that 'the only unmistakable feature of this document was its reek of cheap scent.'

The Fleet retired to its refuelling area at noon on the 2nd April, but bad weather delayed the replenishment and it was still incomplete when Task Force 57 headed for their operational area on Thursday 5th. During these three-day breaks the Squadrons took the opportunity to maintain or replace their aircraft, and to carry out the routine tasks which tended to build up during the hectic operational days. Aircraft which were badly damaged by deck accidents or enemy action were stripped of all valuable components and then unceremoniously tossed over the side. At dusk on the 4th as *Victorious* steamed towards the well-known Sakishima Gunto, three Avengers from 849 – JZ 545, JZ 487 and JZ 370 found a watery grave in this way.

The next day saw the BPF take over once more from the American Task Group and begin all over again the heart-breaking task of neutralising the enemy airfields. Raids were launched on Hirara, Nobara, Sukhama and Miyara. 849 Avenger Squadron from *Victorious* were briefed to carry out glide bomb attacks on Hirara but had a poor start to the day. Of the six aircraft scheduled to go, the Commanding Officer's aircraft went unserviceable and number two – Sub Lieutenant Brown – created a minor flying sensation on deck when he attempted to fly off. As the Flight Deck Officer dropped his flag, Brown let off his brakes and roared off up the deck. Unfortunately his starboard brake jammed on causing the aircraft to slew to the right and, in spite of all his efforts, the aircraft flew headlong into the island. Happily the pilot and crew survived with only minor injuries, a nasty shock and a very bent aeroplane. The remaining aircraft carried out the sortie without loss and landed back on at 1415 to complete the day's flying for the squadron.

At dusk that day a force of enemy aircraft was picked up and intercepted by the CAP, but one aircraft evaded its pursuers and went for *Illustrious*. The carrier took violent avoiding action and had a lucky escape, for only slight damage was caused when the enemy's wing tip caught the island.

This was the only Kamikaze attack on the Force who continued to attack the runways of the airfields, and targets of opportunity throughout the 7th. That evening Captain Denny broadcast at 2100 to the ships company and gave them news that there would possibly be a change of plan for the next period of operations and that, with luck, the British carriers would strike Formosa.

In fact the Americans had been suffering heavily from massed attacks by waves of Kamikaze planes, flown by dedicated and skilled pilots of the Japanese Navy. It was believed that they were flying from the airfields of Shinchiku and Matsuyama in the northern part of Formosa, using them as fuelling bases before launching off to attack the American ships off Okinawa. By the end of the Okinawa campaign, in which the Japanese launched literally hundreds of these death missions, the total cost to the Americans was a staggering 36 ships sunk and a further 368 damaged. The death and destruction could not be allowed to continue and so on the 9th April Admiral Spruance, USN, the Commander US 5th Fleet, asked Task Force 57 to strike at enemy airfields in Formosa on the 11th and 12th and try to relieve the pressure.

So it was that under the codename of Operation 'Oolong', the carriers of the BPF headed for their new theatre of operations with promises of more excitement and action. Inevitably bad weather delayed the first day of operations, but on the 12th the conditions improved sufficiently for the action to begin. In Position 202 degrees Yonakumi Shima 30 miles, the first day was full of incident and the opening move was made by the enemy. At five-past-seven the CAP of Seafires intercepted four Zekes, splashed one and, shortly afterwards, the carriers launched their first strike.

One force of twenty-four bombers escorted by fighters hit Shinchiku airfield, while a similar force heading for Matsuyama met bad weather and went for the alternative target of Kirrun harbour. It was on this day that the Fireflies from *Indefatigable* scored one of their most notable achievements. Two aircraft over Yonakumi Shima caught a flight of Jap 'Sonia' light bombers and a journalist wrote an eye-witness account of the encounter:

Killed a plane a minute. Two North of England Navy pilots flying Fairey Fireflies from the carrier *Indefatigable* bagged four Jap planes in as many minutes in a spectacular dogfight at almost water level in the Pacific early in April. The pilots, Sub Lieutenant Walter Thompson, of Cleator Moor, Cumberland, and Sub Lieutenant Philip Stott, of Liverpool, were escorting an American flying-boat rescuing ditched air crews from dangerous waters around Jap held islands in the Formosa area, when Thompson's Observer, Sub Lieutenant Eric Miller, of Newcastle, spotted five Japanese Sonias a few miles away. Closing immediately the Fireflies attacked at such close range that Thompson's windscreen was covered with blazing oil when one of his victims tried to get down to sea level. The fifth Sonia escaped into the clouds.

The Japs attempted another strike against the Fleet later in the day, but as before the CAP successfully thwarted their efforts and the raid was turned back. Lieutenant Commander

J.B. Edmundson of *Victorious* was CAP leader and flying his Corsair II – P139 – off Formosa, when he sighted two 'Zekes' and a 'Val' at 7,000 feet:

> The enemy aircraft were flying very slowly at about 120 knots and one of them was carrying out the most erratic and peculiar evasion. Two aircraft escaped, but the Zeke we splashed dived down to sea level instead of going up into the cloud which was the obvious evasion. If stories of doping are true, then I reckon that this pilot was well and truely doped.

The next day the strikes were again mounted on the two enemy airfields of Matsuyama and Shinchiku, and the following debrief report from *Victorious'* 849 Squadron illustrates a typical mission. Major R.C. Hay, the Air Group Leader, reported:

> We took off to strike Matsuyama airfield, Formosa at 0645 and departed at 0705 – surely a record! A landfall was made at 0730 with visibility of 30 miles and 10/10ths cloud at 6,000 feet. Cloud deteriorated over the hills so I ordered the strike to proceed round the coast. This they did, climbing to 8,000 feet. Unfortunately a solid layer of cloud built up right over the airfield and prevented a detailed examination of the target. The cloud layer was 1,000 feet thick with a base of 3,000 feet. I informed strike leader D.R. Foster and orbited overhead looking for a gap – he eventually decided to bomb after diving through cloud. From down below I observed many bombs striking the airfield until it was covered in brown smoke and dust. There was no flak before the bombing, but the moment the bombers appeared below 3,000 feet. every gun went into action. They were obviously waiting. On withdrawal one Avenger bombed a factory. I caught a passenger train which was skulking in a tunnel but rather carelessly had left the engine sticking out. We then shot up a few junks and went on to Giran where approximately twelve aircraft of various types were spotted. One twin-engined plane was strafed but failed to burn.
> Considering the weather I think the strike was a fine

piece of work. There was no jamming and radio discipline was excellent. No enemy aircraft were seen airborne.

Lieutenant Chute from *Victorious* was on a strafing raid against Matsuyama Airfield in Formosa that day and found the anti-aircraft fire fairly uncomfortable. In response to a plea from the pilots, tracer had been mixed in with the other ammunition for their machine guns. Chute attacked an ack-ack position which was firing at them. 'It had the desired effect. They ducked or dived for cover.'

And so the cycle went on — two days of strikes, withdrawal to replenish and then back to the area again. On the 13th April the Fleet learned with deep regret of the death of the American President Roosevelt — a staunch friend of the British and a great leader of the American people.

The Fleet reached the enormous harbour of Leyte for a brief respite on 23rd April and exactly 32 days out from Ulithi. Immediately the ships started to make good defects and re-plenish fuel, stores and ammunition from the Fleet Train beginning on the afternoon of the 23rd; aided by good weather replenishment continued throughout the week. At Leyte, the ships found themselves many miles from shore and, because of boat shortage, few libertymen could get ashore; the few days stand-off was less restorative than it might have been. Admiral Rawlings said later: 'Since the libertymen could not get to the beer, I authorised the beer to be brought to them; this innovation proved immensely popular.

The heat and lethargic effect of the climate, which being drier was not quite so marked as at Manus, made conditions even more trying for personnel employed between and below decks, especially on maintenance and boiler cleaning. In *Victorious* there was little time for rest and relaxation and, as one officer said, 'after a day or two most of us, I feel sure, wished ourselves back at sea again.' The Fleet sailed again at 0630 on 1st May with *Formidable* replacing *Illustrious,* to continue once more the neutralisation of the Sakishima Gunto. Operations were again planned with a cycle of two days of strikes followed by two or three for replenishment, but this time the signs of victory were in the air.

Chapter XIII

THE DESPERATE DAYS TO PEACE

By the evening of the 30th April the replenishment of the Fleet was completed thanks to the energy and foresight of the Rear Admiral Commanding Fleet Train. To top up the Fleet on their passage to the north, the Tanker Group sailed from Leyte at 0700 on 30th April, met the carrier force on the 3rd for refuelling and completed the operation by 1500 that day. It was a sultry day with no wind and as the ships headed for the Sakishima Gunto and Part II of Operation 'Iceberg', the officers and men on *Victorious* could not know that they were entering their last hundred days in World War II. In many ways, the next few weeks would prove to be the most dangerous and trying time of all. The war in Europe was coming to an end, but the Japanese — fighting on their own soil — would throw everything into a final, bloody and desperate bid for victory.

On the first strike day, Friday 4th May, a bombardment of the Japanese airfields and anti-aircraft positions on Miyako was carried out by the battleships and cruisers, who detached from the carriers at 1000. *Victorious* went to flying stations just before dawn that day and at 0610, eleven Avengers of 849 Squadron led by Lieutenant Commander Foster took off to attack Miyako Airfield. Although Sub Lieutenant Stalker had to make an emergency landing, the remaining ten aircraft cratered the runways and returned to land on without loss by 0830.

The carriers and their escort of eight destroyers remained some 30 miles to the southward of the area after the departure of the bombarding ships, and the Japanese seized the opportunity of the absence of the heavy ships to launch their attack. At about 1100 three small groups of unidentified aircraft were detected to the westward and shortly afterwards a fourth group was picked up. Fighters immediately intercepted the air attack comprising 16 to 20 aircraft with some of the enemy planes cunningly acting the role of decoys.

This was to be the BPF carriers' first taste of concentrated Kamikaze attacks by determined enemy pilots, and they knew that they were in for trouble. There were no contacts on the radar screens within 20 miles when at 1131, a Zeke was seen diving from a great height on to HMS *Formidable* and was engaged by every gun that would fire. Analysis now shows that this group escaped detection, either because the few radar sets in the ships were busily tracking the decoys, or else because the enemy made a low approach at sea level before climbing very high at about 15 miles range. Whatever the cause, the effect was very frightening to the spectators on the flight deck of *Formidable* and, although repeatedly hit by close-range weapons, the suicide pilot slammed his aircraft into the flight deck near the island structure. It appeared to release a bomb just before striking the deck and the resultant explosion started a large fire in the deck park of aircraft, killed 8 men and wounded 47 more, damaged 11 aircraft beyond repair and holed and dented the flight deck to a depth of two feet. In spite of the blazing fires and bomb splinters which had pierced the ship right through to the inner bottom and damaged the centre boiler room, by 1700 the ship was again able to fly on 13 of her Corsairs and earned the praise and admiration of the Fleet.

Three minutes later, a Zeke flying from forward to aft off the starboard bow of HMS *Indomitable* was engaged by the carrier's 4.5-inch guns and temporarily disappeared in cloud. In no time it reappeared in a steep 60-degree dive at the ship from the starboard beam. The Force was turning to starboard at the time and the Captain of *Indomitable* put his helm hard over. The plane continued in its death dive and was heavily engaged by the ship's guns, which succeeded in hitting the plane and setting it on fire.

Then, at the last moment, the Kamikaze flattened out from his terrifyingly steep dive, deck-landed on his belly on the flight deck at a few hundred knots and not surprisingly bounded over the side carrying the radar arrays of the port midships directors with him. As the Captain said in his report of the incident:

Very little damage was done except to the ship's radars and his bomb appeared to explode shortly after the plane submerged.

No sooner had that excitement passed than another Zeke selected the unfortunate *Indomitable* as his personal target. This time the combined anti-aircraft fire from the carrier and the escorting HMS *Quality* had the desired effect; hit hard and often the Jap burst into flames and crashed into the sea about 10 yards off the bow of the carrier. Meanwhile the CAP dispatched two more Zekes as they commenced their dives and thus ended a short but hectic engagement with the 'Divine Winds'.

The bombarding force rejoined the carriers at 1420 that afternoon just after a Jill and a Val had fallen to the guns of the patrolling fighters. During the afternoon several more enemy aircraft were intercepted and, at 1515, Corsairs from *Victorious* splashed a Judy to the north of the Force. It was not until 1720, as the Fleet was withdrawing for the night, that another attack became evident. The Jap planes approached and at 1721 a Judy believed to be the 'Gestapo' of the group was shot down from 24,000 feet to the east. The enemy employed a homing reconnaissance plane – nicknamed 'Gestapo' – whose job was to locate the force and then home in the Kamikaze volunteers, but on this occasion they lost their airborne homing aid and the raids were successfully intercepted. A few minutes after the Judy had been destroyed, Seafires from HMS *Indefatigable* intercepted four Zekes to the south and shot down three. At 1820 Corsairs from *Victorious* found and splashed yet another Zeke to end a day which had been full of incident, and one which had cost the enemy 14 aircraft shot down against our losses of one Avenger on a strike and fourteen other aircraft destroyed by their Kamikaze hits.

The Fleet withdrew to replenish on the 6th, completed by 1400 on the 7th and late that night heard the gratifying news of peace in Europe. It was almost exactly four years to the day that *Victorious* had been in commission, and a large proportion of that time had been spent in the hard, bitter North Atlantic. Now that war was over, but the struggle against Japan would go on with renewed vigour until she too was crushed.

Victorious at Portsmouth January 1958. The long modernisation is over and the new angled deck awaits sea trials and the arrival of her aircraft.

Top left: a Sea Vixen lands aboard.

Top right: a Scimitar landing on.

An extract from the log of *Victorious'* 849 Squadron for Tuesday 8th May reads:

Once again the undaunted BPF approached Miyako area, and cries of joy were heard when it was announced that Plan 'Queen' was in operation. This meant no strikes for 849, but a bombardment by the battleships. *King George V* and *Howe* left at 1000 with bags of cover, and at 1300 commenced the bombardment, joining up again about 1530.

May 9th was a better day from the weather point of view and initial reconnaissance flights reported that runways were repaired and again serviceable. Four bomber strikes were flown off during the day, two to each island of Miyako and Ishigaki. All runways were re-cratered and a direct hit was scored on one aircraft on the ground at Miyako. A motor transport park at Ishigaki was attacked and three vehicles were destroyed, while low-flying fighters discovered a Val hidden in a cave. Firing neatly through the entrance, they were rewarded by an explosion and sheets of flame as the aircraft burned out in its hideaway.

Commander Hay recalls that at this time the pilots were getting pretty fed up with the frustrating and seemingly unending routine of cratering Jap airfields. Day after day the same task and as the enemy were past masters in the art of camouflage, seldom was anything seen. As a delightful diversion to counter the boredom, Ronnie Hay devised a tactic which caught the enemy literally 'with his trousers down'. Taking off with his three escorting Corsairs for the early morning recon-naissance, he used to go and sit over the Jap airfields at 5,000 feet just watching and waiting.

The Japs were just like anyone else first thing in the morning, and he watched with great interest as they came out of their hideaways and made for the little square boxes with sun shutters over the top. When all the cubicles were occupied, he would swoop down, deliver a quick burst of canon fire and observe the few lucky survivors race for cover. One can imagine the shock and horror of this invasion of their privacy, but perhaps the Japs merely wondered at the poor quality of their rice.

At 1645 on the afternoon of the 9th, the Japanese launched another of their determined Kamikaze attacks and this time it was *Victorious* who was to be the main target. Enemy aircraft were detected flying very fast and very low some 22 miles to the westward. A CAP of four Seafires managed to intercept the Jap planes at 15 miles, but allowed themselves to be decoyed away by one aircraft which they shot down. Meanwhile another group of four enemy planes evaded a second CAP of Seafires, and after climbing to 3,000 feet made straight for the Fleet.

From 1650 onwards, the Fleet was under almost continuous attack and carried out emergency turns at 22 knots. One minute after such a turn of 60 degrees to starboard was executed, a Zeke made a shallow 10-degree dive onto HMS *Victorious* from her starboard quarter. Captain Denny of *Victorious* recalls the attack:

> Our first Kamikaze that day started from almost astern of us and my turn put him on my beam. He tried to pull up and start again, but he was not quick enough. I crossed ahead of him pretty close and his wheels touched the flight deck at right angles. The undercarriage sheared off and the plane broke up, sliding eighty feet across the flight deck to crash over the side and onto the 4.5-inch guns.
>
> From the first moment I started to swing the ship, he had been trying to adjust and steer up the flight deck — which would have given him the whole length in which to drop his stick down and hit — but he didn't make it.[1]

In fact the enemy was well hit by close range weapons and, added to that, *Victorious* was a very slippery and evasive target. Captain Denny goes on to say:

> Our anti-aircraft fire was pretty effective and the *Victorious* was an immensely handy ship to handle, with a big rudder. I could spin her round quite rapidly and I managed to ruin both my Kamikaze attacks that day. They aimed originally for between the lifts — with American ships they could open up the flight deck and go right through to the hangar space below; but eventually they found that this didn't work with the British carriers — they had armoured flight decks.[1]

[1] Quoted from Peter Smith's *Task Force 57* (William Kimber, 1969).

The Jap pilot hit the deck near the forward lift and exploded. He smashed a 4.5-inch gun turret, holed the flight deck, put the forward accelerator out of action and started a fire which was quickly brought under control.

Six minutes later another Divine Wind enthusiast made a shallow power glide from astern on HMS *Victorious*. An eye-witness summed up the feelings of everyone on board who experienced these attacks by saying:

They were very frightening and seemed almost unstoppable. You could hit them with gunfire time and time again but still they came on. Perhaps the most frightening of all was the nasty feeling that he was actually aiming at you personally. It made you feel most uncomfortable and rather vulnerable.

Apart from the difficulty of identifying the difference between a conventional raid and a Kamikaze attack, there was the question of mounting and co-ordinating an effective anti-aircraft defence. The CAP fighters could intercept the enemy outside the Fleet's gunfire barrage, but frequently chased their victim right on to the target. This hindered the ship's gunnery and invited the inevitable accidents. There again, the degree of competence of enemy pilots varied considerably and this in turn affected the success of the attack. Although the Kamikaze aircraft tended to enter their final dives somewhat earlier than the conventional dive-bomber, Captain Denny remembers:

Each pilot would react differently; there appeared to be no set formula for an attack, other than the aiming point and run-in. One could never tell whether one was up against a first class pilot or not, until the moment one swung the ship and watched the pilot's reactions. If one's timing was good, and the pilot was forced to re-think his attack, the majority of them would veer in at a lower angle which at once reduced their effectiveness if they did hit. If one could lead an enemy pilot to make a large alteration of course, or if he failed to make an alteration at all, one felt secure that he would not score a hit. The fatal thing to do was for the carrier to steer a straight course, for in that case he would always get you. In the cases where more than one aircraft approached, in all cases they would make separate attacks. One could watch them pick their targets, through a good pair of glasses, and as soon as the leading aircraft went into a dive, his wingmen would open up on either side of him for a different approach, hoping to hit you no matter which way you turned.[1]

The second Kamikaze, though heavily hit by the fire from *Victorious'* guns, ploughed on to hit a glancing blow on the flight deck aft. The effect of the impact and probably the anti-aircraft fire coupled with his speed, caused the aircraft to go over the side of the ship burning furiously. Although the attack was spectacular, this time the damage was not so serious and was confined to one arrester unit out of action, a 40-mm gun director destroyed and four Corsairs damaged beyond repair.

The total casualties from the two attacks on *Victorious* amounted to three killed and nineteen wounded but it was not over; within the minute, a third suicide aircraft made a pass at the carrier, but shifted target at the last moment to aim at the battleship *Howe* ahead. This time the Kamikaze was hit at longer range, and continued to absorb punishment until he crashed in flames 100 yards from the *Howe* after passing over the quarterdeck.

Thus ended the rather brief but hectic few minutes for *Victorious,* and though her aircraft operating ability was somewhat impaired, she managed to land on five Corsairs of her CAP at 1830. Steward Joseph Landers and Able Seaman Joseph Edward Cann had been killed in the action and Able Seaman Albert Biss died later of wounds, but the ship continued to operate until she was able to effect repairs in Sydney in June. Her luck still held!

The enemy continued to hurl themselves at the British forces and at 1705, a fourth Kamikaze approached HMS *Formidable* and then appeared to head for *Indomitable*. It was engaged by the guns of both ships without apparent results, and at the last

[1] Quoted from Peter Smith's *Task Force 57* (William Kimber, 1969).

moment turned and dived into the after deck park of HMS *Formidable*.

This time the results were more dramatic and somewhat more devastating, for there was a large explosion and fire and a great deal of smoke. The Captain reduced the speed of the ship to 15 knots to assist in fire fighting and the blaze was brought under control by 1720. As far as damage was concerned, the Jap plane had destroyed six Corsairs and one Avenger on deck, but more unfortunately for the carrier, a rivet had been blown out of the flight deck and this allowed burning petrol to fall into the hangar. Because the sprinkler system. had to be turned on, a further three Avengers and eight Corsairs were damaged. After this assault only 15 Avengers and Corsairs were serviceable out of her complement of 54 aircraft, though her casualties of one killed and a few injured were mercifully light.

When Task Force 57 resumed action on 12th May after the usual two days refuelling, Admiral Rawlings moved the launching position of the carriers further eastward. Temporary repairs to *Victorious* and *Formidable* enabled both ships to remain sufficiently operational to complete the programme of strikes, but the whole question of an effective defence continued to worry the command. The Japs had demonstrated an apparent change of tactics in their attacks of the 9th May, and had abandoned the previous practice of a high approach in favour of a low one. This greatly reduced the length of radar warning available and made interception by fighters much more difficult – as well as reducing the time that the gunners had to bring the Kamikaze planes under effective anti-aircraft fire.

The problems were discussed and countermeasures instituted and the change proved so effective, that no further serious attacks were made on the force. Two groups of Radar Warning Pickets each consisting of a 6-inch cruiser and destroyer, were stationed 12 miles north-west and south-west of the fleet to increase the range of detection. Destroyers were stationed astern of each carrier to afford more gun protection in what appeared to be the enemy's favourite position for attacking carriers, and lastly, the AA protection of the carriers was boosted by closing the cruisers and battleships to within one mile of the carriers when an attack developed.

The strikes continued and the airfields of Sakishima Gunto were cratered and useless by day, repaired and serviceable by the next morning. The fighters made the usual Ramrod sweeps of enemy airfields and on the last attack of the day on the 16th May, Sub Lieutenant Whyte of *Victorious* caught a troop convoy of four lorry loads of Japanese soldiers. In a brisk series of strafing runs all four of the lorries and most of their occupants were destroyed, but with ironic justice his number two was hit by the troops who had been passengers in the trucks and ditched three miles from Miyako. The lifeguard submarine USS *Bluefish* was informed and made a daring and skilful rescue by picking up the pilot during the night.

Losses from enemy action were comparatively light, but there were always other dangers and at 0747 the next day, a Corsair flown by Sub Lieutenant Hardiman made an emergency landing on HMS *Victorious*. The aircraft came in much too fast and removed two arrester wires, then ploughed on up the deck and through both barriers, burst into flames and, seriously damaging 2 Corsairs and 1 Avenger in the deck park forward, plunged like a flaming torch over the side. The pilot was unfortunately killed in the crash, and Lieutenant Banning and Petty Officer Groves of the Flight Deck Party were also killed. Although the ship rigged emergency 'Jury Barriers', both were removed in aircraft crashes later that afternoon. As a result 20 aircraft from the ship had to be accommodated in other carriers, causing congestion and offering three very attractive targets of deck-parked aircraft to any passing Kamikaze pilot: fortunately they were conspicuous by their absence throughout the day.

On the 18th May, self-inflicted disaster was to strike the carrier *Formidable* whilst she was fuelling and exchanging aircraft. At 1103 she was observed to be on fire and it soon reached serious proportions. Someone in the cockpit of a Corsair in the hangar accidentally fired its guns into an Avenger which exploded; fighting the fire that followed was made more difficult by the fact that the fire curtains were out of action due to earlier enemy Kamikaze attacks. It was extinguished eventually by drenching the hangar at a cost of 7 Avengers and 21 Corsairs damaged or destroyed, but by evening the ship was capable of operating again.

A different kind of accident occurred on the 20th, when in dense fog the *Quilliam* was badly damaged in collision with the *Indomitable* and had to be towed to the fuelling area. The *Indomitable* was detached on the 22nd to Sydney via Manus to expedite repairs in order to ensure that four carriers would be available for the final operations against the main Japanese islands which were to take place after Okinawa was secured. The final day of strikes was on Friday 25th May 1945 and an officer in 849 Squadron in *Victorious* wrote:

> Loud cries greeted Commander C.E.A. Owen, DSC (Ops), when he told us that today's strikes were the last before returning to Sydney. At 0850 the CO, Lieutenant Commander Foster, led a strike of nine aircraft from 849 and twelve from 810 Squadron (*Implacable*) to attack runways and dispersals at Ishigaki Airfield. Photographs confirmed direct hits and all aircraft landed 'midst sighs of relief at 1220. Just for luck, Lieutenant Swain from 849 led another strike of seven aircraft to our old friend Miyako. They took off at 1400, bombed Nobara Airfield and returned safely to land on at 1645.

Thus ended Operations 'Iceberg' and 'Oolong' and a great party was held that evening to celebrate. Captain Denny gave a talk to the assembled squadrons that evening to congratulate them on their fine work and, particularly, to congratulate the ground crews on the way in which aircraft serviceability had been maintained. After these final strikes the Fleet dispersed to their rear bases for major storing and repairs before undertaking the final operations. Two days laters when Admiral Spruance relinquished command of the Fifth Fleet to Admiral Halsey he signalled to Admiral Rawlings:

> I wish to express to you and to the officers and men under your command, my appreciation of the fine work you have done and the splendid spirit of co-operation in which you have done it. To the American portion of the Fifth Fleet, Task Force 57 has typified the great traditions of the Royal Navy.

In his report, Admiral Spruance stated that the British Pacific

Fleet had gained sufficient experience to undertake operations with the US Fast Carrier Force.

Over the whole period of its employment in Operation 'Iceberg', Task Force 57 was at sea for 62 days, broken by eight days re-storing at Leyte. On the 23 strike days the carriers flew 4,691 sorties, dropped 927 tons of bombs and fired 950 rocket projectiles. The number of enemy aircraft destroyed was probably less than the estimate of 100 made by the force. Various other targets than airfields, such as shipping and W/T stations, were attacked. Our aircraft losses totalled 160, including 26 shot down in combat and 72 destroyed operationally; Suicide attacks accounted for 32 destroyed on board their carriers and 30 were lost in the *Formidable*'s hangar fire.

At the end of the Okinawa Campaign, *Victorious* and the other ships of TF57 sailed for Sydney, where she arrived at 1035 on 5th June and that evening secured at 7 Berth, Woolloomooloo. Her aircraft disembarked to the Australian Naval Air Station Nowra at Jervis Bay and for the next three weeks, while the dockyard workers repaired the battle damage, the officers and men enjoyed the hospitality of the city and its people. The Duke of Gloucester visited the ship on the 19th June and one week later *Victorious,* patched up, stored and ready to go, re-embarked her squadrons in Jervis Bay and headed once more for Manus.

This time the BPF were to operate as Task Force 37 under the overall command of Admiral Halsey and the American Third Fleet. On the afternoon of 16th July after refuelling, the massive combined USN/RN fleet left the replenishment area and headed for the final assault on the mainland of Japan. As the most northerly Group of the Third Fleet attacking Kyushu, Task Force 37 were ordered to direct their air strikes against airfields, railways and targets of opportunity. The weather conditions were usually indifferent and only Ramrods were flown on the 17th. The weather was slightly better the next day, but unfortunately *Victorious* found salt-water contamination in her petrol and managed to launch only six Corsairs, until she refuelled again with the Fleet on the 20th.

The continuous bad weather prompted Admiral Halsey to move the area of operations some 400 miles north, to seek an improvement and strike at targets in Japan's Inland Sea. On the morning of the 24th, *Victorious* launched her first Avenger strike at 0900 and this was to prove a great success. The six Avengers of 'A' Flight were led by the CO, Lieutenant Commander Griffith, and were briefed to bomb Okyama Airfield. At the last moment the orders were changed and they were told to go for some tankers sighted just to the south of the original target area. The CO of 849 Squadron reported:

> The weather conditions were very bad and only five of my Avengers reached the target. En route we sighted and attacked a Japanese 'Kobe' Class escort carrier in Shido Wan, off the coast of Shikoku. We scored two hits and the honour went to Sub Lieutenant Cawood.

The original strike was to have consisted of twenty Avengers, eight Seafires, seven Fireflies and four Corsairs, but in the event only six Avengers, two Fireflies and two Corsairs found the target. The escort carrier was later identified as *Kaiyo* and after further attacks by aircraft from all four carriers, she was left with her back broken and sinking.

The attacks went on although for one period at the end of July, the strikes were delayed for nine days due to bad weather.

On the 6th August, the Americans dropped the first Atomic Bomb on the Japanese city of Hiroshima and this was followed three days later by a second which smashed Nagasaki. In the first dreadful attack the enemy lost some 70,000 killed and it took just one more to break their resolve and force them to seek terms for the Allied surrender. The nuclear age was born and a new, horrifying dimension had been added to the destructive power of all-out warfare. By the 10th August, the Japanese had agreed to most of the terms demanded by the Allies, but it was to be another four days until they accepted unconditional surrender; meanwhile, the fight went on.

Victorious entered the launch area again that morning with the other carriers of the BPF and in a series of strikes that lasted from dawn until dusk, they launched yet more attacks against enemy shipping and his aircraft on the airfields ashore. The CO of 849 Squadron collected 'quite an alarming hole in his starboard mainplane', during a strike on Koriyama Airfield, but many targets were hit and all the aircraft returned safely. This was in fact the last day of strikes for *Victorious* since on the 11th, the Fleet withdrew to the refuelling area and, although scheduled to return to the attack on the 12th, a typhoon warning and bad weather cancelled the plan.

At 1300 on Sunday 12th August, the Captain of *Victorious* broadcast to the ship's company and gave them details of the current situation. He told them of acceptance by the Japanese of the Allied terms and went on to say that the battleship *King George V*, with two cruisers and eight destroyers would remain in the operating area with units of the American Fleet, while the carriers withdrew. As *Victorious* headed for Manus and Australia with the other carriers of the BPF, the C-in-C, Admiral Halsey, USN, signalled:

> On the occasion of parting company with some units of Task Force 37 I want all your outfit to know that during this past month the fine co-operative attitude and fighting spirit of the British Force have made as many friends and admirers as there are officers and men in the American section of the team.
>
> While the armistice may still be a few days away, today August 12th sees the end of the British Task Force as we have known it. I have no hesitation in saying that it has written a memorable page in the history of the British Navy.
>
> The time is coming when many of you will be returning to shore life but both to those that leave and those that remain in the service I would say two things. First that you carry with you throughout life a feeling of pride in what you have done out here and the second that you will realise I am profoundly grateful to you all.

For this great ship, the war was over and although the actual 'Peace' was three days away — *Victorious* would not be in at the end. The Engineer Officer of *Victorious*, Commander N. Dalton, summed up the feelings of the ship when he said: 'It was a sad blow to everyone on board, as we had been in every operation and felt we had a prior right to be present. It may have been intended as a reward by releasing *Victorious* at the earliest moment, but we did not see it that way.'

Chapter XIV

MODERNISATION

With the war over and the world at peace, the British Pacific Fleet tackled what was probably its most formidable task. The run down started immediately as the thousands of Hostilities Only officers and men sought to leave the services and return to civilian life and normality, but before ships could be sent home there were the vast numbers of Allied ex-prisoners of war and civilian internees to be considered. These unfortunate people presented the Allies with a major repatriation problem, but with the huge carrier Task Forces in the area, the obvious solution was to utilise their enormous reserves of carrying capacity for this very urgent and humanitarian purpose.

In the case of the BPF there was a large, mobile Commonwealth fleet of ships at immediate readiness, so the carriers disembarked their aircraft and aircrews and with the co-operation of Australian Dockyards, they were quickly converted to carry large numbers of passengers. While the ships were being fitted out for their new role, the Australians held a large Victory Parade in Sydney on 31st August, and contingents from the crews of *Victorious*, *Implacable*, *Formidable*, *Black Prince*, *Grenville* and *Urania* all took part.

The celebrations over, the fleet set about its task of ferrying the thousands upon thousands of ex-POWs back to their homeland, and by the end of October some 70,000 persons had been repatriated to India, Australia and the United Kingdom. The *Victorious* remained in Sydney until 25th September, when she started her long journey to Portsmouth via Fremantle and Colombo. The story that went round the British Pacific Fleet and was to follow the carrier wherever she went, occurred just before she sailed. A portly Commander (S) was standing at the top of her gangway watching some ex-Japanese POW passengers being helped up the brow by sailors. He saw a thin, emaciated man struggling up the gangway clutching a bundle of his few pitiful possessions, and slapping him on the back as he passed said: 'Never mind, old chap, we'll soon have you fattened up and fit again with all the good food on board this ship.' Turning round, the astonished man replied: 'I should bloody well hope so, I've been a sailor on here for two and a half years.'

Victorious entered Portsmouth at a quarter to ten on the morning of Saturday 27th October 1945, and as she secured alongside South Railway Jetty her officers and men realised that they were home. Her rust-streaked sides and the now empty flight deck told their own story — for this very famous and lucky carrier her war was over, but unlike her famous sister ships *Illustrious, Formidable* and *Indefatigable* it was not the beginning of the end, but rather the end of the beginning.

After the usual draft changes had been completed and the men had had their leave, *Victorious* sailed for Plymouth on 31st October to begin a new career as a troop carrier. For the next eighteen months, she made three trips to Australia and the Far East carrying an assortment of passengers. She ferried troops, civilians, Wrens, nurses, VADs, ditched Lend – Lease aircraft and suffered yet more weather damage. She had the usual rudder troubles and spent time in harbour having it repaired, the Dockyard Police searched the ship for an over zealous Dockyard Matey who got himself lost and, finally, on her last trip back to the United Kingdom in January 1947, she carried 'War Brides' and food parcels for Britain.

Victorious sailed to Plymouth arriving on the 14th January and during the trip, some erratic steering enlivened the proceedings in the narrow confines of the Channel, and again pinpointed the old familiar problems. She was put into reserve and it seemed that her future was very much in the balance.

But to return to 1945 — as far as the Navy was concerned the war had brought about many changes. Traditionalists had witnessed the end of a dream, the era of the battleship was over — the leviathan of accepted naval might and power had finally, reluctantly given way to progress. Naval air power had shown its teeth and in every theatre of war the supremacy of the aircraft carrier had been truly established as the new capital ship.

Although the world was now at peace, new and exciting carrier developments were destined to take place in the next ten years. Progress would be fast and furious and although the post-war run down commenced immediately, naval aviation was given its first revolutionary impetus within a very few months.

On 3rd December, 1945, Lieutenant Commander E.M. Brown, MBE, DSC, RNVR, landed his modified Sea Vampire LZ 551 on the deck of *Ocean*. This aircraft heralded the birth of the jet age in naval carrier aviation and was the prelude to an exciting period of invention, trial and development. The Americans had landed an XFR-1 Fireball on the USS *Wake Island* about one month earlier on 6th November, but this aircraft had both piston and jet engines and although it had to rely on its jet when the piston engine unkindly failed, 'Winkle' Brown can rightly claim to be the first on the deck. It was the first deliberate jet deck-landing trial and went off without a hitch.

The new generation of aircraft on the drawing-board or in prototype-form provided many problems for the future, for with their higher landing speeds and greater weights – the old method of landing, stowing and launching the aircraft from an axial deck, then separating them by two barriers had obvious disadvantages. When landing on the deck, by virtue of higher speed and weight, the new generation of aircraft pulled out the arresting wires so far that there was little or no deck left on which to park or stow aircraft. As Captain D.R.F. Campbell so aptly put it:

> The perpetual problem of carrier flight deck geometry is how to provide for the constantly changing requirements of landing, stowing and launching within the confines of a flight deck whose length, breadth and wind speed have not substantially altered in thirty years.

The solution was as simple as it was effective – the angled deck: a new concept that was pure genius and was adopted by both the British and American Navies.

It consisted of angling the landing area of the deck to port of the fore and aft line of the ship so that once more, it left the deck area forward clear for parking. The early trials of the new system involved the inexpensive, simple expedient of buying a can of paint and a brush, then painting a new centre-line angled off to port down the ship's flight deck. In the old days, the pilot who missed the eight or so wires strung across the deck would usually be stopped by one of the two barriers strung protectively across the flight deck abreast the island! If his aircraft bounced over the barriers or carried them away with excessive speed, the next stop was usually assisted by any aircraft parked forward. If this failed, the luckless pilot was finally stopped by the sea as he went over the side. Other than hooking on and catching a wire, whichever other method of stopping was decreed by fate, it was hard on the nerves and costly in aircraft.

The angled deck was to change all that, for with no obstructions in the form of barriers or parked aircraft to worry about, a pilot could miss the wires and go round again and again, or even again, for another try. This was a great step forward and a considerable psychological advantage for pilots, their observers and the flight deck personnel, and a considerable financial saving to the ever watchful Exchequer – particularly as aircraft were getting even more sophisticated and hence costly.

The higher landing and take-off speeds posed yet another problem to be solved. The reflex actions of the batsmen or Deck Landing Control Officers – adequate for the slower piston-type aircraft – were found wanting with the advent of the jet. Commander Nick Goodhart, RN, provided the answer in the form of a mirror landing sight mounted on the deck instead of a batsman. It was a simple device which kept the pilot visually informed of his correct approach angle relative to the deck. Basically the system consists of a large curved mirror flanked by horizontal green datum lights. A white ball of light is reflected into the mirror and providing the pilot lines up the ball of white light between the green datum lights and keeps it there, he knows that he is on the correct approach angle for the deck. The mirror is of course gyro-stabilised so that the movements of the ship will not affect it and the angle of approach can be altered for the approach angles of different types of aircraft. Another innovation was an ingenious gadget known as the Audio ASI – Air Speed Indicator. As the approach speeds of aircraft went up from some 60 knots to over twice that speed, the need for some pilot assistance became obvious. The pilot didn't have time to watch his instruments, re-act to the mirror and correct his altitude on the approach. Invented by a naval doctor, the Audio ASI gives the pilot his aircraft speed by means of a sound signal and means that, instead of constantly checking his cockpit instruments, he can give far more attention to the mirror and thus make a safer landing.

Once the aircraft caught a wire, more problems were encountered. The relatively slow war-time aircraft were light and easily arrested. The fully loaded Seafire weighed about 7,500 pounds whereas the Buccaneer coming in at twice the speed weighed about 40,000 pounds. This meant that the decks had to be strengthened, new and more powerful arrester gear had to be installed and, for take-off, more powerful catapults. Commander C.C. Mitchell, OBE, RNVR, provided the solution for launching aircraft with his invention of the steam catapult. Although it took some ten years to develop, the steam catapult was capable of launching the heaviest aircraft with perfect safety and completed the requirements of the carrier to cope with the technological advance of the jet aircraft.

That briefly then was the story of the progress that influenced carrier thought and development in the ten years or so of post-war aviation. It was the direct cause of a protracted refit and modernisation of *Victorious,* lasting nearly eight long years.

To return to the story of *Victorious,* she had been put into Category 'B' Reserve at Devonport on 16th January 1947 where she remained until 14th July. Although her future had been in some doubt, it was finally decided that she would relieve the battleship *Nelson* as a training ship in the Portland Training Squadron, so she was moved back to Portsmouth for essential repairs and modification. Classrooms were built in the hangar – messdecks and accommodation altered – more boats for instructional purposes were fitted and finally as a fully fledged floating School, she joined the Training Squadron in October 1947 under the command of Captain E.B.K. Stevens.

Her life for the next two years revolved around 'Daily Divisions' and training the new-entry ratings and junior seamen and also – at the beginning of 1949 – basic sea training for Short Service Aviation Cadets. It was all very routine and for most of the time she remained secured to a buoy in Portland Harbour, with only the occasional short cruise to Scotland, the Channel Islands or Gibraltar with the Home Fleet to break the monotony.

It was in February 1948 that the Director of Naval Construction was invited to prepare designs for the modernisation of a fleet carrier. It was to be able to operate aircraft of an all-up weight of 30,000 pounds and the powers that be decided that *Formidable* should be the first carrier to be modernised. To bring the Fleet up to the required standard, other carriers were also scheduled for modernisation, but before *Formidable* was avail- -able plans were changed and *Victorious* was sent to Portsmouth in March 1950. She was relieved of her training task by the battleship *Vanguard* and prepared to start a new lease of life. During the course of the refit, plans to modernise the other two carriers of the 'Illustrious' Class were scrapped – the wisdom of this decision will become apparent as the story unfolds.

The famous carrier was taken in hand by the dockyard authorities on the 10th October 1950, for what was supposed to be a comparatively straightforward task and planned to be completed by mid-1954. The aim of the modernisation was to equip our war-time carriers to cope with the progress of post-war development in both aircraft weapons and techniques.

When the scheme was conceived and plans drawn up, the angled deck had not been thought of; there was no intention to fit new radars and presentations; the requirements for the whole of the next generation of aircraft were still by no means clear and certainly, their sophistication could not be anticipated. As a result, *Victorious* underwent a succession of modernisations within her main modernisation. In 1953 she was altered to have an angled deck, new radar and new boilers; in 1954 she was altered again to have a guided weapon space in the hangar; in 1955 she was altered yet again to have improved airborne radar servicing arrangements; in 1956 she was altered once more and given improved aircraft and servicing arrangements, and fuller

The last sunset at five minutes past seven in the evening on the 13th March 1968. The White Ensign is lowered as two ex-*Victorious* marine buglers loaned from RN Barracks play the notes of the traditional ceremonial Sunset.

Vice Admiral Sir Richard Janvrin, KCB, DSC, salutes his old ship on her last journey. Flying in the last survivor of the famous Swordfish—hero of many a battle—two friends say goodbye.

The Captains of HMS *Victorious* attend the 'Wake'. From left to right: Captain (now Vice Admiral) I. S. McIntosh, CB, DSO, MBE, DSC, RN; Captain J. A. Grindle, CBE, RN; Admiral Sir M. M. Denny, GCB, CBE, DSO; Captain E. B. K. Stevens, DSO, DSC, RN; Rear Admiral N. V. Dickinson, DSO, DSC; and Rear (now Vice) Admiral Sir H. R. B. Janvrin, KCB, DSC.

November 1970: the remains of *Victorious* alongside the wharf at the shipbreaking yard, Fasland, Gareloch.

knowledge of the guided weapon requirements had to be fed in. But this is by no means the complete story, there were still the mirrors, steam catapults and a host of other improvements to be considered and incorporated into the new *Victorious*.

By and large – and with considerable co-operation from the very harassed staffs at Portsmouth Dockyard – *Victorious* kept pace with these changes. It is reported that the pulling out of hair was commonplace among the dockyard officials and as one of those gentlemen pointed out, 'I don't think we had wigs on the National Health in those days – so hair was at a premium.'

Certainly the many changes tried the patience of the numerous departments who attempted to keep pace with progress and new concepts.

Some idea of the magnitude of these changes which Portsmouth Dockyard had to undertake can be gauged from the fact that the ship had to be completely rebuilt from the hangar deck up. The flight deck itself had to be lifted some 4 feet above the original to give a clear hangar height of 17 feet 6 inches. Advantage was taken of these structural alterations to work a complete deck under the flight deck above the hangar, thus providing valuable and much needed additional accommodation space. A four-foot bulge was added to the ship to improve stability and underwater protection; when completed, every compartment in the ship had been gutted and refitted.

When the ship emerged in 1958, she looked very different from the *Victorious* that went into the dockyard in 1950. Obvious differences included lengthening of the flight deck by some 30 feet to a new overall length of 775 feet. Still armoured, it was now strengthened to take the new, very heavy NA 39 aircraft (Buccaneer), and two parallel tracks (BS4 Steam Catapults) 145 feet long were fitted to the forward end of the flight deck, together with the appropriate aircraft positioners and jet blast-deflectors.

The new arresting gear comprised four wires of average span of 80 feet, reeved singly to four Mark 13 units mounted horizontally in compartments on the upper gallery deck. A single emergency barrier using undrawn nylon as the energy absorber was fitted, capable of dealing with speeds up to 120 knots for the new swept-wing aircraft.

Deck landing mirror sights were fitted port and starboard and, because of the angled deck, the port sight had to be mounted well outboard on its own large sponson.

The two hydro-pneumatically operated centreline lifts would each handle a working load of 40,000 pounds. The forward lift was 58 feet by 40 feet, the after lift 54 feet by 34 feet, a combined area of twice that provided by the original lifts. Hydraulically operated main keeps came into operation over the last few inches of travel, aligning the lift flush with the flight deck.

Of course the fully angled deck was the most striking feature of the flight deck. An angle of 8¾ degrees was achieved to port of the centreline by extending the flight deck on the port side outboard for 41 feet over a length of 120 feet. This gave an overhang of some 35½ feet beyond the ship's side supported by an enormous sponson well bracketed into the ship's structure. The upper gallery deck was in fact continued into this sponson to the full extent of the overhang and provided considerable additional accommodation space. To say the least, this extension when viewed from the dock side was impressive although – almost as an afterthought – it necessitated re-routing of the dock-side crane to enable the ship to be moved out of the lock: just one of the small problems facing the now bald and exhausted dockyard officials.

The main hangar was 360 feet long by 65½ feet wide with a clear height of 17 feet 6 inches and divided into two sections by a fire curtain in the middle. Forward of the forward lift was a hangar extension 52 feet long, 62 feet wide with 17 feet 6 inches clear height, equipped to serve as an electronics servicing bay for the Sea Vixen and its attendant black boxes.

Throughout the long refit, as change succeeded change and Plan One inevitably reached Plan Nine, space available for accommodation decreased steadily as the new requirements had to be met. Conversely, the complement increased at about twice the rate, with the introduction of each new weapon, black box, piece of machinery or even aircraft. The full story of the all-absorbing problem may never be known – except to the few. Suffice it to say that a solution was reached by the simple expedient of head-counting. The experts merely tailored the complement to accommodation available, by some very thorough and exhaustive investigations – literally man by man. As one cynical sailor put it, 'you do two men's work, for one man's pay, in half the time, in a quarter of the comfort – but that's progress, ain't it?'

Such was the flexibility and impartiality of the designers, that the officers didn't escape the space economy drive either. Two electrically operated bomb lifts were fitted in the starboard side of the ship to serve the hangar and flight deck, but the after bomb lift had the added, doubtful virtue of providing an alternative supply route from the galley to the Wardroom. This was only an emergency service in the event of the food lift breaking down, but it could provide variety in the menu; as one officer said, 'it was possible to have bomb bangers for breakfast or even rocket rissoles.'

As before, the ship was powered by three sets of steam turbines giving a total of 111,000 shaft horse power and could be steamed from the machinery control room by hydraulic remote controls. New boilers were installed partly because of the short remaining life of the original boilers and partly to provide for the increased demands for steam from additional generators and steam catapults. On the electrical side, the complex new radars demanded even more power, so the main electric generating capacity of the ship was increased from 2,400 kW to 4,200 kW; most of this power, which amounted to nearly twice as much as before, was absorbed by the ever-growing demands for electricity. The almost insatiable demands for electrical power meant that still more generators and conversion machines had to be provided to meet the varied and various requirements for radio, radar, weapon control and communications.

On top of the relatively small island was a very large 30-ton radar aerial. Together with the other sets, the radar fitted in *Victorious* was described as the best ship-borne air defence radar system in the world: a claim that would hold good even by today's standards. Combining early warning and great accuracy of aircraft position and height simultaneously, the complex semi-automatic displays provided the command with instantaneous pictures of the situation in any sector of the sky.

The ship carried nearly 1,000 tons of Avcat fuel for the very thirsty jet aircraft, while for her own protection she was fitted with six twin 3-inch/50s, a new type of anti-aircraft gun supplied by the USA under the Mutual Aid Programme. To provide variety, one solitary six-barrel 40-mm bofors gun was left on the starboard side – a relic of the past and a reliable toy for ship's gunnery department.

This then was the new, modernised *Victorious* as she appeared once more before the critical eye of the public in 1958.

The navy itself could scarcely believe that here at last after eight long years and about £20,000,000, was a British carrier fitted out with all those outstanding British inventions. In an age when one has learned to appreciate the finer points of shapeliness, even a grotesque 27, 48⅓, 27⅓, (Flight deck width in yards, forward, amidships and aft) does not fail to stir the imagination and invite comment and conjecture!

Chapter XV

FOUR MORE COMMISSIONS

Almost three months after *Victorious* had gone into Portsmouth Dockyard for her long modernisation, the North Korean army launched a full scale attack across the 38th Parallel — the time was 0400 and the date the 25th June 1950. Three years later on 23rd June 1953, United Nations representatives and the North Korean and Chinese delegates commenced the long drawn out peace talks, which culminated in an uneasy truce on 27th July and lasts without real solution to this day.

So far as the British Commonwealth participants were concerned, by far the most conspicuous role was played by the Fleet Air Arm and the light fleet carriers. In the golden heyday of Naval aviation, as the period has been called, the performances of these ships and their aircraft were outstanding. It is true that they had virtually no enemy air activity to contend with, but they achieved a remarkable degree of efficiency and professionalism, paving the way for the great changes in aviation which were to follow.

In the Admiralty, the strong aviation lobby — which had gained support and carrier enthusiasts as the result of wartime experience — received even more encouragement and impetus for the cause from successful carrier participation in the Malayan emergency and the ill-fated Suez operation. They served to re-emphasise, if indeed it needed to be re-emphasised, the invaluable role played by carriers in the prosecution of national interests. With a budget that had more than doubled by 1953 to nearly £1,650 million, there was a forceful plea for a new generation of aircraft carriers to form the teeth of the modern Navy, together with the modernisation of existing carriers to meet the changes in carrier warfare.

A much modified HMS *Victorious,* commissioned on 14th January 1958 as the latest carrier for the Royal Navy, sailed from Portsmouth for Preliminary Sea Trials on 3rd February – a glorious day! If ships have souls, *Victorious* must have wondered at the changes in Naval aviation since she last operated aeroplanes at the end of World War II. Little remained of the old *Vic*; she was now fitted out and modernised to cope with that change, to operate the fast modern aeroplanes with which the Navy had been equipped. The roar of the piston engine had given way to the whine of the jet and turboprop, the barriers had gone, her flight deck was lop-sided, she had superb radar and a host of new complex equipments – oh well, that was progress and now she really was the teeth.

A six week period of sea and flying trials brought the first deck landing of the commission when on 23rd June, with much pleasure and the co-operation of Gannet 504, Commander Air, Commander S.J.A. Richardson, RN, caught the first wire. Men poured on board from the various development and trials departments. While aircraft flew on and off the ship, they tested and checked all the flight deck machinery, the arrester wires, the catapults and the mass of new equipment in the ship. Scimitars of No. 700 Carrier Trials Unit, led by Lieutenant Commander P. Lamb – now of Hovercraft fame – created a new first, by carrying out the initial deck landing trials of this latest naval aircraft. The prototype De Havilland Sea Vixen flown by Lieutenant Commander D.P. Norman also arrived from Boscombe Down to make its debut over our latest carrier.

No. 803 Scimitar Squadron (Commander J.D. Russell, RN) were the first fixed wing squadron to be embarked and, arriving in pairs, they joined from NAS Lossiemouth via Yeovilton. The unfortunate accident which cost Commander Russell his life and marred the first landing by a squadron Scimitar, received much publicity in the press. Through no fault of the pilot, the Scimitar went over the side of the carrier and although a very creditable rescue effort was attempted by the planeguard helicopter, flown by Lieutenant R. Duxbury, RN, and crewed by Lieutenant G.R. Fyleman and Leading Seaman Brown. Tragically, the pilot's canopy had jammed and in spite of every effort by the helicopter crew, the attempt was not successful and the aircraft sank before the pilot could be rescued. The remaining squadron aircraft under the command of Lieutenant Commander G.R. Higgs, RN, were safely embarked, followed by No. 893 Sea Venom Squadron (Lieutenant Commander E.V.H. Manuel) from NAS Yeovilton and No. 849 Skyraider 'B' Flight (Lieutenant Commander B.H. Stock, RN) from NAS Culdrose. 824 Squadron of Whirlwind Mark 7 helicopters under the command of Lieutenant Commander J. Trevis, RN, had been embarked since March. So with Sea Venoms, Sea Hawks and Gannets carrying out flying trials, the Flight Deck began to resemble the short runway at London Airport. Finally, with all the trials successfully completed, *Victorious* once more returned to Portsmouth on the 3rd September, to the accompaniment of the heaviest thunderstorm of the year.

At mid-day on Sunday, 28th September, *Victorious* sailed for the Mediterranean on her first operational tour. The wind freshened on Monday whilst on passage through the Bay, and by nightfall was blowing gale force. During the middle watch a wind speed of 72 knots was registered and four of the twenty-man life rafts were carried away and the flight deck catwalk starboard side was damaged.

The next day, the Rock of Gibraltar was to be seen on the horizon, and whilst exercising Scimitars and Venoms on a simulated strike of the Rock, a signal was received from Sir Winston Churchill aboard the Yacht *Christina.* He was about to fly home to England and the signal said he would be delighted to see *Vic*'s aircraft before his departure. The ship duly obliged and, much to his pleasure, the Scimitars beat up North Front just as the Great Man was about to embark in his aircraft.

That evening as the ship passed through the Straits of Gibraltar, two ratings were reported missing. Later it transpired that they were brothers and that the older one had got himself into a spot of trouble on board. Knowing that he would be punished for his crime, he persuaded his younger brother to emigrate. No doubt intrigued by the nearness of the lights and the so-called glamour of Southern Spain, they decided to borrow a life raft and sail away. Together they slipped a twenty-man life raft from the after end of the flight deck, then jumped off after it in search of a new life.

As soon as they were reported missing, a search of the ship was instituted and lookouts were detailed and posted. Unfortunately, the starboard forward catwalk just below the flight deck had been carried away by the recent gales, and the starboard forward lookout hadn't been told and didn't notice. It was pitch dark as he strode across the flight deck and, with gay abandon and binoculars, he leapt into the non-existent catwalk. With a surprised cry and a splash he fell some forty feet into the sea, but his cries did not go unanswered and were heard by some officers on the quarterdeck and the lifebuoy sentry. As he floated past, all four quarterdeck lifebuoys were dropped simultaneously.

Officers and men ran to man the lifeboat, which was quickly lowered and after a short search — ably assisted by the man's cries for help — the unfortunate lookout was recovered and brought back aboard. Taken to the sickbay for a routine medical check up, he assured the Principal Medical Officer that he was 'only in for two years, and didn't want to make a habit of jumping ship.' Undeterred by this minor drama, the ship continued to search for the life raft and its two occupants. Searchlights moved back and forth across the surface of the sea and eventually, about an hour later it was recovered together with its two occupants — fast asleep!

A short stay in Gibraltar and then the ship was off again to Malta where she arrived on Monday 13th October. The ship remained in the area of the Mediterranean until early in the New Year, with exercises, visits to Toulon and Messina and quite a lot of flying to keep her busy. Unfortunately, the amount of flying achieved in this first period was somewhat reduced by the fact that both catapults needed modification and that the helicopters of 824 Squadron were having their problems.

The Whirlwind Mark 7 was the standard anti-submarine helicopter in Naval service. Used in this role, it could either carry an anti-submarine torpedo or submarine detection equipment. At this particular time it was having severe problems staying in the air and, for a while, they were being lost at the rate of about one a fortnight. As one observer put it:

When you released your torpedo, it was a race between the helicopter and the torpedo as to which one hit the water first.

The helicopters were grounded while the problems were ironed out and *Victorious* returned to Portsmouth via Gibraltar, arriving on a cold misty afternoon on the 14th January exactly one year after commissioning.

Sailing again on February 20th, 1959, *Victorious* embarked her squadrons for more exercises throughout the spring and early summer. Visits to various European ports included Oslo, Aarhus in Denmark and even Torquay, but finally the great moment came and the ship set course for America and Exercise 'Riptide' with the US 2nd Fleet. Unfortunately for 824 Squadron, the helicopters were still having their problems and had to be left behind, but she embarked 6 Venoms of 894 Squadron and they remained for three months.

Victorious arrived at Norfolk, Virginia on 10th July and with due ceremony berthed near the mighty USS *Independence,* the latest 60,000-ton aircraft carrier of the 'Forrestal' Class to be commissioned. As one wag remarked: 'You could stick *Victorious* down into the *Independence* hangar, though I believe they wanted us as a seaboat!' Subsequent RN/USN exercises were to show that the best does not always arrive in the biggest package.

The exercise occupied a total of six days and during this period *Victorious* exchanged her aircraft with those of her US counterparts. The American Senior Officers also took the opportunity to see the British carrier during flying operations and, at one stage, no less than one hundred and one gold braided stripes were counted in the *Victorious'* Operations Room − possibly a world record, but in any event a hell of a crush!

There is no doubt that the American visitors to the ship were most impressed by everything they saw in *Victorious,* though she and the Royal Navy lacked the highly developed, robust and thoroughbred aeroplanes of our American allies; all the new developments had been incorporated into the ship during her long modernisation, and they were particularly impressed by her new Type 984 radar and the high degree of automation. When it came to aircraft, well that was a different story; the point was made by one American airman who on looking over the Scimitar remarked: 'God dammit, only the British could build a plane with so much power to fly sub-sonic.' And another added rather incredulously: 'You mean you make your own aircraft?'

The famous McDonnell Phantom was designed with two General Electric J79 turbo-jets each giving 9,600 pounds of static thrust, whereas the Scimitar had two Rolls-Royce Avon 202 turbojets, each producing some 11,250 pounds of static thrust — with the former capable of speeds up to twice that of sound, the comparison in performance between these two aircraft doesn't need elaboration. After the exercise and the subsequent 'post mortem', the ship headed for Boston and New York before returning to the United Kindgom. It is tactful and customary naval tradition to be silent about the activities of a ship during a strictly Flag-showing, social visit. However, they must have gone out of their way to cultivate that Olde English Charm, to impress the locals and reinforce the popular image of the English Tar: 'One little boy was convinced the Admiral's name was Nelson', but this reaction was by no means unanimous, since one New York taximan thought *Victorious* was a French carrier and he was 'very impressed with the high standard of English'.

On the ship's return to Portsmouth for what the Americans call 'R and R' (Rest and Recuperation) and the British call anything from a bottom-scrape to a refit, the ship's company bade farewell to Captain Coke and welcomed their new Commanding Officer, Captain Janvrin. The period was a fairly hectic one from the domestic point of view for on the 11th September the RN Film Corporation gave a big dinner aboard to thank leading members of the Film Industry for all the support and help received. Among leading personalities present on this great occasion were Lord Mountbatten, Mr Shouras of 20th Century Fox, Mr Jack Warner of Warner Brothers and, representing the acting profession, Mr Jack Hawkins of *The Cruel Sea* and Mr Kenneth More of *Reach for the Sky* — an appropriate combination in any aircraft carrier.

Exercise 'Blue Frost' scheduled for the late autumn had no

connection with that other well-known TV personality, but was concerned with providing air support for the 'enemy', who landed in Norway both from the sea and air. International Drama was soon to hit the headlines when after a very long trip at altitude, the crew of a Skyraider from *Victorious* began to consider the question of returning to the ship. A variety of small problems were to frustrate this plan and at half-past-one in the afternoon on a bright September day, lost and out of fuel, the Skyraider ditched near a fishing boat.

The crew of the Russian Trawler *Mozyr* were very surprised to see a large dark blue aircraft fly right over them, waggle its wings and then fall in the sea about a mile away.

The crew of three were out in less time than it takes to say Comrade and were sitting in their dinghies riding the fairly large swell before the tail of the aircraft finally disappeared beneath the water. The aircrew kept their dinghies tied together and, to amuse themselves, let off flares to guide the trawler to their position. The pilot, Lieutenant Barry Hartwell, recalls the moment of rescue:

It was a shock to see the hammer and sickle prominently displayed on the funnel as the ship circled us. We waved, but it appeared to be steaming off and leaving us and the cloud of depression rising over those three dinghies must have been visible for miles. However, with a feeling of great relief we saw the trawler turn back and come towards us again. At the second attempt she managed to get to us and we were pulled inboard. The fishermen at first thought that we were American, but by saying 'English' and 'British' loudly for some time we managed to alter this impression and their attitude towards us thawed noticeably.

The welcome was typically Russian and, in the Captain's cabin, the Political Commissar smiled, thoughtfully tapped his pistol and then — shrugging, he put it away in a drawer. On the bulkhead of the cabin was a picture of what seemed to be a young girl. 'Your daughter?' the pilot managed to convey to the Skipper. 'That is Lenin!' was the Russian reply.

The trawler was one of a fleet being shepherded by a large

depot ship *Atlantika* and, next morning, they were rowed across to their new home. Going over the side in a cargo net and with their minds mostly on safety, the airmen looked down and saw a most attractive young Russian girl. Russian ships carry quite a few women on board, mostly for cooking, nursing and other domestic chores. By and large, they were rather matronly in stature and approachability and not nearly as attractive as this one, even though she happened to be gutting a herring at the time.

Communications were established eventually between the Russians and the Admiralty and HMS *Urchin;* Commander D.J. Bent, DSC, RN, of the Fishery Protection Squadron was sent to pick them up. With a photo of the ship, eighty cigarettes, a tin of vitamin pills and a picture postcard of roses, they each took their leave of the Russians and eventually reached Devonport and *Victorious.*

During their absence, *Victorious* had conducted an intensive search for the aircraft survivors and then for the Russian ship which had picked them up: 117 sorties in which no less than 35,000 square miles of sea were covered. However, the latter part of the search was to prove fruitless because of an error in the position passed by the Admiralty. The moral of this story was pointed out by an officer in the ship who said: 'When a Russian says he is so many degrees *West,* he does not mean *East.*'

Meanwhile back in *Victorious,* after a Radio Luxembourg *Take Your Pick* programme held and recorded in the hangar, the ship continued with flying exercises and trials in the Channel, and Lieutenant Commander G.R. Higgs of 803 Squadron completed the first ever successful night deck landing in the Scimitar. After Christmas leave, the ship sailed once again from Portsmouth on the 16th January to carry out the initial deck landing trials of the new NA 39 (Buccaneer) Naval Strike Aeroplane. Two aircraft were made available for the trials – one from the firm Blackburn and General Aircraft, piloted by the firm's test pilot, Lieutenant Commander D. Whitehead, AFC, RN (Retd) and Lieutenant Commander E.A. Anson, RN, and the other from the Naval Test Squadron at Boscombe Down, piloted by Commander Price and Lieutenant Commander Evans,

RN. Weather conditions were not always helpful, but during the seven days of the trial, three reasonable days saw the NA 39 complete successfully 31 launches and landings.

After yet more flying, *Victorious* went on a courtesy visit to Hamburg. It was a huge success and voted to be the best of the commission. Large crowds gathered on the River Elbe to witness the arrival and so many people attempted to drive to the river banks, that traffic in the city was brought to a standstill. On Friday 26th February 1960, *Victorious* secured alongside Pitch House Jetty in Portsmouth to undergo a six month mini-refit, thus ending her first new commission which had lasted just over two years.

After the refit, her life from 1960 consisted of three more commissions and a long refit from 2nd April 1962 until 12th June 1963. Most of her time was spent East of Suez with the odd 'Crisis' to liven up the proceedings. The first of these occurred on 30th June 1961 when the British Government pledged its support to the newly independent Kuwait against the threats of General Kassam's revolutionary Iraqi Government.

Victorious was on her way to Hong Kong when, on 29th June, she was ordered to 'proceed to the Persian Gulf with all dispatch'. After a very hot month in the Gulf she was relieved by *Centaur* on 31st July and proceeded for a thankful rest to Mombasa. The Army revolt in Tanganyika in January 1965 provided a timely break from the Malaysia and Indonesia 'Confrontation', and she successfully assisted in restoring order before heading once more for Singapore and the Con-frontation – which from the aircrews' point of view was a full scale flying programme in a war setting.

In 1963, Indonesia waged a violent propaganda campaign against Malaysia and followed it up with infiltration of Indonesian troops into Singapore and Borneo. It lasted for three years and although the commando ships and helicopter squadrons bore the brunt of the British defensive operations, *Victorious* and the other fixed wing carriers provided invaluable air search and support.

The highlight of the 1964 commission was a trip to Japan in May of that year. As the ship secured in Yokosuka Naval Base, the ship's company poured ashore to find out if all the stories told about past visits were true: they were! Many made excursions to Yokohama, Tokyo, the area around Fuji-yama and a few of the more hardened veterans attempted a full tour of the 275 bars alleged to be in Yokosuka.

Inevitably the *Victorious* gave a reception for the local Japanese dignitaries and American naval units in the area, and Lieutenant Roy Massey recalls the sensation caused by one of the Japanese guests whom he had been asked to look after by the Captain. The Japanese gentleman explained that he was very happy to be aboard the mighty *Victorious,* because his brother had once landed on her – his brother, he added, had been a Kamikaze pilot!

It was in the cold dank days of November 1965 that the ship's company for the 8th Commission of this veteran aircraft carrier began to form. In the five months that followed they came singly and in batches, until on a spring afternoon of April 7th, 1966, in 'C' Hangar, *Victorious* was commissioned. No commissioning is complete without its cake, and in front of a goodly muster of Admirals, dignitaries, wives, sweethearts, families, friends and the ship's company it was cut by the Captain's wife, Mrs D.L. Davenport, ably assisted by the youngest rating on board.

On 8th July 1966 a group of ex-*Victorious* officers slipped the head rope and the great carrier headed once more for the Far East. Through the now familiar Canal to the Red Sea, Indian Ocean and Malacca Straits, to sample again the delights of such ports as Singapore, Hong Kong, Sydney and Perth.

It was in Sydney that the ship acquired its own Firefly aircraft, a veteran of the Korean War. It was purchased through the generosity of the officers of *Victorious* and RAN Air Station Nowra and presented to the Fleet Air Arm Museum on the carrier's return. As Robert Rodwell stated in the 1966 December issue of *Flight International.*

The point has not been lost on the Naval Air Command at home that this enterprise is probably the only occasion in which a strike carrier has bought its own strike aircraft. The occurrence suggests other possibilities in the defence field which might be eagerly studied by the Treasury.

Victorious only just made it through the Canal before the six-day war in June 1967, when she was en route for the United Kingdom; she was delayed and ordered to remain in Malta to see how the situation developed.

In spite of Colonel Nasser's accusations that *Victorious* was actively helping the Israeli forces, she remained at anchor in Grand Harbour under the watchful eye of a Russian minesweeper for nearly two weeks, much to the annoyance of the wives back home.

The *Victorious* entered Portsmouth Harbour for her great welcome home from the anxious wives and relatives on 21st June 1967. The squadron had bade farewell and flown ashore, but on her flight deck – one Gannet and the veteran Firefly remained to see the great lady in her moment of triumph. She was to undertake another refit before her last commission.

Chapter XVI

THE LAST SUNSET

Ships very quickly settle down into the routine of a dockyard refit and *Victorious* was no exception. Once the welcome home celebrations were over and the first leave party had got away, the rest of the ship's company and the dockyard maties soon got on with the task. There was quite a lot to be done below decks, particularly in the boiler rooms where the boilers needed re-tubing and that troublesome rudder had to be fixed once and for all.

She commissioned again in August 1967, while the refit was still in progress, and over the next few weeks her ship's company were busily working and learning to live together. Preparations were going ahead and were well in hand for the formal re-commissioning ceremony planned for November. Commander Jeffrey Lloyd, RN, known with respect and affection throughout the ship as the 'Angry Ant', because of his small size and seemingly tireless energy, seemed well pleased with the progress that was being made.

With about a fortnight to go to the great day, the first disaster struck. *Victorious* was again in the dry dock in Portsmouth Dockyard because of the old recurring fault in her rudder. It had still not been cured, so she had been docked down again. This was inconvenient, but posed no real problem and certainly would not delay the ship.

Until the first of November the officers and ship's company had been living out of the ship. They had been accommodated in the adjacent depot ship and old aircraft carrier, HMS *Centaur*.

When a ship goes into dry dock, it is usual for the officers and men to move out and live elsewhere and the ship's company of *Victorious* conformed to the standard practice; HMS *Centaur* had provided a congenial and comfortable temporary home for the crew of *Victorious*. But now most of the officers and men had moved back on board. In the next few weeks they would buckle down to the enormous task of tiddlying up the ship, clearing up the compartments, passageways and messdecks and getting the ship ready for sea. It was a daunting task, but no one from the Command downwards doubted that the job would be completed on time – and barring some unforeseen complications nothing would stop them. But something did stop them and that something was an accident. The chief culprit in a drama that was soon to be enacted in *Victorious* was an ordinary, simple hot-water urn. It was sited on the bar of Number 13 Chief Petty Officers' Mess and was extensively used by the Chiefs to provide constant hot water. On the evening of Friday 10th November the urn was not working and was reported as defective, so an electrical rating came up to the mess to sort things out and repair it. He diagnosed the trouble to be a faulty plug, replaced it and left.

An accomplice in the plot was the dockyard temporary firemain. It was rigged and used for supplying ships during the dockings period in dry dock, but a section of it had been removed some days earlier. The ship's main firemain was still intact, but because the ship was in dry dock and there was no sea water, it was supplied instead from the dockyard fresh water supply. In the event of fire, however, it would need to be replaced by sea water supplied at much higher pressure, so for this eventuality, two water pumps were positioned by the Dockyard at the seaward end of the dry dock.

The next day was Saturday and, as usual, a high proportion of the ship's complement was ashore for the night or had gone on weekend leave. But for Captain Ed Brown, the next few hours would very much change his life and his career. A cruel stroke of fate would rob him of his chance to command an aircraft carrier, for he was designated to relieve Ian McIntosh as the next Commanding Officer of *Victorious*.

The morning watch which started at 0400 on Saturday 11th November 1967 was much like any other for one of Her Majesty's Ships in Dry Dock undergoing a routine docking and refit. The dark mass of the ship nestled in the large, oblong well that formed the dry dock as she waited for the start of another day; waited for the army of dockyard workers to come aboard at daybreak. They would pour aboard in their hundreds and begin again the race against time, the race to get the work finished by the appointed date, so that *Victorious* could sail for her last operational commission at sea. Under the existing Defence plans, she was scheduled to be scrapped in 1971, so this would be her last major refit and, if all went according to plan, she would meet her date and sail on time.

The stage was now set for the final scene. The audience was asleep and no one stirred aboard the *Victorious*, except for the Quartermasters on duty at the gangways and the occasional dutyman on his rounds or tour of the ship. The subdued hum of machinery seemed to accentuate the silence and provided the background to the two men who talked at the gangway. The Quartermaster looked at the clock hanging on the quarterdeck bulkhead – half past four – time was dragging and it would soon be time for him to go on his rounds. Slowly the minutes ticked away – twenty to five, quarter to five and then ten minutes to five.

Shortly before five o'clock the Quartermaster left the Bosun's Mate in charge of the gangway and started off his rounds of the sleeping ship. This routine inspection was carried out at set times throughout the night to ensure that all was well in the ship. Torch in hand, he set off on his regular and well-known route. Up ladders, along the maze of passageways, through doors and hatches and down yet more ladders, looking particularly for signs of fire and checking the security of messdecks and compartments. As he reached the long passageway known as the Burma Road or the Hall of Mirrors on Number Two Deck he looked at his watch – 0515 – all was well and he prepared to return to the Quarterdeck. Just as he turned to leave he thought he smelt something – a peculiar smell. He sniffed again – yes, it was unusual and it smelt rather like burning rubber. He stopped outside the Chief Petty Officers No. 13 Mess on Two Deck and decided to take a look around. He searched the area but found nothing suspicious, and certainly nothing burning or even smouldering, so with a final look around he went on his way.

Forty-five minutes later that first faint, tell-tale warning smell had turned to smoke, flame and ultimate tragedy. At 0600 smoke was seen coming out of a vent above 13 Mess door and almost simultaneously Chief Petty Officer T. Catterson who had been asleep in an adjoining bunk space discovered the fire and gave the alarm.

Within minutes the ship's fire party were galvanised into action. They were backed up by the Dockyard Fire Brigade who arrived at nine minutes past six, followed just two minutes later by the Portsmouth City Fire Brigade. The blaze got a good hold while the ship's fire party attacked it with gas/water extinguishers and, tragically, attempts to get water from the firemain failed. Within minutes the dense smoke and heat drove the fire party aft and it was not long before they had to clear the area. The Dockyard and City Fire Brigades obtained water from shore hydrants, managing to bring the fire under control by ten past eleven and finally extinguishing it by 1230, but not before one of her ship's company had tragically lost his life.

A subsequent Board of Inquiry concluded that the hot water urn in Number 13 Mess had probably boiled dry and, because it had no safety cut-out, the insulated supply cable had overheated. This in turn started a fire which spread rapidly, due to the ignition of combustible material used in do-it-yourself improvements, which the enthusiasts of the Mess had employed to decorate their bar.

Within hours of the disaster, the men turned to with a will to clear up the mess and begin again the task of getting the ship ready for the 24th November in a race against the clock. Petty Officer Tony Cox summed up the ship's company reaction at the time with the words 'It's a terrible tragedy to lose a shipmate, but let's get the ship to sea again.' The sailors rose to the occasion, cleaning scraping and painting, while the dockyard cut away the buckled bulkheads, assessed the extent of the fire and prepared to repair the damage.

As the days ticked by, great progress was made and the morale remained at a high pitch. While the men worked and strove to hide the scars, rumours began to circulate and the ship began to hum with speculation. As usual, it seemed that the press had got the news about the future of *Victorious* before the Captain, so of course he was unable to confirm or deny the many buzzes that were going around the ship. Finally the blow fell, for on the 23rd November 1967 the Captain was informed that *Victorious* would not re-commission. With a heavy heart, he cleared lower deck in the hangar and told the ship's company the news. As a victim of the economic crisis, serious manning problems within the Royal Navy and current Government policy, *Victorious* would not sail again and would be scrapped.

It seemed that the ship which had survived through a long hard war, that had withstood the onslaught of enemy bombs and Kamikazes, that had evaded the submarine torpedoes and enemy mines, was to succumb to a relatively minor fire, lack of resolve or interest in the Navy and the decision of a post-war Socialist Government. The preparations for the re-commissioning ceremony were too far advanced, for on the morrow all the guests would arrive. Captain McIntosh decided that the event would go ahead as planned, but that it would take the form of a wake. The farewell celebrations that followed were attended by no less than six Captains of *Victorious* – a great tribute to the *Vic* and a fitting climax to her career.

After the last guest had gone, the ship took on a strange silence, almost as if the life were slowly draining out of her. Men began the slow and painful task of de-storing and, gradually, her ship's company began to depart. Nearly a thousand men were drafted to the carrier *Hermes* just a few yards away at South Railway Jetty. As Chief Regulator Paddy Mooney led his eighty or so Flight Deck Party over the gangway of *Victorious* for the last time, he halted them, 'Let's give three cheers to the good old fighting lady', he said. To the utter astonishment of the Officer of the Watch and the Gangway Staff, eighty lusty voices gave three rousing cheers in a final, solemn and very touching tribute.

The men who toiled and formed the Flight Deck Party were hard-working, loyal and extremely fond of their ship, but now they were in *Hermes* and things were different. Their new ship needed chain guardrails and there were none in store, so being opportunists and extremely capable men, they took advantage of a heaven sent gift. One evening they crept stealthily back aboard *Victorious* and borrowed the guardrail chains round the edge of the liftwells and flight deck, considerably replacing them with tatty-looking string. As the few men remaining stripped each compartment and stowed everything on the Flight deck, it took on the appearance of Steptoe's Yard, piled high with mounds of machinery, stores and fittings. But by the end of March, the destoring was completed, the ship had been de-commissioned and sadly, transferred to the Senior Officer Reserve Ships.

At five minutes past seven on the evening 13th March 1968 *Victorious* finally ended her career as a Naval ship. As the few remaining officers and men together with a handful of the press gathered on the Flight Deck to witness this last ceremony, three Sea Vixens of 893 Squadron and three Buccaneers of 801 Squadron paid their own noisy farewell. As the roar of their jet engines died away, two ex-*Victorious* Royal Marine buglars came to attention. 'Sunset, sir.' In the watery dusk, the moving notes of the Ceremonial Sun-Set echoed over the forlorn and empty flight-deck of *Victorious*. Down below she was a hollow shell and the noisy, throbbing roar of her machinery was stilled – her heartbeat stopped for ever. Slowly, very slowly the large white ensign was lowered for the last time and the small gathering of officers, men and press representatives saluted in silent tribute to the end of a legend. As the notes died away, the commissioning pendant was struck and handed to Captain Ian McIntosh.

A lot of tributes were paid to the *Vic* on her last day in the Navy; typical of many was one which read:

1. From Cdr (Air), Cdr (AE) and Lt Cdr (Ops) 1963/64 Commission.
2. English Hymnal No. 407 First Verse. Last line.

Translated it read 'Almighty *Victorious* thy great name we praise'. Another from the Flag Officer Naval Air Command:

On behalf of all in the Naval Air Command I salute a great lady on her premature retirement after twenty-seven years magnificent service spanning almost the entire life of the Fleet Air Arm.

Good luck and God speed to all the Ship's Company.

It seems a shame to many that this carrier which not only

took part in so many of the famous actions of World War II, but typified Naval Aviation at its best, could not have been spared to end her days as a memorial museum and a lasting tribute to the Navy and the Fleet Air Arm. But it was not to be and she was placed on the disposal list for scrap and sold in July 1969.

It was almost a year later that *Victorious* left Portsmouth on her last, sad journey to the Breaker's Yard. On the 11th July 1969, the ship was pulled and pushed by tugs to start her long journey to Scotland, to the Shipbreaking Industries Yard at Faslane on the Gare Loch. As the ship was towed out of Portsmouth, Flag Officer Naval Air Command, Vice Admiral Sir Richard Janvrin, KCB, DSC, paid his own farewell tribute. Together with Lieutenant Commander E.J. Trounson, RN, as the pilot, he flew in the last remaining Swordfish aircraft to salute the Navy's oldest carrier, the ship he commanded in 1959 and 1960.

The skeleton crew of a handful or so of ratings who formed the towing crew, added their own epitaph to the story as they left Portsmouth for the last time and on a souvenir of the trip they wrote:

Ashes to ashes and dust to dust
If the Navy don't want her — Gillette must.

It was late one evening in July 1970. The sun struggled against the lengthening shadows as it dipped towards the horizon and, in front, the still waters of the Gare Loch rippled in the evening breeze. All was quiet, the workers had gone home, the noise of tearing metal and clattering machinery was stilled and, like sentinels, the dockside cranes stood their silent guard. A few yards away, I could see the dismembered, mutilated remains of *Victorious*, as she floated alongside the wharf of the breaker's yard. No longer recognisable as an aircraft carrier, the few remaining feet of rusted metal which floated on the water looked more like a submerged wreck, waiting for time and the elements to erase the shattered remains and hide her scars. But for *Victorious*, men with modern techniques and armed with cutters and cranes would hasten the process of nature, would systematically rip her to bits and remove every trace.

As I watched, a solitary seagull wheeled overhead peering at the large whale-like shape below. Then with undercarriage selected down, it made a slow and cautious approach upwind, to land with precision and perfection on the stern. The seagull perched quietly for a few moments to survey the scene — adjusted his position, then boosted himself off to join his friends. Like thousands of his human counterparts before him, he could now boast that he too had flown from *Victorious* — a boast that future generations of seagulls and humans will envy!

Now *Victorious* is a memory and the future of the Fleet Air Arm lies in the balance. The carriers will be replaced by land based aeroplanes and the hard, bitter lessons gained from fifty odd years of naval aviation will again be forgotten. If we are to lose fixed-wing air power at sea and all that that implies, it is certain that in the future, some sadder and wiser government will regret the folly of their predecessors and — who knows — perhaps even envy that seagull his boast!

APPENDIX I

GENERAL

1. The following Staff Requirements have been compiled for an aircraft carrier to meet the decision to build a fully protected carrier.

2. The carrier should be fitted as a Flagship.

REQUIREMENTS

3. **Displacement.** This must not exceed the Treaty limitation of 23,000 tons.

4. **Speed.** An emergency speed of 30 knots at deep load draught with an operational speed of 29 knots.

   With one boiler not steaming, the figures should be:

Emergency	– 29 knots
Operational	– 28 knots

5. **Endurance**
   a. Sufficient to steam 150 hours at 16 knots with steam for 30 knots;
      plus 80 hours at 25 knots with steam for 30 knots;
      plus 8 hours at full speed.
      All on the hypothesis of 6 months out of dock.

   b. An addition of about 35% (E in C being consulted in this matter) to allow for abnormal consumption due to weather, damage and oil left in tanks.

   c. As much additional fuel as the tonnage and space available permit.

   Note: The endurance of *Ark Royal* is estimated at 12,000 miles at 14 knots for 6 months out of dock and satisfies the above requirements. It is believed that an endurance of 11,000 miles at 14 knots would be sufficient.

6. **Manoeuvrability.** As high a speed of turning under rudder as is possible without causing the ship to heel unduly, is required, so as to shorten the time of turning into wind for flying operations.

7. **Armament.** Designs of large carriers forwarded on M.F.O. 363/36 showed an armament of 16 – 5.25 HA/LA guns in twin W.D. mountings sited in four groups of four guns each. This mounting has now been discarded as the weight and size of the 5.25 turret mounting precludes it being fitted on a ship of this displacement and protection. Armament is, therefore, proposed as follows:

   16 – 4.5 inch HA/LA guns in W.D. twin mountings in four groups of four guns each; each group to be capable of separate control on either HA or LA targets. The whole broadside of 8 guns also to be capable of control from either director on that side (as for *Ark Royal*). It is desirable that the guns should be capable of fire across the deck at as low elevations as possible.

Supply of ammunition should be by two endless chain hoists per mounting. Owing to the impracticability of siting the magazines below the guns, horizontal conveyors will be required.

Adequate ready-use stowage is required at the gun positions.

The question of blast upon aircraft ranged on deck should be considered when the positions for the mountings are chosen.

6 – 8 barrelled Mk M Pompoms. To be sited as clear of the blast of the 4.5-inch mountings as good arcs of fire will permit. At least two of these mountings should be capable of fire through as wide an arc as possible either side of the fore and aft line ahead and two similarly through the fore and aft line astern.

0.5 inch Multiple Machine Guns. A minimum of four 0.5-inch multiple machine guns to be fitted giving adequate ahead and astern fire and command over the flight deck.

80 degrees elevation.

Lewis Guns. As many Lewis Guns for which space can be found, and which can be manned, should be fitted.

They should be mounted where they can engage aircraft attacking the flight deck with M.Gs or low bombing.

8. Protection – Above water.

Flight Deck. As large an area of the flight deck as possible should be of not less than 3-inch NC armour. This would give protection as follows:

Against 6-inch plunging fire (100-lb projectile) below 23,000 yards

Against bombs   500lb dive bomb

                    500lb S.A.P. bomb from 7,000 feet

                    250lb S.A.P. bomb from 11,500 feet

                    1000lb A.P. bomb   4,500 feet

                                    (calculated only)

Side. Side belt protection to the sides and ends of the hangars and to the magazine and machinery compartments should be 4½-inch C armour.

This protects against:

Deck. Where not protected against bombs or plunging fire by the armoured flight deck, the magazines and machinery compartments should be given a 3-inch deck.

Consideration should be given to protection of the hangar floor from splinters of shell bursting below and outside the 4½-inch side protection.

Steering Gear. The steering gear should be protected by not less than 3-inch NC armour, sides and deck.

Bridges. Bullet proof plating should be fitted to the bridge – plotting positions and observers' offices in bridge structure.

Protection – Under water

Under water protection should be provided against 750-lb underwater charge in contact with the side.

Venting of explosions (occurring under the ship's bottom) should be arranged where practicable.

9. **Ammunition Stowage**

4.5 inch. A minimum of 400 rounds per gun and as much additional as can be arranged.

Mk M Pom-Poms. A minimum of 1,800 rounds per barrel.

0.5 inch M.Gs. A minimum of 2,500 rounds per barrel.

10. *Habitability.* The flying complement for which accommodation is required is estimated to be 78 Officers and 347 other ranks.

The ship's complement is estimated at 840 Officers and other ranks.

11. **Number of Aircraft to be carried**
    36 aircraft of present T.S.R. dimensions.

12. **Number and disposition of Aircraft lifts**
    Two lifts (45ft x 22ft) at forward and after end of hangar.

13. **Bomb Stowage**
    The following are the number and types of bombs to be stowed. Bulk stowage should be fitted if practicable for 500-lb, 250-lb and 100-lb bombs:

	Aircraft	Bombs carried per Aircraft	Loads	Total Bombs	Round Figures
500-lb	30 T.S.R.	3	1	90	100[1]
S.A.P.	6 F.D.B.	1	1	6	
'B'	30 T.S.R.	6	1	180	200[1]
	6 F.D.B.	1	1	6	
250-lb	30 T.S.R.	6	3	540	550
S.A.P.	6 F.D.B.	2		36	
100 lb	30 T.S.R.	6	2	360	400
A/S	6 F.D.B.	2		24	
20lb	30 T.S.R.	12	1	360	600
	6 F.D.B.	8	5	240	
Practice	30 T.S.R.	8	10	2400	3000[2]
	6 F.D.B.	8		480	
4.5-inch Parachute Flares	30 T.S.R.	10 per aircraft			300
Smoke or Flame Floats 12½-lb)	30 T.S.R.	8	10	2400	2400
Flame Floats 4½-lb)	30 T.S.R.	30 per aircraft			900

[1] The stowage of the two types should be interchangeable. Lifts should be large enough to take the 'B' bomb, which is of greater diameter than the S.A.P.
[2] Cases only. Can be stowed anywhere convenient.

It is desirable that a proportion of all types of bombs should be stowed aft in a second bomb room.

14. Torpedo Stowage and Parking Space

Consideration should be given to the possibility of stowing a proportion of torpedoes in armoured recesses in the hangar wall. If this can be done, provision of mantlets in the parking space would not be necessary and arming and re-arming would be more expeditious.

The parking space should be arranged as in *Ark Royal*.

Stowage is required for 45 18-inch Mk XII torpedoes.

15. Bomb Lifts

Bomb lifts should be fitted from each bombroom direct to the flight deck, with an unloading position at the hangar level.

The bomb lifts should be of sufficient size to take the 'B' bomb.

Each lift should be capable of supplying 72 500-lb bombs in 20 minutes.

16. Arresting Gear and Crash Barrier

Six in number arresting wires should be provided.

A crash barrier is required. The position of this barrier cannot be accurately determined until the effect of the streamlined stern of the flight deck has been tested in *Ark Royal*, as this affects the ability of pilots to land further aft in existing carriers.

17. Accelerators

One accelerator is required.

18. Parking Space

The span of the aircraft will be 50 feet. Parking with their possible effect upon the close range weapons mounted abreast the island on the port side.

19. Cranes

Two in number are required and should be sited abaft the island one on each side.

20. Wind Breaker

A wind breaker is required at the fore end of the foremost lift.

21. Night Landing Illuminations of Flight Deck

This question is under investigation especially over the area covered by the 3-inch armour on the flight deck.

22. Bridge Structure

Offices are required as in *Ark Royal*.

23. **Petrol and Oil Stowage**

   a.   A petrol stowage of 50,000 gallons is required.

   The petrol stowage should be well subdivided.

   b.   Oil stowage is required for 2,000 gallons of oil for aero engines.

24. **Communications**

   As for *Ark Royal,* with H/F. D/F. (See S.D.029/36).

25. **Homing Beacon**
   A homing beacon fitted on the island mast is required.

SUMMARY OF MAIN REQUIREMENTS

Type	Island Type
Displacement	Not greater than 23,000 tons
Speed	Emergency — 30 knots at deep load draught
	Emergency — 29 knots with one boiler not steaming
Endurance	11,000 miles at 14 knots, 6 months out of dock (See paragraph 5)
Armament	16 — 4.5 inch HA/LA in twin mountings in four groups of four guns
	6 — Mk M.2 pdr. pom-poms 8-barrell
	Minimum of 4 — 0.5 inch M.M.Gs

Protection

Above Water	To Flight Deck	3 inch NC
	To Side	4½ inch C
	To Deck	3 inch NC
	To Steering Gear	3 inch NC
	To Bridges	Bullet proof
Under Water	Against 750 lb contact charge	

Accommodation — (Estimate for 1265 Officers and other ranks)

Number of aircraft to be carried	36
Arresting Wires	6
Accelerators	1
Lifts — Aircraft	2
Lifts — Bombs	3
Cranes	2
Petrol Stowage	50,000 gallons
Oil Stowage (for aero engines)	2,000 gallons

AUTHOR'S NOTE: Abbreviations used in this staff requirement are amplified for the benefit of the reader as follows:—

E. in C.	Engineer in Chief
HA/LA	High Angle/Low Angle (Guns or targets)
W.D.	War Department
M.Gs	Machine Guns
N.C.	Nickel Chrome Armour
C.	Chrome Armour
S.A.P.	Semi Armour Piercing
A.P.	Armour Piercing
T.S.R.	Torpedo/Strike/Reconnaissance Aircraft
F.D.B.	Fighter/Dive/Bomber
H/F D/F	High Frequency Direction Finding (Equipment)

APPENDIX II
APPROVAL TO BUILD HMS VICTORIOUS

The following letter was written by the Admiralty to Vickers-Armstrong accepting their tender to build *Victorious*. It shows how costs have risen in the last thirty years and I have added a few 1970 prices for comparison as footnotes.

To
Vickers-Armstrong
High Walker-on-Tyne   13 April 1937
Gentlemen,

With further reference to Admiralty letters dated 13th and 16th January, C.P.450/37, I have to inform you that your tenders dated 31st December 1936 are accepted for the construction and completion in all respects of the hull and machinery of TWO aircraft carriers for H.M. Navy as follows:

HMS *Illustrious*
HMS *Victorious*

(to be constructed at High Walker-on-Tyne, the machinery to be built by the Wallsend Slipway and Engineering Company, Ltd)

(i)   Hull and as referred to in para 2 (i) of
letter of invitation to tender

£1,690,100

(ii)   Main Machinery Boilers and Auxiliary Machinery
as referred to in para 2 (ii) of letter of
invitation to tender

702,121

(iii)   Auxiliary Machinery as referred to in para 2 (iii)
of letter of invitation to tender

67,000
(Token figure)

I am, Gentlemen
Your obedient servant

Director of Navy Contracts

Notes:
1. The total cost for *Victorious* in 1937 was estimated to be £2,396,000 with an extra £17,950 for insurance.
2. The final cost of the ship after fitting out in 1941 came out to about £6,500,000.
3. The cost of the refit in 1950-58 which meant a virtual rebuild from the waterline up and a host of new equipment came to about £20,000,000.
4. A 'new generation' carrier today would cost about £100,000,000, but included in this figure would be the amount of money needed to provide her costly air group of modern aircraft.
5. By comparison, a static airfield ashore with ancillary equipment and aircraft costs about the same.

APPENDIX III

HMS VICTORIOUS – COMMISSIONED 29.3.41
OFFICERS IN COMMAND

	FROM	TO
Capt. Henry C. Bovell, CBE, DSO, RN	15.10.40	28.11.42
Capt. Lachlan D. Mackintosh, DSO, DSC, RN	25.11.42	21.10.43
Cmdr. R.C.V. Ross, DSO, RN	1.11.43	7.12.43
Capt. Michael M. Denny, CB, CBE, RN	8.12.43	14. 8.45
Capt. John C. Annesley, DSO, RN	15. 8.45	19. 7.47
Cmdr. Albert H.F. Hunt, RN	12. 7.47	30. 9.47
Capt. E.B.K. Stevens, DSO, DSC, RN	1.10.47	24. 5.48
Capt. Norman V. Dickinson, DSO, DSC, RN	25. 5.48	15. 7.49
Capt. John A. Grindle, CBE, RN.	16. 7.49	31. 3.50
Cmdr. G. Gwinner, DSO, DSC, RN	31. 3.50	30. 6.50

HMS *Victorious* was paid off on 30th June 1950 and Commander Gwinner, RN, left the ship in October of that year. She remained in Portsmouth Dockyard until she was re-commissioned after her long modernisation on the 14th January 1958.

Capt. Charles P. Coke, DSO, RN	1. 1.58	11. 8.59
Capt. Hugh R.B. Janvrin, DSC, RN	12. 8.59	21.12.60
Capt. John M.D. Gray, OBE, ADC, RN	22.12.60	1. 5.62
Cmdr. Peter G.R. Mitchell, MVO, RN	2. 5.62	23. 7.62
Cmdr. Cecil R.P.C. Branson, RN	24. 7.62	31. 3.63
Capt. Peter M. Compston, RN	1. 4.63	9.10.64
Capt. Dudley L. Davenport, OBE, RN	9.10.64	12. 9.66
Capt. Ian S. McIntosh, DSO, MBE, DSC, RN	12. 9.66	31. 3.68

APPENDIX IV

SQUADRONS AND AIRCRAFT EMBARKED IN
HMS VICTORIOUS BETWEEN 1941-1967

800Z   Six Fulmars. Embarked, 9 May 1941; *Bismarck*, 24/25 May 1941; one aircraft lost. Malta Reinforcement Operation. Disbanded, 21 June 1941.
Commanding Officer – Lieutenant Commander J.A.D. Wroughton, RN.

825   Nine Swordfish. Embarked February 1941. Attacked *Bismarck* 23/24 May 1941 securing one hit. Transferred to HMS *Ark Royal* 11 June 1941.
Commanding Officer – Lieutenant (A) E. Esmonde, RN.

820   Twelve Swordfish. Embarked 13 June 1941. Re-armed with twelve Albacores 27 June 1941. Disembarked 30 November 1941.
Commanding Officers –
    Lieutenant Commander J.A. Stewart-Moore, RN, June 1941
    Lieutenant Commander W. Elliott, RN, July 1941

809   Twelve Fulmars. Embarked 12 July 1941. Attack on Petsamo 30 July 1941, shot down 4 Me Bf 109s for the loss of 3 aircraft. Malta convoy Operations 10/12 August 1942. Shot down 2 enemy aircraft. Squadron reduced to six aircraft 24 August 1942. Squadron earmarked for Army Co-operation Training and 'Torch'. Equipped 6 Fulmar II Ps and embarked *Victorious* 19 October 1942. Disembarked 23 November 1942.
Commanding Officers –
    Lieutenant Commander V.C. Campbell, RN, July 1941
    Lieutenant E.C. Savage, RN, October 1941
    Captain R.C. Hay, DSC, RM, 24 August 1942

827   Twelve Albacores. Embarked 2 July 1941. During attack on shipping at Kirkenes six aircraft were lost. Disembarked 7 August 1941 to reform. Temporarily embarked from HMS *Furious* 30 March 1944 for attack on *Tirpitz*. Scored ten hits in conjunction with 830 Squadron. Re-embarked in HMS *Furious*, 21 April 1944.
Commanding Officers –
    Lieutenant Commander J.A. Stewart-Moore, RN, 1941
    Lieutenant Commander K.H. Gibney, RN, 1944

828   Nine Albacores. Embarked 3 July 1941. Disembarked 15 August 1941.
Commanding Officer – Lieutenant L.A. Cubitt, RN, March 1941.

817   Nine Albacores. Embarked 21 July 1941. Attack on Petsamo 30
                July 1941. Disembarked December 1942.
                Commanding Officers –
                    Lieutenant Commander D. Sanderson, RN, August 1941;
                    Lieutenant G.R. Beer, RN, March 1942

832   Twelve Albacores. Embarked 14 August 1941. Took part in attack
                on *Tirpitz* 9 March 1942. Re-armed with fifteen Avengers January
                1943. Transferred temporarily to USS *Saratoga* 27 June 1943.
                Re-embarked 25 July 1943. Disembarked 27 September 1943.
                Commanding Officers –
                    Lieutenant Commander A.J.P. Plugge, RN, April 1941;
                    Lieutenant Commander W.J. Lucas, RN, February 1942
                    Lieutenant Commander F.K.A. Lowe, RN, June 1943

885   Six Sea Hurricanes. Embarked 25 June 1942. Malta Convoys.
                Disembarked 28 August 1942.
                Commanding Officer – Lieutenant R.H.P. Carver, RN, June 1942.

884   Six Fulmars. Embarked 23 July 1942. Malta Convoys (Operation
                'Pedestal') and rearmed with six Seafires in September. Took part
                in Operation 'Torch' North African Landings and disembarked 23
                November 1942.
                Commanding Officer – Lieutenant Commander N.G. Hallett, RN.

882   Twelve Wildcats. Embarked 7 October 1942. Supported North
                African Landings. Disembarked 27 September 1943.
                Commanding Officers –
                    Lieutenant Commander H.J.F. Lane, RN, July 1941
                    Lieutenant Commander E.A. Shaw, RN, December 1942

896   Six Wildcats. Embarked 3 February 1943. Pacific Operations.
                Disembarked 27 September 1943.
                Commanding Officers –
                    Lieutenant Commander J.C.M. Harman, RN, November 1942
                    Lieutenant Commander B.H.C. Nation, RN, March 1943

898   Twelve Wildcats. Embarked 3 February 1943. Pacific Operations.
                Disembarked 27 September 1943.
                Commanding Officer –
                    Lieutenant I.L.F. Lowe, RN, February 1943

829   Twelve Barracudas. Embarked 12 February 1944 to take part in
                the *Tirpitz* raids and then attacks against German shipping off the
                coast of Norway. Disembarked on 9 June 1944.
                Commanding Officers –
                    Lieutenant Commander G.P.C. Williams, RN
                    Lieutenant Commander D. Phillips, RN, March 1944
                    Lieutenant Commander V. Rance, RN

831   Twelve Barracudas. Embarked 12 February to 16 February for
           Deck landing trials. Embarked 11 May 1944. Took part in attacks
           on *Tirpitz* 15 May 1944. Sailed to join Eastern Fleet on 12 June.
           Took part in attacks at Sabang, and Cement Works at Indaroeng.
           Disembarked in Ceylon September 1944. Disbanded 15 December
           1944.
           Commanding Officers —
             Lieutenant Commander V. Rance, RN, January 1944
             Lieutenant Commander Brooks, RN, March 1944
             Lieutenant Commander J.L. Fisher, RN, May 1944

1834   Fourteen Corsairs. Embarked 12 February 1944 to take part in
           attack on *Tirpitz* as escort and top cover. Increased to 18 Corsair
           IIs in September 1944 and took part in raids on Sigli, Car Nicobar,
           Pangkalan Brandan, Palembang (shot down 10 Japanese aircraft
           with 1836 Squadron), Sakishima Gunto, Formosa and Tokyo area.
           The squadron disembarked to Maryborough, Queensland from 23
           August until 25 September 1945. Re-embarked in *Victorious* and
           arrived in UK on 31 October and disbanded.
           Commanding Officers —
             Lieutenant Commander P.N. Charlton, RN, December 1943
             Lieutenant Commander R.D.B. Hopkins, RN, November 1944
             Lieutenant J.G. Baldwin, RN, June 1945

1836   Fourteen Corsairs. Embarked 8 March 1944 as escort and top
           cover for attack on *Tirpitz*. Increased to 18 Corsairs in September
           1944 and with 1834 remained the two *Victorious* fighter
           squadrons embarked till the end of the war with Japan. Took part
           in all the raids and returned in the ship on 31 October 1945 to
           disband.
           Commanding Officers —
             Lieutenant Commander C.C. Tomkinson, RN, August 1943
             Lieutenant Commander J.B. Edmundson, RN, March 1945
             Lieutenant Commander G. Baldwin, RN, June 1945

822   Twelve Barracudas. Embarked 11th September 1944 for the
           attack on Railway Centre at Sigli, Sumatra. Disembarked to
           Katukurunda on 20th September 1944.
           Commanding Officer — Lieutenant Commander Watson, RN.

849   Nineteen Avengers. Embarked 19 December 1944 and remained
           with the ship until the end of the Pacific War. Many of the
           squadron officers left in August 1945 in Sydney, but the
           remainder came home with the ship and the Squadron finally
           disbanded in October 1945.
           Commanding Officers —
             Lieutenant Commander D.R. Foster, RN, September 1944
             Lieutenant Commander A.J. Griffith, RN, June 1945

SAR Two Walrus. Embarked in *Victorious* in November 1944 and remained with ship until the end of the War. On 10 August 1945, W3085 ditched when chasing a pilot and, as it couldn't take off, the Walrus was eventually sunk by gunfire.
Pilots – Flight Lieutenant D.R. Howard and Flying Officer B.L. Ada, RAAF.
Observers – Sub Lieutenants J. Wilson, R. Humphries and A. Braithwaite, RNVR.

POST MODERNISATION – SQUADRONS EMBARKED

803 Eight Scimitar F.Mk 1s. Squadron re-commissioned on 3 June 1958 and embarked 25 September 1958. Unfortunately the CO, Commander J.D. Russell, RN, was tragically killed on the first 'land on' and the Senior Pilot took command. The establishment of aircraft went up to twelve Scimitars on 30th June 1959 and the Squadron gave a display at the Farnborough Air Show in the same year. They finally disembarked from the ship on 2 April 1962 and then went to HMS *Hermes*.
Commanding Officers –
  Commander J.D. Russell, RN, 3 June 1958
  Lieutenant Commander G.R. Higgs, RN, 26 September 1958
  Lieutenant Commander A.J. Leahy, MBE, DSC, RN, 21 December 1959
  Lieutenant Commander T.C.S. Leece, RN, 18 December 1960

893 Fourteen Sea Venom Mk 21. This squadron commissioned in January 1956 and was in action at Suez. It embarked in *Victorious* on 25 September 1958 and had the distinction of becoming the first Royal Navy Squadron to carry Firestreak guided missiles on Modified Sea Venom (FAW 23) aircraft. The squadron paid off in February 1960 and reformed with twelve Sea Vixen FAW MK 1 aircraft in September that year. The squadron was embarked in *Victorious* for three out of her four post-modernisation commissions and with twelve Sea Vixen FAW Mk 2s embarked for the last time on 19 April 1966 and disembarked on 13 June 1967.
Commanding Officers –
  Lieutenant Commander E.V.H. Manuel, RN, 28 September 1958
  Lieutenant Commander K.E. Kemp, RN, 14 December 1962
  Lieutenant Commander D.J. Melhuish, RN, 28 June 1964
  Lieutenant Commander J.A. Sanderson, RN, 22 November 1964
  Lieutenant Commander S. Idiens, RN, 22 January 1965
  Lieutenant Commander G.P. Carne, RN, 4 November 1965

894 Six Sea Venoms embarked in May 1959 when 824 Whirlwind Squadron were disembarked for gear box troubles. Squadron remained with ship for trip to America and disembarked on 22 August 1959.
Commanding Officer – Lieutenant Commander W.G. Black, RN.

824   Eight Whirlwind Mark 7s reformed in April 1958 and embarked for *Victorious'* first commission but disembarked with gear box trouble in the Mediterranean in the summer of 1958 before the visit by *Victorious* to the States. The squadron disbanded in April 1959 and reformed again in November of that year.
Commanding Officer — Lieutenant Commander J. Trevis, RN.

825   Eight Whirlwind Mk 7s. Squadron reformed on 16th August 1960 and embarked on 18 October 1960 finally disembarking on 27 March 1962 after Exercise 'Dawn Breeze' and disbanded.
Commanding Officer — Lieutenant Commander J. Ashton, RN.

892   Eleven Sea Vixen Mark 1s embarked 21 October 1960, disembarked 30 March 1962.
Commanding Officers —
Lieutenant Commander D.M.A.H. Hamilton, RN, 1 April 1960
Lieutenant Commander A. Gray, RN, 1 June 1961

801   Ten Buccaneer Mark 1s. Embarked for third commission of *Victorious* 1963-64. Reformed 10 Buccaneer Mark 2s and embarked on 19 April 1966 for the ship's last commission. They disembarked on 13 June 1967 from the Mediterranean direct to Lossiemouth.
Commanding Officers —
Lieutenant Commander E.R. Anson, RN, 17 July 1962
Lieutenant Commander P.H. Perks, RN, 17 April 1964
Lieutenant Commander A.J. White, RN, 15 August 1964
Lieutenant Commander J.F.H.C. de Winton, RN, 19 December 1964
Lieutenant Commander M.C. Clapp, RN, 22 November 1965

849   The Squadron was reformed at Culdrose in July 1952 and consisted of the Headquarters and a number of Flights. A flight of four aircraft would be allocated to whichever carriers were in commission and in the 1950s the aircraft were the Douglas Skyraider AEW (AD4W). The first Flight to embark in *Victorious* after her modernisation was 849B Flight of 4 Skyraiders which joined the ship on 26 September 1958 and completed the first commission. In 1960 the Squadron re-equipped with the Fairey Gannet AEW Mk 3 and for the next three commissions, a Flight of four Gannets was allocated on each occasion.
Commanding Officers —
First Commission 849B Flight — Lieutenant Commander B.H. Stock, RN.
Second Commission 849B Flight — Lieutenant Commander A.D. Levy, RN.
Third Commission 849A Flight —
Lieutenant Commander M.J.F. Rawlinson, RN, and
Lieutenant Commander J.E. Nash, RN.

Fourth Commission 849A Flight —
Lieutenant Commander J.E. Nash, RN, and
Lieutenant Commander W.M. Forbes, RN.

814   Eight Wessex HAS Mk 1's. Squadron reformed on 24th November 1961 at RN Air Station Culdrose and embarked in *Victorious* from RAF Khormaksar, Aden on 26th August 1963. They disembarked to Culdrose on 26th July 1965 and re-embarked for Vic's last commission on 12th April 1966. The Squadron left the ship on her last commission as she returned to Portsmouth on 19th June 1967.

Commanding Officers —
Lieutenant Commander L.J.B. Reynolds, RN, 24 November 1961
Lieutenant Commander J.G. Brigham, RN, 26 August 1963
Lieutenant Commander J.G. Beyfus, RN, 23 September 1963
Lieutenant Commander P.J. Lynn, RN, 24 September 1964
Lieutenant Commander N.K.L. Whitwam, RN, 26 October 1965
Lieutenant Commander M.C.S. Apps, RN, 17 January 1966

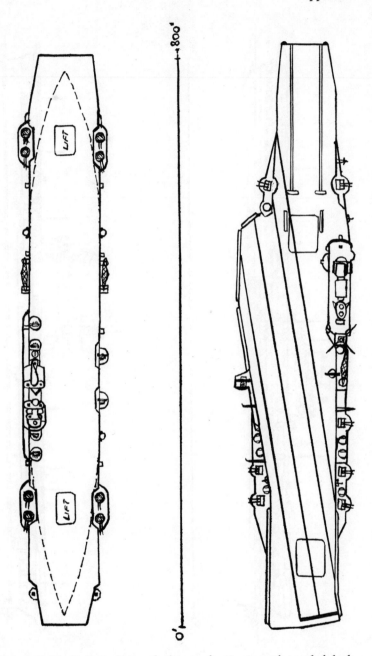

Plan view of the carrier before and after modernisation. The angled deck greatly alters the shape of the ship

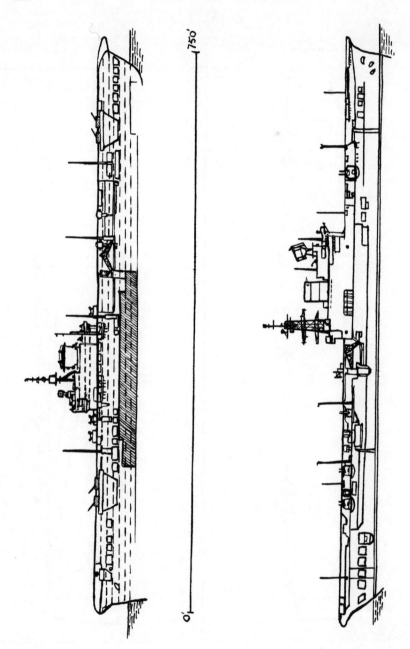

HMS *Victorious* in 1941 and, below, as she appeared after her modernisation in 1958

INDEX

INDEX OF SHIP'S NAMES